Academic Librarianship:

Yesterday, Today, and Tomorrow

Edited by Robert Stueart

Neal-Schuman Publishers, Inc.

Published by Neal-Schuman Publishers, Inc.
23 Cornelia Street
New York, NY 10014

Printed and bound in the United States of America.

Library of Congress Cataloging in Publication Data
Main entry under title:

Academic librarianship.

  Bibliography: p.
  Includes index.
  1. Libraries, University and college – Addresses, essays, lectures. 2. Ellsworth, Ralph Eugene, 1907-   – Addresses, essays, lectures. 3. College librarians – United States – Biography – Addresses, essays, lectures. I. Stueart, Robert D. II. Webb, William H.
Z675.U5A32   027.7   81-18866
ISBN O-918212-52-9   AACR2

To Ralph —
Effective Leader, Able Administrator,
Enlightened Teacher, Early Pioneer,
Dedicated Advocate, Wise Counselor,
True Friend, and Mean "Snooker" Player

Contents

Preface

This volume is dedicated to Ralph E. Ellsworth, with a deep sense of gratitude on the part of so many colleagues and friends whose professional and personal lives have been touched by this great person.

What better tribute to his 50 years in academic librarianship than for colleagues, all of whom have worked closely with Ralph and most of whom have worked for Ralph, to write chapters on their own areas of interest and expertise – this expertise covering many areas of academic librarianship, the field to which Ralph has dedicated his professional life. Perhaps his greatest contribution has been in the development of others, as this volume will illustrate. The old adage "One who develops ten people is greater than one who does the work of ten" certainly applies here. Developing people to their fullest potential is one of the highest challenges of management, and Ralph has done it with style. He is a giant in this respect.

In light of that, the first chapter, by Ms. Marjorie A. Broward, currently a consultant in information management in Sydney, Australia is intended to set the stage for the tribute that follows. Marge worked with Ralph at the University of Iowa in the early 1950s and was later recruited by him to become Head of the newly formed Business Library at the University of Colorado. This chapter is on "mentoring," which has come to be recognized as an important, perhaps even essential phenomenon among academic library managers. Ralph, over the years, has done his share of mentoring.

The second chapter, by Dr. Edward R. Johnson, is a bio-bibliographic essay on Ralph. Ed got his start in the profession as a staff member at the University of Colorado while Ralph was director. This chapter elucidates Ralph's professional activities – writing, consulting, and professional leadership. It concisely illustrates his impact on the academic library profession.

The remaining chapters in this volume relate to issues that are facing academic librarianship today. Interestingly, these same issues have been with the profession for some time, as is evident in Ralph's writings over the years. Therefore, each chapter is introduced by a quote from Dr. Ellsworth's extensive writings on all of the subjects. Each issue's current concern is then addressed by the authors, who, in some cases, give a historical perspective to Ralph's own contributions in the area as well as discussing the current concerns.

The chapter on library organizations is by Dr. Richard M. Dougherty, a frequent writer and consultant on scientific management and currently Director of the University of Michigan Libraries, who worked as Associate Director with Ralph at Colorado. Dr. Ellsworth Mason, who succeeded Ralph as Director of Libraries at the University of Colorado, has worked closely with him on a number of projects and, like Ralph, is a recognized authority on library buildings, the topic of his essay in this volume.

Mr. John Lubans, Jr., currently Associate Director of the University of Houston Libraries, served with Ralph as Assistant Director for Public Services at Colorado. John, a much-sought-after speaker and author in the area of library instruction, has written the essay on that topic for this volume. Who better to write on the topic "Centralized Cataloging" than Mr. Joseph H. Howard, Assistant Librarian for Processing Services of the Library of Congress, and, for several years, a colleague of Ralph's at Colorado, where he became Associate Director? Joe's co-author is Ms. Judith G. Schmidt, Technical Officer of the Processing Services Department of the Library of Congress. The essay "Interlibrary Cooperation" was authored by Dr. Joe A. Hewitt, Associate University Librarian for Technical Services at the University of North Carolina. Joe was recruited directly from library school to Colorado, under Ralph's encouragement.

Two people who worked with Ralph at the University of Iowa, Mr. Dale M. Bentz, currently University Librarian at Iowa, and Mr. Frank Hanlin, Bibliographer at Iowa, have co-authored the chapter "Collection Development," which relates Ralph's contributions to our current knowledge and state of the art. The censorship essay has been written by Ms. Abigail Studdiford, currently a doctoral student at Rutgers University and Executive Director of the New Jersey Library Association, and previously Associate Director of Libraries at Princeton University. Abby went to Colorado as Head of Acquisitions during Ralph's tenure.

The librarian as scholar is a topic with which Ralph was very concerned and to which he committed much time and effort. Dr. LeMoyne W. Anderson, Director of Libraries at Colorado State University and a long time coworker with Ralph on the evaluation of academic librarians, is a well-qualified advocate in this essay. On a similar note, the "Role of the Academic Library Within the Institution" is written by Mr. Clyde C. Walton, currently Director of Libraries at the University of Colorado, and a person who worked closely with Ralph at Iowa.

Mr. W. Carl Jackson, formerly Dean of Library Services at Indiana University, worked with Ralph both at Iowa, as Head of the Order Department, and later at Colorado, as Associate Director. As one long involved in the American Library Association and the Association of Research Libraries, Carl brings his expertise and ideas about the national organizations—how they meet research librarians' needs, an issue on which Ralph's outspokenness served as a catalyst. The final chapter, written by the editor, Dean of the Graduate School of Library and Information Science at Simmons College, is the "Education of Academic Librarians." I began my library career under Ralph's tutelage at the University of Colorado and was fortunate enough to work in a series of positions at Colorado, ending up in administration.

One other person who has contributed significantly to this volume is Mr. William H. Webb, recently retired Assistant University Librarian for Collection Development at the University of California at San Diego. Bill, who was appointed University Bibliographer at Colorado by Ralph, has performed much of the editorial work on this volume and prepared the index.

The purpose of *Academic Librarianship*, then, is to discuss the major issues facing academic librarianship as it moves into the 1980s, with a realization that those issues in fact are not so different from those of 20 or 30 years ago and may not be that different from those of 20 years from now.

The editor is appreciative of a small grant from the Hollowell Research Fund of Simmons College for help with data gathering.

Mentoring—The Subtle Factor

Marjorie Broward
Consultant in Information Management
Sydney, Australia

"Much Ado About Mentors," the title of a recent *Harvard Business Review* article, aptly describes the widespread emerging interest in the concept of mentoring. From Homer's first conscious effort at mentoring, down to the present, man has assumed responsibility for counseling, coaching, and sponsoring younger persons. There have been mentors and protégés in philosophy, in the military, in the sporting world, in the arts, where novices study with their masters, and certainly in business.

According to Levinson,[1] a mentor may fill any or all of five functions—that of teacher, sponsor, host and guide, exemplar, and/or counselor. By believing in the young person, by providing guidance in the ways of the organization, and by facilitating advancement, the mentor represents a happy blend of parent and peer. A similar definition, provided by Lynn Cullum, states that mentorship involves the functions of both coach and godfather. She says,

> The coach can be an intellectual mentor who helps set the standard of professional performance, meet it, and set the next standard. Or the coach can be a cultural mentor who introduces you to the environment, and provides a sort of interpretation. A godfather brings you along, promotes you, makes sure you get rewards. He watches out for your interests and will not promote you too far or too fast.[2]

In the above-mentioned article "Much Ado About Mentors," Roche[3] discusses the results of a 1977 survey of over 1200 top executives. In this sample it was found that nearly two-thirds had mentors and that those who have had one earn more money at a

1

younger age and are happier with their career progress than those who have not. A broad survey of the literature on the subject yields some generalizations about mentors: a person seldom becomes a mentor before entering his or her forties; the mentor is usually ten to fifteen years older than the protégé; the relationship usually lasts two to four years; the number of mentors is growing; male mentors with female protégés often find the relationship hampered by the sexual dynamics of the situation; and executives who were once protégés are more likely to become mentors themselves. Levinson[4] found that the relationship often ends with strong conflict when the protégé feels his own individuality and independence are threatened, but Roche[5] found that mentor relationships often developed into lengthy friendships.

Shapiro et al., writing in the *Sloan Management Review*, suggest that this system of professional patronage and sponsorship is comprised of a range of advisory/guiding personae. They suggest that the patron relationship is a continuum ranging from mentors through sponsors and guides to peer pals. The mentor relationship is the most intense and paternalistic, while the sponsors are helpful but less powerful in career advancement. Guides may be secretaries or administrative assistants who will help to explain the system and ward off pitfalls, while peer pals help one another with advice and support. The authors also point out that "peer pals and guides are more congruent with the feminist notion of women helping other women within an egalitarian framework. While mentors frequently introduce (and introject) their protégés to established networks, peer pals often create their own 'new order' networks."[6]

What does this brief discussion of mentorship have to do with this book of essays? With the exception of Anderson and Mason, who worked with Ralph on committees and as consultants, all of the librarian/contributors held library positions under Ralph Ellsworth's directorship at either the University of Iowa or the University of Colorado. In the 1950s and 1960s, when most of these colleagues began working with Ellsworth, the term "mentoring" was unrecognized in the library world. The increased attention given to mentoring in the business world, especially in relation to women and other minorities, makes one wonder how prevalent mentors are in librarianship. In particular, is there a connection between the working environment Ellsworth created with his personal leadership style and the fact that so many of his former staff members have gone on to both positions of top management in research libraries and leadership positions in professional associations? It cannot be a coincidence that so many who have worked for Ralph have gone so far.

Differences between managers and leaders is pointed out by Abraham Zaleznik, who states: "A bureaucratic society which breeds managers may stifle young leaders who need mentors and emotional interchange to develop. Most societies are caught between two conflicting needs: one for managers to maintain the balance of operations and one for leaders to create new approaches and new areas to explore."[7] Those librarians who have worked for and with Ellsworth would probably be unanimous in their characterization of Ralph as a leader more than a manager. Certainly the following distinction by Zaleznik is relevant to the application of this leadership theory to Ellsworth: "For people who become managers the instinct for survival dominates their need for risk and their ability to tolerate mundane, practical work assists their survival. The same cannot be said for leaders who sometimes react to mundane work as to an affliction."[8]

As a leader, Ralph was prepared to accept the risks involved in creating new approaches. Whether it was setting up a faculty coffee lounge in the library, arranging the undergraduate library according to the chronological periods of history, providing a separate "Honors" collection, instituting what was probably the first divisional plan for an academic library, undertaking one of the first massive conversions to the Library of Congress classification, developing a faculty delivery service, or extending academic library service to industry, he was willing to give a new idea a fair go. One of the hazards of mentoring is that the mentor puts himself or herself at risk by supporting a protégé. Ralph was willing to back and support his staff in developing innovative methods for improving service to the university community. At times he was impetuous, teaching by the example of how not to handle a situation, but always he was a visionary with boundless enthusiasm. A characteristic of successful mentoring is the strong, emotional exchange of ideas, whereby the younger person is encouraged to challenge the ideas of his or her mentor. Ellsworth was always prepared to listen to the criticisms and the contributions of his staff but just as quick to ask penetrating "how?" and "why?" questions to make certain the suggestions were well thought out and could be implemented. He recognized that the final decision and the final responsibility was his.

While no poll has been taken, it is probably safe to assume that the contributors to this volume could all identify the mentoring functions Ralph performed for them as a teacher, sponsor, counselor, and friend. Since it has been shown that persons who were once protégés are most likely to become mentors themselves, the influence of Ellsworth can be expected to broaden in ever-increasing circles. His contributions to academic and research librarianship are recognized throughtout this volume; his influence is likely to continue for many decades.

FOOTNOTES

1. D. J. Levinson et al., *The Seasons of a Man's Life* New York: Knopf, 1978.
2. "Women finally get mentors of their own," *Business Week (October 23, 1978): 79.*
3. C. R. Roche, *"Much ado about mentors," Harvard Business Review* (January/February 1979): 14-28.
4. Levinson, Op. Cit.
5. Roche, Op. Cit.
6. Eileen Shapiro et al., "Moving up: Role models, mentors and the 'patron system,' *Sloan Management Review* (Spring 1978): 51-57.
7. Abraham Zaleznik, "Managers and leaders: are they different?" *Harvard Business Review* (May/June 1977): 78.
8. Ibid., p. 72.

*W*e are like mountain climbers in unexplored territory, who, at great cost, gain one peak, only to discover that it is merely a shoulder to another, distant, higher, and more formidable range. — **Ralph Ellsworth**. Ellsworth on Ellsworth: An Unchronological, Mostly True Account of Some Moments of Contact Between "Library Science" and Me Since Our Confluence in 1931, with Appropriate Sidelights. *Metuchen, N.J.: Scarecrow Press, 1980.*

Ralph E. Ellsworth,
A Bio-Bibliography

Edward R. Johnson, Director
North Texas State University
Denton, Texas

I have known Ralph Eugene Ellsworth for nearly 20 years, beginning with my early days as a student assistant in the old Social Science Library at the University of Colorado. We did not become better acquainted, however, until some nine years ago when I conducted the research for a doctoral dissertation on the subject-divisional plan and first interviewed him. During the course of doing further research for a biographical study of Ellsworth, I had the privilege of corresponding and conversing with him several times, spending an afternoon fly fishing with him on the North St. Vrain Creek, near his cabin, and interviewing him at his home in Boulder. I also had the pleasure of interviewing a number of his former associates, several of whom have contributed chapters to this collection of essays. They all speak of him in the highest terms and with great affection.

Although Ralph was obviously somewhat uncomfortable with the prospect of a biographical study, it was clearly only discomfort at the prospect of prolonged personal attention, and not an unwillingness to review his life and career with me. On the contrary, my impression of Ellsworth, which was reinforced after prowling in the archives of three universities and listening to the recollections and opinions of several of his colleagues, was one of a man who is extraordinarily open and frank about himself and his views.

Interviewing Ellsworth and reading his correspondence of nearly four decades was an interesting, stimulating, and frequently entertaining experience. He is not shy about expressing orally or in writing his opinions on many subjects, ranging from politics and religion to librarianship. Ellsworth is an extrovert who is not afraid of raising a cloud of dust. As expected, I found a man of strong convictions who obviously enjoys poking occassional fun at some of the pomposities and personalities in the world of academia and librarianship. I also discovered someone who has many friends who admire him highly and about whom he cares deeply. Those who know him, perhaps especially those who do not always see eye to eye with him, agree that Ralph Ellsworth's long career in academic librarianship is a significant one in the history of the profession. To appreciate his contributions and impact, however, also requires an understanding of the influence of his strong personality.

Ellsworth has recently written his autobiography, entitled *Ellsworth on Ellsworth.* It was published by Scarecrow Press, which has published several of his other books over the years. It is also, typically, brief; brief enough to leave us with many questions. From whom, for example, did he inherit his skeptical streak and his well-known sense of humor? Also, his heritage, still reflected in his physical appearance, is Scandinavian, but about that part of his background he tells us little. In a recent review of Ellsworth's autobiography, David Laird agrees that "this slender volume of memories hardly seems adequate for a man whose image is bigger than life. "Yet," he adds, "as I read it, I began to feel a rightness about it for it is, like Ralph, the unvarnished truth."[1]

Ralph was born on a farm in Iowa, on September 22, 1907. Even though the Ellsworth family had to struggle as the result of depressions in the early 1920s, Ralph did well in school while holding down a part-time job. As a typical rural midwesterner, he had to help with the chores, but he enjoyed them. He loved the outdoors but by high school had also become a voracious reader. This habit, developed early, stood him in good stead when he enrolled at Oberlin College. (Oberlin is also the alma mater of at least one other distinguished academic librarian – Keyes Metcalf.) Ellsworth worked his way through college, with various odd jobs.

After graduation from Oberlin and a brief stint in a Cleveland book store, Ellsworth enrolled in the Western Reserve University library school in 1930. He received a bachelor's degree in library science in 1931. That same year, in September, he married Theda Chapman, whom he had met at Oberlin. He and his bride soon got their first view of the West, when they moved to Alamosa, Colorado. Ellsworth had obtained a library position there despite the economic depression.

Ralph launched his half century of academic librarianship at small and isolated Adams State College. The school had a library staff of one—Ellsworth. In 1934 he entered the Ph.D. program of the influential Graduate Library School (GLS) of the University of Chicago. This was an important period for the GLS. Under the leadership of Louis Round Wilson, it moved away from the traditionally technical orientation of American library schools of the time. Ellsworth chose to write his dissertation under the direction of Douglas Waples, whom he considered "a great man." Many alumni of the GLS went on to make their impact on librarianship, not the least of whom was Ralph Ellsworth.

About the GLS, Ellsworth wrote to his long-time friend (and fellow GLS alumnus) Richard Logsdon:

> Instead of the tiresome, practical courses in preparing one for work in a library, it was evident at once that the spirit of inquiry, research, was the center of focus on GLS. One knew immediately that he wouldn't be better prepared for jobs but that he would be involved in creating new knowledge.[2]

In 1937 Professor William Randall, of the GLS, who had been consulting with the University of Colorado about its library, recommended Ellsworth for the vacant post of associate librarian. After accepting the offer from Colorado, the position of director of libraries became vacant upon the death of the incumbent and Ellsworth was offered that position instead. The Ellsworths moved to Boulder, and at the age of 30, Ralph Ellsworth began his 34 years as an academic library administrator.

From 1937 to 1943 he led the University of Colorado libraries through several major changes. Although he inherited a set of plans for a new library building and had little to say about its design, he enthusiastically plunged into learning about the planning of libraries. He soon became interested in the concept of unit, or modular (as it was called later), construction as a way of making academic libraries more flexible and easily expandable. He had quickly determined that academic library buildings lacked these desirable qualities.

He was particularly intrigued by the work of Angus Snead Mac-Donald, an architect and designer of library shelving. MacDonald was a well-known advocate of the unit construction idea, and Ellsworth saw its potential benefits for planning libraries. He was unable, however, to convince the University of Colorado administration to consider any possibility but the traditional "fixed-function" type of building, already planned. As an alternative, Ellsworth developed a new concept of organizing the collections and services in the library: the subject-divisional plan.

The Norlin Library opened in 1940, with its collection organized into subject divisions: science, social science, and humanities. The divisions consisted of core collections of the most important books and journals in those subjects. Separate rooms were also provided for lower-division students, documents, browsing, and music. The subject-divisional concept had two important benefits for library users. First, it was designed to assist undergraduate students in using a large and complicated university library. Second, it emphasized in-depth subject assistance to other, more sophisticated, users of the library.

The subject-divisional plan had a number of precursors that Ellsworth studied and adapted, so it was not entirely unique. He, however, became convinced of its benefits and was the first librarian to advocate the plan's widespread adoption in academic libraries. He was in large part responsible for initiating and propagating the subject-divisional plan, which became one of the most important and popular concepts in academic librarianship in the twentieth century.

He still wanted to design a modular library, so when, in 1943, the University of Iowa asked him to become director of libraries and to plan its new library, he eagerly accepted the assignment. He served Iowa as its librarian from 1943 to 1958. Ellsworth's goal for Iowa was to design a library building with the maximum possible flexibility and functionality. He did not want an architectural monument such as those common to academic libraries in the late nineteenth and early twentieth centuries. In 1951 Ellsworth's modular library at the University of Iowa opened its doors. Although its exterior was unexciting, the interior achieved the goals of openness, functionality, and flexibility through the use of movable partitions rather than load-bearing walls.

The University of Iowa library attracted considerable national attention from prominent academic librarians. The Cooperative Committee for Library Building Planning of the Association of Research Libraries, of which Ellsworth was an active member, studied his ideas with care. Ellsworth and Donald Bean had published a pamphlet in 1948 entitled *Modular Planning for Small University Libraries* that had already alerted the academic library profession to his ideas. The University of Iowa Library was significant for showing librarians and architects a new approach to building design and planning. By the beginning of the 1950s Ellsworth was thus well established as a library consultant.

In some 40 years Ellsworth consulted on over 200 academic library projects. It is impossible to list all these projects, as the records are not complete and even Ellsworth is not sure of their exact number.[3] (Most of the papers relating to his consulting activities are now housed in the Center for the Study of Library Architecture, at the University of Denver School of Library and Information Management, as is his extensive collection of photographic slides.)

In the early 1960s, one librarian who benefited from Ralph's advice and expertise called him "the best library consultant in the country . . . ."[4] Ellsworth's high reputation brought him more requests for jobs than he could handle, and he referred many to other librarians. As a result, he was instrumental in launching the successful careers of several librarians as consultants and planners. A list of these names reads as a veritable "who's who" of academic librarians. Ellsworth's reputation today is undimmed. Indeed, according to Laird:

> In the West his image is, among some academic types, almost mystical. His imposing six-foot-plus frame and shock of white hair with full beard of the same color do not detract from that image. We could easily imagine him, dressed in a robe, as Gandolf helping Frodo Bagginses through our trials.[5]

Ralph was no less influential in other areas of academic librarianship. He was an extraordinarily active professional, and served vigorously both the American Library Association and the Association of Research Libraries. He served on numerous ALA committees, several of which he chaired, and was twice elected president of ALA's Association of College and Research Libraries (in 1951–52 and 1960–61.) He ran unsuccessfully for the ALA presidency in 1952. Characteristically, Ellsworth was both highly active in and critical of ALA. In ARL he was equally active and influential. He chaired the important Cooperative Committee for Planning Large University Libraries and was instrumental in the development of the national plan for microfilming and providing bibliographic access to doctoral dissertations through University Microfilms. Ellsworth was also deeply involved with the establishment of the Midwest Inter-Library Center (now the Center for Research Libraries). After the field of library planning, however, he is best known for his tireless efforts over many years on behalf of a national plan for centralized cataloging.

Western Reserve University honored Ellsworth in 1956, for his contributions to academic librarianship, with an honorary doctorate. In 1958 he returned to Boulder to direct the University of Colorado libraries. During his years in Colorado, he further enhanced his status as a preeminent librarian and library consultant, through his participation in a number of projects outside the United States. He lectured and wrote widely during this period as well. He retired as a library administrator in 1972 but has continued to be active as writer and consultant.

Ralph and Theda Ellsworth live in Boulder today, and their love of Colorado has not lessened. They continue to improve their cabin in the mountains, and Ellsworth remains an avid fly fisherman and fly tier. He is as outspoken on the subject of fishing and conservation as he is on other topics. "Many of our best streams have been dammed and turned into reservoirs," Ellsworth writes in his autobiography. "Thus, mobs of slobs can now enjoy sitting in their boats on their fat bottoms, drinking beer and throwing the cans into the water. . . ."[6] To his friends and colleagues who know of his strong convictions, these comments are vintage Ellsworth. The Ellsworths have loved Colorado for 50 years. Their two sons are also Westerners: Peter is now an energy education consultant in Wyoming, and David is a wood sculptor living in Colorado.

Ralph Ellsworth has contributed prolifically to the literature of academic librarianship. During his fifty-year career, he has produced numerous publications, some twelve books and over 80 articles in all. He has written on many subjects, ranging from intellectual freedom to higher education. Perhaps the most noteworthy of his publications are those on library-building planning, library cooperation, centralized cataloging, the intellectual role of librarians, and the role of the American Library Association. Ralph's writing style, like the man himself, is direct and to the point, sometimes blunt, irreverent, even provocative. He has not hesitated to express his opinions openly or to criticize his fellow librarians, administrators, or others when he believed they deserved it. Above all, Ralph's intention in these writings was to push academic librarians, sometimes hard, to accept their proper role as intellectuals and to make decisions on important national academic and professional matters.

Ralph's enormous influence on the field of library-building planning tends to overshadow his other activities. They were equally important, however. Through the force of his personality and the effect of his extensive publications, Ellsworth was prominently involved in many important library developments at all levels. The scope and depth of the ideas he has contributed to academic librarianship during his career can be seen in the bibliography in Appendix I. His consultantships are listed in Appendix II.

FOOTNOTES

1. W. David Laird, "Review of *Ellsworth on Ellsworth,*" *College and Research Libraries,* v. 42, no. 2 (March 1981): 155.
2. Ralph E. Ellsworth, letter to Richard L. Logsdon, January 31, 1979. (Copy in the author's possession.)
3. Ralph E. Ellsworth, interview with author, Boulder, Colorado, April 21, 1980.
4. Logsdon, *op. cit.*
5. Laird, *op. cit.*
6. *Ralph E. Ellsworth, Ellsworth on Ellsworth: An Unchronological, Mostly True Account of Some Moments of Contact Between "Library Science" and Me Since Our Confluence in 1931, with Appropriate Sidelights.* Metuchen, N.J.: Scarecrow, 1980, p. 146.

We heads of college and university libraries have been unforgivably slow in applying principles of scientific management to our libraries. The bigger the library, the worse the situation seems to be. . . . In our efforts to be above the little things, we forgot that our libraries were becoming large organizations and that they could become very inefficient and expensive and very wasteful of scarce human talent. — **Ralph Ellsworth.** *"The Library's Life Style: A Review of the Last 35 Years,"* Michigan Libraries, *v. 36, no. 3 (Autumn 1970):29.*

A Revisionist View
of Scientific Management

Richard M. Dougherty, Director
University of Michigan Libraries
Ann Arbor, Michigan

The fiber of tax-supported organizations in the United States is being severely tested as the demand for services continues to rise, while budgets have stabilized or declined. Libraries have not been exempted from this service/budget squeeze. Almost every issue of *Library Journal (LJ)*, *Hotline*, or *American Libraries* brings fresh reports of budget cutbacks. It is painfully apparent, judging by the proliferation of tax revolts at the state level, millage rejections at the local level, and the growing pressure for federal tax relief, that society is less willing to tax itself to support programs from general tax revenues than has been the case in recent years.

For libraries, this growing fiscal conservatism in societal attitudes could not have come at a more inopportune time. Libraries must begin to retool for the future; the "Channel 2000" experiment conducted by Online Computer Library Center, Inc. (OCLC) with a group of citizens in Columbus, Ohio, reported in an issue of *American Libraries*, is only one portent of the future.[1] Although libraries will continue to collect and make available the traditional printed resources, an information organization whose role remains static as society moves into the age of information is in fact atrophying functionally. The rapid growth in the number of independent information brokers is only one indication of how many organizations and individuals presently require information they themselves find difficult to obtain.

There is a possibility that library budgets will enjoy very little

17

growth in economic terms during the 1980s; consequently, if libraries are to retool for the future, strategies must be found to free resources to fund new initiatives. There are basically two available strategies. First, new programs can be funded by either improving the efficiency of current procedures or by adopting labor-saving technologies or both, and second, by reordering the priorities of existing activities.

Technology offers one attractive potential for offsetting the rate of rise in operating costs and for improving operational efficiency. Fred Kilgour, very early in his tenure as director of what was then the Ohio College Library Center, directed attention to the relationship between worker productivity and technology. He described this relationship thus:

> Output per man hour of labor input is the generally accepted measure of productivity. To increase productivity in libraries, librarians must employ an innovative technology that has the potential for dynamically increasing productivity at an essentially steady percentage rate at least equal to the rate of increases in costs. The only technology which can achieve these goals is computerization with its attendant facets, particularly comprehensive system design.[2]

Kilgour was convinced libraries could drastically improve productivity by adopting computerized cataloging. The phenomenal success of OCLC during the seventies has confirmed Kilgour's faith in a library concept that was largely untested in 1969. In fact, a simple comparison for the period 1974–1980 between OCLC's basic First-Time-Use (FTU) charges for a typical library in Michigan and the Consumer Price Index (CPI) reveals the clarity with which Kilgour saw the future. In 1974, the OCLC FTU charge for a non-Ohio library was $1.87; by 1980/81 the comparable charge was $1.40, not an increase but an actual decrease,[3] whereas the CPI for the comparable period rose 47 percent[4] and the level of beginning librarians' salaries increased 31 percent[5]

It can be safely assumed libraries will increasingly rely on new technologies as they become available, to improve operational efficiency. But if organizations such as libraries are to remain vigorous in the years ahead, more attention needs to be paid to improving operational performance and efficiency. Proponents of scientific management, one of the early twentieth-century schools of management theory, developed management tools designed for the purpose of improving efficiency. Paradoxically, library managers have largely ignored those tools. Although scientific management as a management philosophy fell into disfavor two generations ago, the tools developed by the pioneers of scientific management can still assist perceptive managers who desire to reallocate resources. Through judicious application of scientific management tools, a contemporary library manager should be able to strengthen justifications for existing basic library services such as original cataloging, reference services, and bibliographical instruction, and free funds from existing activities for redeployment to activities of greater immediacy or import.

The seeds of current societal dissatisfactions toward tax-supported agencies are rooted in the events of the last thirty years. From World War II through the mid-sixties, the American economy was the envy of most civilized nations. The country's almost uninterrupted economic growth enabled governmental agencies to initiate and extend a variety of important social programs, including expanded Medicaid, Social Security benefits, and Medicare. The general social euphoria unfortunately diverted attention from the reality that the nation's industrial technologies were slowly becoming obsolete. Our products were gradually becoming less competitive in world markets. This obsolescence did not occur overnight, and it did not surprise economists who had been issuing warnings for years. But the prolonged period of prosperity contributed to management, labor, and government officials' collective failure to stress improved organizational efficiency as a national priority. In other words, organizational efficiency wasn't a concern, because funds to accommodate growth always seemed to be available.

There were other factors, mostly negative, which have contributed to the current social climate of negativism and cynicism. Management has not always behaved in a socially responsible manner, and the average citizen views himself as being virtually powerless to fight the abuses of large bureaucracies. How often have companies violated the environment either through carelessness or through conduct which verged on criminal neglect? The highly publicized PBB incident in Michigan in which a fire-retardant chemical was inadvertently mixed with cattle feed, which led to the slaughtering of hundreds of thousands of cattle, is only one tragic example.

The general perception that industry has not been sufficiently concerned about the health and welfare of citizens has led to a proliferation of government regulations designed to protect citizens. Some would argue that the cure has become worse than the ailment.

The strained relationship between the auto industry and federal regulators provides a striking case study. Industry officials paid scant attention to safety precautions, prompting the government to impose a variety of regulations which industry now alleges has unduly inflated the cost of automobiles. The Chrysler Corporation repeatedly blamed its woes on governmental interference, but neither Chrysler nor the other manufacturers can absolve themselves from their own shortsightedness and avarice. Industry cannot blame government regulators for their decision to ignore the changing tastes of consumers, following the 1974 Arab oil embargo. Instead of tooling up to produce well-designed, gas-efficient cars, they continued to turn out highly profitable gas hogs which soon became a glut on the market, thus affording foreign manufacturers the opportunity to capture larger shares of the domestic auto market. Neither government nor industry is blameless, but the strained relations which now exist between the auto industry and government typify the current corporate/government environment. Ironically, it is the consumer who will pay higher prices as the auto industry retools at a cost of billions of dollars.

Labor unions have also contributed to the current climate of negativism. Wages and benefits have been bargained upward with little consideration of worker productivity. Often, companies simply passed on to consumers the costs of generous wage settlements. Because the higher wages were not compensated for by higher productivity, the increased wages contributed to the general inflationary economy. In this country, management and labor traditionally have viewed themselves as adversaries, which may have been tolerable during the prolonged periods of economic growth, but is a posture no longer in the best interests of either party during this period of limited economic expansion.

Public officials cannot claim ignorance; they were forewarned: even in the late 1960s, grumblings from taxpayers could be heard in many communities. But the dissatisfaction did not register sufficiently high on the voter Richter scale until inflation in some states drove property tax assessments out of control. The tax reform measure, Proposition 13 in California, Proposition 2½ in Massachusetts, has come to symbolize voter unrest and resentfulness toward government. However, the fact that most radical tax measures have failed at the ballot box indicates people are still willing to pay for social services if the services are responsive to community needs and if public officials act responsibly.

Tax-supported organizations must work to regain voter confidence. This rebuilding process may take years to accomplish. Words like "accountability," "productivity," "quality control," and "profit sharing," which so often have been little more than vacuous slogans, may assume new importance. These concepts can serve to fabricate new relationships between public and private sectors, between labor and management, and between government officials and their electorates. The Chrysler recovery, if successful, will be attributable to new attitudes and relationships among the three sectors.

SCIENTIFIC MANAGEMENT

Another way to forge changed attitudes is to create a different working environment. In recent years, considerable attention has been paid to issues such as management styles, particularly participatory management, management by objectives (MBO), and other techniques designed to assist workers in achieving their maximum potential. One eminent student of management once made the following observation about organizations with which he was familiar:

> . . .Managerial decisions were based on hunch, intuition, past experience, or rule-of-thumb evaluation; that virtually no overall studies were made to incorporate a total-flow concept of work among departments; that workers were ineptly placed at tasks for which they had little or no ability or aptitude; and, finally, that management apparently disregarded the obvious truth that excellence in performance and operation would mean a reward to both management and labor.[6]

Although the management of many contemporary organizations matches this profile of corporate performance, and these observations might have been offered by contemporary management theorists such as Douglas McGregor, Rensis Likert, or Peter Drucker, this assessment was attributed to Frederick W. Taylor, at the beginning of the 20th century.

Ironically, Taylor could also have been referring to most contemporary libraries, even though management of large libraries was given special emphasis throughout the last decade.[7] However, most efforts have focused on improving planning procedures and expanding staff participation in library decision-making. Less attention has been paid to the goals and objectives of library programs and operations. Library services are infrequently formulated with a view of costs and benefits to those who are served or to those who pay for the services. Basic activities have been performed with little attention to operational efficiency. In many respects, the current state of library management reflects the general malaise of management-and-worker relations in most public and private organizations.

The contributions of Douglas McGregor, Chris Argyris, Rensis Likert, and others have enriched our understanding of what motivates workers and how workers can contribute to an organization's strength and vitality.[8] Prior to the work of McGregor, many people assumed the average person possessed an inherent dislike for work and had to be coerced to put forth an adequate day's work toward a company's goal. Pay incentives were often viewed as the principal mechanism for motivating workers.[9] McGregor and others found that workers actually desired to participate in the affairs affecting them and were willing to assume responsibility and to contribute to the formulation and achievement of organizational goals and objectives.

The recent focus on the human aspects of management discredited much of the philosophy expounded by the proponents of scientific management, yet the outright dismissal of the principles and techniques of scientific management may have been tantamount to "throwing out the baby with the bath water." Many of the principles postulated by scientific-management advocates are relevant to contemporary organizations. In light of the growing interest in improving organizational performance, the time seems propitious to reexamine scientific management in light of current needs and attitudes.

Before turning to the principles themselves, a brief review of Frederick Taylor himself might serve to place his accomplishments in clearer perspective. Frederick W. Taylor began his career in 1878, with the Midvale Steel Company. Although Taylor is generally credited as being the Father of Scientific Management, several papers on management written by Henry R. Towne, president of the Yale and Towne Manufacturing Company in the 1880s, undoubtedly influenced Taylor's life work. It was Taylor's experiments with time management at the Midvale Steel Plant that gained for him worldwide attention. Taylor's methods came to be both revered and reviled by public officials. Louis Brandeis, prior to his appointment to the Supreme Court, called Taylor "a really great man – great not only in mental capacity but in character" and that his accomplishments were due to this fortunate combination of ability and character.[10] Georges Clemenceau was sufficiently influenced by Taylor's work to order each agency of the French government to establish a planning department modeled after Taylor's recommended model. Even Lenin embraced aspects of Taylor's philosophy, although he was driven by different motivations. Lenin exhorted his comrades to "organize in Russia the study and teaching of the Taylor system and systematically try it out and adopt it to our own ends."[11]

But Taylorism became anathema to organized unions, and Samuel Gompers became one of his principal antagonists. Gompers railed at the "prospect of men turned into robots by the Circe's wand of Taylorism. . . ."[12]

Although Taylor viewed himself as being concerned about the plight of the common laborer and professed belief that workers should share in the profits brought about by increased productivity, there seems to be little doubt he approached problems with a prevailing bias toward management. Upton Sinclair chided Taylor for this bias, in a letter to the *American Magazine*. In referring to the Midvale pig-iron handlers, Sinclair wrote, "They had formerly been getting $1.15 an hour: [Taylor] paid them $1.85 . . . I shall not soon forget the picture which he gave us of the poor old laborer who was trying to build his pitiful little home after hours, and who was induced to give 362 [sic] percent more service for 61 percent more pay."[13]

In spite of bitter opposition to some of Taylor's ideas, many of his principles are now taken for granted by planners and organizers of factory and office work. No less than Peter Drucker, one of the best-known contemporary students of management, has recognized the lasting contributions of Taylor to Western industrialization.[14]

Taylor's philosophy of management was much deeper than some students of management seem willing to acknowledge. Taylor's philosophy was formed from experiences which extended over a number of years. He did recognize the difference between the philosophical aspects of management and the mechanisms for implementing his philosophy. He believed it was necessary to develop management as a science, and this could be accomplished through the scientific selection, education, and training of workers. And in order to achieve high productivity, he recognized the importance and necessity to create an intimate, friendly spirit of cooperation between management and workers.[15]

To implement his philosophy, Taylor formulated a variety of practical mechanisms. Although some of them are obviously dated or inappropriate for organizations such as libraries—e.g., differential hourly rates and the like—the following guides, even though introduced over 70 years ago, are remarkably applicable to contemporary library management.[16]

1. Standardization of all tools and implements
2. Time study
3. Planning rooms or departments
4. Slide rules and similar time-saving implements
5. Instruction cards for workmen
6. Mnemonic systems for classifying manufactured products and implements used in manufacturing
7. Routing systems

Librarians have long endeavored to standardize basic forms, catalog cards, and typewriter keyboards, and today librarians are working to standardize computer command languages, terminal protocols, and so on. Some libraries have recently established planning offices. Of course, hand-held calculators and microcomputers have replaced slide rules, but the principle is the same. Thorough training of staff is even more important today than it was in Taylor's day. Librarians have always been classifiers at heart, and no less than the Dewey decimal system incorporates mnemonic features to distinguish among categories of books. Finally, organizational communication networks are more sophisticated than the internal routing systems envisioned by Taylor, but the need is no less important. In many respects, one of Taylor's greatest contributions to Western industrialization was to provide managers with a framework for thinking about work.

Taylor's work greatly influenced others in the field of scientific management. Two of the best known were the Gilbreths, Frank and Lillian, who achieved a sort of incidental fame from a Hollywood depiction of their lives in *Cheaper by the Dozen*. Taylor had developed timing techniques, whereupon the Gilbreths developed a series of analytical tools to describe the tasks actually performed. The flow-process chart and micromotion analysis are numbered among their contributions. The Gilbreths' philosophy in many respects mirrored Taylor's own desire to improve work efficiency and to discover the best way to perform a task.[17]

The analytical tools developed by the pioneers of scientific management can be used to analyze complex work procedures. For instance, before an organization automates a procedure or a set of procedures, it should have thoroughly analyzed its existing manual procedures. The data collected can be used to eliminate unnecessary tasks and reorganize those tasks which remain, and the data collected can serve as the basis for specifications of the automated system. A manager need not adopt Taylorism as a management philosophy to reap its benefits.

Current societal attitudes toward work and productivity have evolved over a long period of time. Even now, attitudes toward work are continually changing. Daniel Bell, in his view of the future, warns that society has already entered the post-industrial age.[18] If Bell is prescient and his vision of the future materializes, traditional attitudes toward work will change even more drastically as future generations join the work force.

Academic libraries have been buffered from the wrath of tax-payers, but library directors and library operations have not escaped the attention of budget officers. And the future does not bode well, since campus libraries consume a significant share of an institution's discretionary income and they are so labor-intensive. These two characteristics make libraries an inviting target for academic officers who are scrambling to balance institutional budgets. Budget reviews have already become a normal fact of academic life.

Librarians should begin now to identify which activities are most essential and which activities may be the most vulnerable to budget cuts. Although the vulnerability factor will depend largely on local circumstances, among the likely candidates will be activities costing more, or those that are the most difficult to justify.

Original cataloging of monographs and serials, data-base services, preservation, collection development, and bibliographic instruction are all professional activities that satisfy these two criteria. Most librarians would maintain that these activities are core professional activities, and while few librarians would argue with that perception, the future of these services may depend more on the views of faculty and academic administrators than on librarians who are viewed as interested parties. In a time of budgetary crisis, faculty tend to defend a library's book budget because they perceive it to be in their best interest to do so; but how many faculty will climb the barricades to defend the continuation of reference service or bibliographic instruction? Although there are documented instances of faculty and/or administrators coming to the defense of library services, all too often this has not been the case.

Library managers are beginning to pay more attention to the attitudes of faculty and administrators as they develop plans for library services. But even in the most supportive environment, a library's case will be immeasurably strengthened if it can provide evidence demonstrating the efficiency of its operations and the effectiveness of its services to users. It is in this connection that the tools developed by Taylor and his followers can be put to good use. In order to illustrate first why some library services may be vulnerable to budget cuts, and second, the value of analytical tools for collecting evidence to explain and defend these activities, some hypothetical scenarios will be constructed pertaining to three high-cost, basic library activities: original cataloging, reference and information services, and bibliographic instruction.

Original Cataloging

Cataloging of monographs requires mastery of complex and detailed rules. Primarily it is catalogers who are most interested in the subtleties and nuances of cataloging. It was the catalogers who were the primary motivators behind the creation of the second edition of the *Anglo-American Cataloging Code*. It is librarians, again principally catalogers, who are most concerned with the impact of the *Code* on existing cataloging records. Most users of catalogs are not even aware of the bibliographic subtleties so important to catalogers. Most students and faculty who search for books, limit their searches to author or title. This assertion is supported by studies on catalog use. One suspects that books presenting more formidable bibliographical entry challenges – e.g., corporate reports, government documents – often languish on the shelves undisturbed.

Librarians, particularly catalogers, will assert that original cataloging provides an overall cohesiveness to a collection. But often they seem to forget that catalogs are not intended for catalogers but rather are intended to assist library patrons. Ultimately, it is the library patron who will determine the value of the card catalog, and ironically, it may be a faculty user of the catalog who later becomes a vice president, budget officer, or president, who renders the decision. If the former faculty member didn't use the library, or used the library but really viewed the catalog as an unnecessary appendage, the library director may have a tough time justifying the high cost of maintaining either existing catalogs or convincing this doubting Thomas that the initial cost of implementing a new form of catalogs – i.e., COM catalog or on-line catalog – is worthwhile.

Reference Services

Library-school graduates often aspire to reference positions upon graduation. For many, reference service is the sine qua non of librarianship. But how much of reference work is truly professional? How might reference work be viewed by our faculty member who just consulted the card catalog? Not enough attention has been paid to the impressions of those who leave the desk. Were they well served? Was the information provided correct? Did an overly qualified person provide the service? These are not easy questions to answer. Most librarians readily acknowledge that many questions posed are directional or require searches of only a single reference work to obtain a needed fact. And many would probably acknowledge that the information provided is not always complete, accurate, or current. The question of performance is not an academic one, since there is a growing body of evidence dealing with the quality of service provided. And there is no need to reiterate the arguments pro and con on how reference desks should be staffed.[19] What librarians must not do is to underestimate the importance of the attitudes of those who leave the reference room.

Bibliographic Instruction

Bibliographic instruction is a growing area of service specialization. Most libraries now offer programs of orientation and instruction. Some programs focus on orientation for new students, whereas others focus on guiding graduate students and faculty through the intellectual structure of specialized disciplines. Numerous articles have described specific instruction programs, and others have documented quantitatively how bibliographic instruction has improved the quality of library performance. Does our skeptical former faculty member care about improved library performance? Wouldn't evidence that library instruction has improved a student's educational experience or enhanced his ability to exploit information services long after graduation be more convincing? Shouldn't justification for bibliographic instruction be more closely related to the impact of one's educational or job performance than on library performance?

THE TOOLS OF SCIENTIFIC MANAGEMENT

The foregoing scenarios are admittedly oversimplified and employ hyperbole, but they describe experiences which have touched more than one director. To document the value and/or justify the costs of these library activities, the tools of scientific management can be employed. They can be used to improve the efficiency of existing operations, redesign procedures, alter staffing patterns, train workers, and improve the performance of individual librarians.[20]

Tools such as the flow diagram, the flow-process chart, and the form-process chart can be employed to analyze a variety of library procedures. The decision chart, decision tree, and decision tables developed to analyze work involving "yes" and "no" decisions can be used to analyze complex reference and search procedures. Work sampling and diary study techniques can be used to determine how catalogs are actually used and to establish the number and type of errors that may have crept into a catalog. Sampling techniques can measure periods of peak activity at a reference desk and gather information which provides insights on the proper staffing ratios between professionals and nonprofessional desk assistants. The flow diagram can be used to plan and organize a "ready" reference collection.

Tools such as the flow-process chart, decision tree, and decision tables can be used by instruction specialists to design programs that most clearly explain the intricacies of searching for information either in libraries or in reference tools.[21]

However, establishing the qualitative value of activities such as bibliographic instruction will be difficult, probably as difficult as establishing the value of a quality education. For instance, we don't know to what extent bibliographic instruction provided at a four-year college might prepare a student who undertakes graduate study at a large university. Or, how important is it to society that an undergraduate student be "bibliographically literate" upon graduation? A longitudinal study designed to answer such questions will require the application of statistical techniques coupled with those of survey research, in addition to the tools of scientific management.

SUMMARY

The quality of library services can be enhanced through the proper application of scientific management tools. There are those who believe it is antithetical for a professional to speak in terms of production and productivity, because such conversations may carry with them the stigma of the blue-collar laborer, but the need to collect quantitative data in libraries in order to improve operational performance and the quality of management decision making was never more compelling. Increasing staff efficiency and performance has not received wide attention from practicing professionals in recent years. However, the growing awareness that society expects more from its tax-supported agencies may gradually alter the attitudes of managers.

Adversarial relationships are not a natural outcome of scientific management; adversarial relationships, on the contrary, are the outcome of mismanagement. Managers should aim to create an organizational environment in which staff can participate meaningfully in decision making, and in which decisions are not based upon hunch and intuition, but rather are based on rational judgments and objective data. Possibly even Samuel Gompers and Frederick Taylor would have agreed on this last point.

FOOTNOTES

1. " 'Channel 2000' View Data Test Shows Promise for Future Libraries," *American Libraries*, v. 12, no. 6 (June 1981): 303-305.
2. Frederick G. Kilgour, "The Economic Goal of Library Automation," *College and Research Libraries*, v. 30, no. 4 (July 1969):310.
3. "Trustees Set 1975/76 First-Time-Use Charges," *OCLC Newsletter*, no. 83 (June 27, 1975):1.
4. U.S. Bureau of the Census, *Statistical Abstract of the United States: 1980* (10th ed.). Washington, D.C.: Government Printing Office, 1980, p. 487.
5. Carol Learmont, "Placement and Salaries 1979: Wider Horizons," *Library Journal*, v. 105, no. 19 (November 1, 1980):2276.
6. Claude S. George, Jr., *The History of Management Thought.* Englewood Cliffs, N.J.: Prentice-Hall, 1968, p. 87.
7. *The Management Review Analysis Program*, a process developed by the Association of Research Libraries' Office of Management Studies, typifies the concern librarians have placed on improving the quality of management in academic libraries.
8. Douglas McGregor, *The Human Side of Enterprise.* New York: McGraw-Hill, 1960, Chris Argyris, *Integrating the Individual and the Organization.* New York: Wiley, 1964, Rensis Likert, *New Patterns of Management.* New York: McGraw-Hill, 1961.
9. McGregor, *op. cit.*, pp. 33-44.
10. Sudhir Kakar, *Frederick Taylor: A Study in Personality and Innovation.* Cambridge, Mass.: MIT Press, 1970, p. 2.

11. *Ibid.,* p. 3.
12. Spencer Klaw, "Frederick Winslow Taylor: The Messiah of Time and Motion," *American Heritage,* v. 30 (August 1979):32.
13. *Ibid.,* p. 38.
14. Peter Drucker, *Management: Tasks, Responsibilities, Practices.* New York: Harper & Row, 1973, p. 24.
15. George, *op. cit.,* p. 89.
16. George, *op. cit.,* p. 91.
17. George, *op. cit.,* pp. 98-99.
18. Daniel Bell, *The Coming of the Post-Industrial Society: A Venture into Social Forecasting.* New York: Basic Books, 1976.
19. See Thomas Childers, "The Test of Reference," *Library Journal,* v. 105, no. 8 (April 15, 1980): 924-928; Egill A. Halldorsson and Marjorie E. Murfin, "The Performance of Professionals and Nonprofessionals in Reference Interview," *College and Research Libraries,* v. 38, no. 5 (September 1977):385-395; Dorman Smith, "A Matter of Confidence," *Library Journal,* v. 97, no. 7 (April 1, 1972):1239-1240, for reports on studies involving quality of service and personnel providing reference service.
20. Richard M. Dougherty and Fred J. Heinritz, *Scientific Management of Library Operations,* (2nd ed.). Metuchen, N.J.: Scarecrow, 1981.
21. See Tom Kirk, "Problems in Library Instruction in Four-Year Colleges," in *Educating the Library User,* ed. by John Lubans. New York: Bowker, 1974, pp. 83-103; William Garvey and Belver C. Griffith, "Scientific Communication: Its Role in the Conduct of Research and Creation of Knowledge," *American Psychologist,* v. 26 (April 1971): 349-362; John McGregor and Raymond McInnis, "Integrating Classroom Instruction and Library Research," *Journal of Higher Education,* v. 48 (January/February 1977):17-38.

Many university presidents and other planning officials today firmly believe that a combination of the computer and microfiche will minimize or even eliminate the need for large library buildings . . . They all seem to have found relief from fund-raising problems for buildings in the writings of McLuhan, Licklider and Miller. – **Ralph Ellsworth**. *"Some Observations on the Architectural Style, Size and Cost of Libraries,"* Journal of Academic Librarianship, *v. 1, no. 5 (November 1975):19.*

Once More Into the Breach; or Tilting Windmills

Ellsworth Mason, Head of Rare Books
University of Colorado Libraries
Boulder, Colorado

It's like the many-headed Hydra of yore; strike off one head, and two more sprout from the bloody stump.[1] In 1970 the University of Denver sloughed off a good library-building consultant when Ralph Ellsworth told the vice-chancellor that, no, you couldn't put it all in a shoebox and run it with a nickel, even with micro-chips. That was the last instance of Ralph's Complaint (not to be confused with Portnoy's) that this author encountered, but now, 11 years later, the State University System of Florida has commissioned an expensive consulting firm to study its space needs and report in detail on "alternative technologies" to alleviate them. Florida at this point in history is a reasonable state engaged in many good things in higher education.[2] But a bet could be wagered that somewhere in that organizational pile sits a little man[3] who is certain that in a few years, libraries will be able to put it all into a shoe box.[4]

Ralph Ellsworth always approached building planning from a very broad perspective. As Bill Fyfe of the Chicago Office of Perkins and Will observed in an in-house resume of the Institute for the Training of Library Building Consultants, financed by the Educational Facilities Laboratories and held in Boulder in 1964, Ralph's approach is essentially as broad as campus planning.[5] Some of his greatest contributions to library buildings consisted in lateralizing fools, or incapacitating them by mousetrapping, or maneuvering them so that they fought one another, leaving the field wide open for the sane space planners to proceed unmolested. Those of us who followed in Ralph's tracks were amazed at what he could sometimes accomplish by an emphatic gesture or a strategic roar, or other devices to which he could resort when his great natural charm did not carry the day.

When Ralph went to consult on the Hofstra University Library (a two-story 20,000-square-foot building that had originally built vertical space on the second floor to add a second stack level but had neglected to supply walls and foundations strong enough to hold the added weight), Hofstra had just officially converted from a college to a university. The year before, the library committee had pronounced the library space adequate, and a new library committee had launched a quite radical proposal that a small addition be made to the existing building. With no hesitation, Ralph proclaimed in a ringing voice (I was told when I became director, shortly thereafter), "Forget about it; it's a *disaster!* Now, what Hofstra needs is *this* kind of building," which he proposed to describe in very large terms. We ended up with 125,000 square feet.

Despite this remarkable ability, Ralph, as the quotation at the head of this chapter indicates, has had to cope with ideas still held tenaciously by clients that all reasonable men would have thought long discredited. The remarkable discontinuity of human experience, the "unremembering hearts and heads" of W. B. Yeats's poetry, has always been powerful enough to cancel out a very large part of the educational effort of every generation. Not only is the wheel continually reinvented, but it seems that we are condemned each time to go through all the old preliminary stages, first trying out the three-sided wheel, then the square wheel, then the hexagon, and octagon, until finally we discover the deep satisfaction of the round, each stage in the progression heralded as a breakthrough.[6]

At times there occur very sharp breaks with what we have learned in the past. The latest of these occurred during the decade after 1965, and its fallout is still with us. As a result, many of the issues that Ralph and others battled through to a more or less successful conclusion from 1945 to 1965 have now once again raised their ugly heads.

MONUMENTALITY

This term refers not only to an imposing building made of fine materials, but, in the pre-modular sense, to a building handed to the architect as his baby, of brick and mortar as the architect's palette, with which he can express himself in terms of beauty, to glorify someone (usually) or something (occasionally), without regard for the library functions enclosed. This concept of building libraries had some validity when libraries' only requirements were high ceilings to provide enough air space, and large windows to provide enough light (when libraries were closed at night), and a few small offices and desks. This author ran such a library, vintage 1896, at Colorado College and can report its nearly complete success in keeping the students away in the 1950s.

Ralph was at the very head of the movement against monumentality, and one of the earliest to perceive the long-term implications of Angus Snead MacDonald's advocacy of a new type of structure for libraries in the 1930s, comprised of load-bearing columns arranged in regular bays that completely eliminated load-bearing walls, thus making changes in internal compartmentalization of the building easy instead of impossible. Quite ironically, the first library that he planned was a massively monumental building.

When Ralph became Librarian of the University of Colorado in 1937, he was already aware of MacDonald's new concept, at least for libraries. But he was new on the job, a comparatively young man, and the university was already committed to a monumental building. In recent years of underfunding at the University of Colorado, it has been pleasant to think back to a time when a much smaller and less affluent population stretched itself grandly to build a university as a center of pride. Part of this process required the importation of a prestigious and highly gifted architect from New York named Charles Klauder to set an architectural style that would serve, with a wide range of variations, to signal the importance of higher education and hold the campus together by the similarity of its buildings. In addition, this style had to relate to the natural beauties of the mountains, dominated by the sharply upthrust rock of the Flatiron Mountains which overlook the entire campus less than a mile away.

To these requirements, Klauder, who knew nothing except monumentality, responded with magnificent success.[7] His buildings, faced in a carefully planned pattern of flat Colorado fieldstone, in a varied light-brown tone, have a lovely texture that carries a further distance than most. This facing, and a red-tiled roofing, carried over from building to building as the campus grew, achieve a more complete feeling of integration than that of any of the older universities in the country. Klauder's buildings are handsome and imposing; the early ones are full of delightful architectural details. His fieldstone walls are a foot and a half thick, and both the inner and outer walls of his larger buildings are load-bearing.

Norlin Library was the fourth Klauder building planned for the University of Colorado and by far his most impressive when it opened, in 1939. This massive five-story building is approached from its broadest side up a flight of wide steps, across a wide limestone plaza, past huge limestone pillars supporting a frieze that bears, cut into limestone, this paraphrase of Cicero: "Who Knows Only His Own Generation Remains Always a Child," through marble-framed bronze doors, over which is the inscription cut in stone: "Enter Here the Timeless Fellowship of the Human Spirit." Flanking the main entrance at a distance on the plaza, butted into the face of the building, are two huge semicircular marble basins, each with three stylized lion heads above with mouths open to pour water into the basins, now inoperable.

Directly inside the entrance is a series of pillars 18 inches in diameter, and at each end of the entrance lobby, running from basement to attic, are two huge main staircases, oval in cross-section, with handsome ornamental handrails that make a grand design when viewed down their center stairwell from the upper floors. Those fixed outer and inner walls, and those grand staircases, and those entrance-lobby columns, and the tier-built stacks behind the entrance lobby, posed major problems in running this library when Ralph Ellsworth returned, in 1958, to take it over for a second time, after 15 years away from it.[8]

Little of Norlin Library reflects the convictions of Ralph Ellsworth, and if anything was needed to solidify his commitment to modular construction, five years of running Norlin, which was already resisting physical changes before he left, certainly did it. His next building at the State University of Iowa, was the first sizable modular library built in this country. It threw as offspring the first modular library built in Europe,[9] and Ralph's book written with Donald Bean, in 1948, was the first book on modular library planning.[10]

By 1960 the understanding that all library buildings of any size should be modular buildings was complete and accepted as a given fact by all good architects, although there has been one lapse, a kind of menopausal pregnancy in the history of monumentality, in a fixed-function library by John Johansen built for Clark University in 1969. Librarians in this country take modularity so much for granted that it may seem strange that monumental buildings, or major elements inherent in the old monuments, are still with us.

However, modular libraries are to a great extent a response to the demand for open access to library collections, a policy that is general only in the United States. England has only recently begun to catch up. In a study of recent British academic library buildings, Anthony Vaughan, a significant voice in British librarianship, regards modular libraries "as being situated in space and time as a specific response to a specific view of academic librarianship" which is not shared, as he points out, by most Continental librarians or by a range of architects who consider it more important to provide social spaces for readers than functional spaces for librarians.[11]

If one can accept this view of modular buildings as a specific answer to specific conditions that may change in the future, then one will not be surprised that atavisms of monumentality or library elements that always accompanied monumentality continued throughout the sixties and seventies and are returning for serious consideration once again. The most numerous of these, in the experience of this author, involves the use of tier-built stacks. Before mingling of readers and books was common practice, tier-built stacks were used to save the costs of floor loads, with all the book weight being absorbed on a slab at the bottom of the stack and very light floor loads provided for seating and work and traffic areas. These buildings, of course, were much cheaper to build than later buildings with 150-pound live load floors throughout the building.

In renovations of the University of Colorado, the Ohio State University, and the Texas A & M University libraries in the 1970s, tier-built stacks were newly installed in two libraries, and old ones retained in the third, because of budgetary and floor-space restrictions. The University of Colorado librarians were under pressure from the very top university administrators to retain entirely the old ten floors of tier-built stacks, ultimate removal of which would have turned that building into one that was pleasant to be in and easy to use. The triple-tier stacks that were built in the new addition to the original building not only make about half a million volumes easily accessible; the use of wood end panels throughout also makes them quite pleasant to use.

One can expect more and more use of tier-built stacks in the future, possibly accompanied by lighter floor loads for the surrounding seating, which the three buildings discussed here did not have. The lack of uniform floor loads in the building will, of course, limit changes that can be made in the building in the future, especially the ability to convert reader space to stack space, the most frequent conversion observed over the past two decades.

This author has had to argue not infrequently over the past ten years in favor of totally uniform floor loads for libraries. Everyone, except librarians who have seen dozens of radical space-use changes in a period of five years, is sure that there are some locations in a building that will never be used for shelving. I have seen one not quite completely modular library seriously impeded in planning an addition and renovation, because the entrance-traffic and circulation-desk areas were supported by columns that, although spaced in a modular fashion, were built below normal strength for the rest of the building. The reason, which was thought obvious then and is wrong now, was that no one would ever use that area for book shelving. Last year I encountered opposition to uniform floor loads for libraries from both architects and state officials in Florida. As academic budgets continue to contract, this will become an increasingly serious problem for library planners.

Monumental staircases were installed in a number of libraries in the 1970s bearing disabilities in their future of a major kind when radical space shifts are needed. They sometimes are a major architectural feature of the building (U.S. Air Force Academy, the Countway Library of Medicine at Harvard), but more often are an architect's bullheaded folly (Colorado State University, Arizona State University).

And, of course, monumental buildings, but without fixed walls, have continued to be built whenever the university's focus in the project is not the library itself. Some buildings in the 1970s were aimed at fund raising (New York University, Bobst Library), Hollywood Drama (University of California, San Diego), or the architect's reputation (University of Chicago Law Library, by Saarinen; Northwestern University, by Skidmore, Owings and Merrill; and Yeshiva University, by Armand Bartos). All of these, though modular buildings, incorporate major disabilities, because the focus in their planning was not on creating a building that would reach out to help library users or the staff that serves them. A nicely balanced pair, one on each coast, are the Bobst Library at New York University, with a 100-foot-square hole in the middle of it, from its floor to its ceiling ten stories above, and the University of California, San Diego, which has a nearly solid core area of about the same size in the middle of it.

Libraries are always headed for trouble whenever a university hires an architect with a lofty reputation in order to drape their enterprise with the glory of his name. In such cases, the architect will call the shots and grandly dismiss anything that would stifle the architect's fancy, as Klauder put it to the University of Colorado 50 years ago. While one would think that lack of money would shut off this kind of trend, there is underway at present a very large addition to a central university library building – whose corncob gothic style defies addition – coping with the requirement of the administrator who obtained funds for it: it had to be the tallest building on campus, a requirement that is working mightily against the building's success. With the ever-increasing disappearance of assertive library directors, who are no longer prized by university presidents, situations in which the architect will overbear the library planners will become more common.

The acceptance of modular construction instead of monumental construction produced much cheaper buildings, not only because of the decrease in ornamentation used, a factor that led, in its turn, to some extremely sterile buildings, but because it used much lower ceilings, incorporating any given square footage in a greatly reduced cubic footage. For every foot of vertical rise of a building that can be omitted, a significant percentage of reduction in construction costs and a comparable reduction in heating and cooling costs are realized.

The ability to use eight- to eight-and-a-half-foot ceilings depended on engineering developments in air-handling systems that pumped air throughout a building, removing its dependence on the air volume within rooms (the reason for high ceilings), and in electric lighting systems that could provide good reading light far removed from exterior windows. Both of these technologies contained problems of their own, which we thought had been solved in the 1960s but which are now returning.

AIR-HANDLING SYSTEMS

Older buildings used very high windows to provide light for daytime reading. They were also the only effective means to freshen air, by opening them, since seepage of air provides too low a rate of turnover to maintain an adequate oxygen supply for any highly populated reading room.[12] These large and heavy windows were usually double-hung, that slid up to open; between their weight, some wood warpage through weathering, and the friction that resulted from the accumulation of years' of grime, they were always hard to open.

Even more romantic, they often let birds flutter in, since the large openings of the windows were usually left unscreened. At Coburn Library, Colorado College, the lower sills of the windows were about at waist height. For air relief, they were opened about a foot on nice days, and with predictable regularity, birds would come in and immediately fly to the upper part of the room, which had a 20-foot ceiling. They then began what often turned out to be a week's fluttering to get out again, sometimes at the upper part of the windows, where they were far above the reach of librarians standing on ladders, and sometimes winging their merry way across the free airspace of the room, would en route drip their favors on objects below – sometimes books and sometimes people. (Their end was often mysterious; they simply disappeared. It was assumed that they had found the window opening by themselves, and to my knowledge no corpses or skeletons were ever found in that building. Usually they would tire themselves by struggling until they slid down to the lower reaches of the window shades and we could catch them and release them a ways from the library building, hoping they would head in another direction.)

The windows facing west in this building exposed a 40-square-foot glass panel to the Colorado sun for about three hours of the afternoon, and even window shades did not greatly alleviate the heat, since once the glass heated up, it radiated its heat right through the shades.[13] It was partly to alleviate problems like these that forced-ventilation air-supply systems were developed, complete with chilling to provide what was called "air conditioning." These systems had their own problems, which, in libraries, were pretty well resolved, in terms of knowing what should be done, by 1965. One problem was the mentality of the clients, who – in relatively temperate breezy areas, such as the upper Pacific coast, or dry areas, such as Colorado – believed, in contradiction to their skin feeling, that they did not need chilling in their systems. In a sweep of coastal high-school libraries below San Francisco, this author found that this was everywhere a tenet of faith. Within the next ten years, about half of these libraries, always parts of school buildings, lapsed into heresy and installed chilling.

In Colorado, a lame-duck governor of the state, with wisdom that would have been questioned by Solomon, issued a fiat in 1971 forbidding any new public building constructed in that fair state to install chilling in its air-handling system. This fiat still stands, and the first library built within its constrictions measured the temperature at 138 degrees in one corner of its main floor during its first summer of operation. One result of this restriction is the use of swamp coolers that reduce temperatures by the evaporation of water dripped across the path of moving air. This it does reasonably well. It also increases the humidity in the building well above the mold point. But, although the need for chilling systems in library buildings is acknowledged, since they are mainly used in summers, budgets increasingly convince library administrators that they are unnecessary, to the detriment of library use.

It is also known that in humid areas of this country, which includes nearly everywhere, humidity-removal units are required to keep humidity below the mold point (about 70 percent relative humidity), since mold, often in barely perceptible form, has destroyed more books throughout history than anything else except the acid inherent in paper.[14] Air-conditioning systems pass incoming air over chilled coils, to cool it. This process of reducing the temperature of air makes it lose a considerable amount of its moisture, but in areas where the outside humidity frequently rises above 70 percent, the moisture content of a building will gradually rise above 70 percent and remain there until the heat in the building is turned on in the fall, if no humidity-removal equipment is used in the air-handling system.

Humidity removal requires heating of the moist air before it is chilled. To budget and plant directors, the idea of preheating air before it is chilled has always been horrifying, and in the present academic budget squeeze, the chances of having units installed are miniscule. Exactly at a time when preservation of books is becoming a national concern, libraries are moving to conditions that are less and less satisfactory for preserving them.

During the 1960s, filtration systems for keeping dust and noxious gases out of buildings were developed to a highly efficient level. Dust can be minimized by using a good pad prefilter, to catch larger dust particles, backed by bag filters that provide a range of filtration efficient up to 95 percent. Properly designed electronic filters can achieve about that same level of filtration. To remove noxious gases requires passing the air through an activated charcoal filter as well.

Every barrier in the form of filters placed in the air flow slows down the passage of air and requires more powerful fans, which are more expensive to buy and more expensive to run. All filters must be replaced at regulary scheduled intervals, since serious damage to air-conditioning equipment can result from clogged filters, and good filters are expensive. For all these cost reasons, getting a proper filtration system installed in a library's air-handling system was always a matter of skillfully persuading the decision makers who controlled the planning. In the present academic condition of empty coffers, it has become nearly impossible. One more blow to book preservation nationally.

During the 1960s, there was universal acceptance of the use of overhead air diffusers in air-handling systems. These diffusers, if well designed, offered the great advantages of supplying tempered air comfortably and of being available in place for supplying air to rooms that were enclosed after the building was originally constructed. They were an important element in achieving convertibility in any building. In rooms that required a high rate of air exchange (heat-producing rooms), air-supply ceilings were used. Tempered air flows into the room through thousands of inlets in the ceiling.

To supply overhead diffusing of either kind, an elaborate and expensive system of air ducts must be installed, tailor-made, within the dropped ceilings of buildings, and the cost of metal-working labor is extremely high. The alternative is to throw air from the edge of an area directly across the area through long, narrow lateral ducts located somewhere above head level. This method requires a much smaller system of ducts and is much cheaper, but it tends to produce more noise of air passage, and the variation of temperatures achieved from the point of discharge of the air to the extreme edge of its flow is considerable. In addition, this system makes it impossible to enclose open areas of a building without providing a separate system of ducts and diffusers in the ceiling of the new room, thus militating, through cost, against making building changes. Nevertheless, with all of its disadvantages, this system (which we knew in the 1960s was the less desirable) is beginning to be used increasingly in buildings.[15]

In the 1960s, it was universal practice to use a central source for air distribution for the entire building. Unusually large buildings would have two systems, one in the basement and one on the top floor. In either case, the noise and maintenance disturbances were located far from any library work or use areas. These systems required very large vertical riser ducts to connect on each floor with the system of horizontal ducts that led to ceiling diffusers. They also required very large distribution fans, expensive to buy and to run, and very large amounts of floor space and even larger amounts of cubic space in the building.

The alternative, which central air distribution replaced, was a system of dispersed air-distribution units, located in four to six small mechanical rooms on each floor of the building, each feeding a portion of the floor through a simplified system of ducts, usually unconcealed and usually provided with lateral-throw air ducts, as already described above. A dispersed-unit system of air distribution is much cheaper than a central air-distribution system. If properly provided with quiet fan units and proper wall and door insulation and sound suppressors at the mechanical-room end of the horizontal ducts, they provide a satisfactory system, whose sound intrusion on reading and work areas will be minimal, although the frequent tromping in and out for maintenance must be endured.

The comfort provided by such systems is far less uniform than that of a central air-diffusion system. Nevertheless, they are now being used frequently in library buildings, to save money, and the necessary sound-suppressing requirements are not being provided in many cases, with serious sound intrusions on reading areas the result.

LIGHTING

Keyes Metcalf has given a full account of our gradual creep into higher-intensity library illumination in the United States during this century. There is no question but that our reactions to library lighting intensities are conditioned to a considerable degree by those we commonly encounter in our daily life outside the library. Nevertheless, there have been considerable improvements in the handling of lighting in libraries over the past 50 years. My four undergraduate years at Yale, from 1934 to 1938, were spent under wretchedly bad lighting conditions. The study lamp on my dormitory desk was so tall (and I was so short) that it blared continuously in my eyes, with the most rampant form of glare. I didn't understand until much later why I always felt uncomfortable while studying in my room. In the Sterling Memorial Library, only one year old in 1934, the lighting intensity on the reading tables of its great Reference Reading Room was about five footcandles, although the quality was reasonably good. Not only did the room feel gloomy, with a vast area of darkness in the upper part of the high-ceilinged room; the remarkably rich and fine details of wood carving and stone carving located throughout that room were largely obscured.[16] In the stacks between aisles were incandescent 40-watt bulbs set into white enamelled open cages in the ceiling that provided no more than 20 footcandles on the average, and made those stack areas always feel dim and dingy, brand-new though they were. The best lighting was that provided by low-wattage bulbs in standing reading lamps that flanked lounge chairs in the recreational reading room of that building, and these low-intensity local lights produced the effect of a conservative New York gentleman's club, which the architect probably intended, for people who did not want to be disturbed and didn't want to see much except the page they were reading. During the period when such inadequate lighting was provided, it was a rare book that was printed in a type size that would be considered reasonably large by today's standards.

While proper design of the lighting fixtures and their placement in a room could always achieve good quality with incandescent lighting fixtures, my impression is that light quality was taken even more casually by those who used incandescent fixtures than by those who used fluorescent fixtures. The difficulties inherent in their use were quickly alleviated by the virtual disappearance of incandescent lighting in public buildings in a few short years, caused by the drastic increase in the efficiency of the use of electrical current by fluorescent tubes and by the dramatic decrease in the heat that they produced. Since the cost of electricity was one of the more important factors that limited the number of incandescent fixtures formerly used, and since the cost of the chilling equipment used in air-conditioned buildings depends on their heat load, the large advantages of fluorescent fixtures quickly took over the field of building lighting.[17] The ability to run them at greatly reduced cost led to a willingness to provide more fixtures in a building, exactly at a time when the area on a floor of a typical building was greatly expanding. The willingness and the need coinciding, the use of general ambient lighting in buildings was made possible.[18]

By the 1960s, the provision of general ambient lighting throughout library reading areas was general practice, and very little local lighting was provided except in library work areas. This was partly because of the bad conditions previously generated by local lighting; partly because of persistent propaganda by the electric lighting companies, which became outrageously excessive at one point in the 1960s; partly because of the national affluence; but to a considerable degree, it was because of the clear realization that the internal feeling of the building, and the contribution that architectural details and interior design could make to it, depended largely on providing general lighting. With one exception – the addition of undershelf lights to carrels to help avert shadows – it was hard to sell local lighting to library planners even when it was desirable for special uses or special esthetic effects in limited areas of the library.

General lighting was also valued for the flexibility it added to the building. If properly planned, it allowed any area to be converted to a reading area, without changing lighting fixtures. The concept of lighting flexibility was so firmly embedded that at the University of Guelph, in Canada, stack lights were hung on the stacks and carrel lights in the carrels, to the exclusion of general lighting in a large part of the ceiling areas of the building, which approximated the uncomfortable dimness of parts of the upper floors.[19]

The effect of general lighting on the feeling of a building depends on the light sources having been arranged so they are as unobtrusive as possible, and on the proper-colored fluorescent tubes having been used to enhance the interior design, which in almost all cases requires the use of warm white tubes. Over the past decade, these elements, which were known to be highly desirable, have come undone. In almost every library I have visited in recent years, a number of the lighting fixtures have been left dark to save energy. The esthetic result is about the equivalent of a gap-toothed smile on a ten-year old. This is especially true when the dark spots on the ceiling are not in a regular pattern, which is usually the case, plant-department employees not being hired for their art talent.

In addition, in almost every case I have noted, the fluorescent tubes have been a mixture of warm white and daylight-colored tubes. When used exclusively, either of these tubes appears almost colorless, the daylight producing a harsher, slightly whiter effect. But when they are used in juxtaposition (most horrifying when mixed in the same fixture), they emphasize their difference, the warm white appearing an unpleasant orange-yellow, and the daylight an unpleasant greenish blue. Since daylight tubes are about half the price of warm white tubes, they are bound to oust the latter throughout the land. The result will be to flatten the effect of the color scheme and the feeling of shapes in the building considerably, thus effectively throwing away half the cost of the interior design.

One possible way out of this dilemma, which is otherwise unavoidable through institutional plant policy, is for the library director to raise two or three thousand dollars a year in gift money, to cover the additional cost of the warm white tubes that will have to be replaced annually. But worse may be hard upon us, since very recently much cheaper phosphors have been developed for use in manufacturing fluorescent tubes that will be even cheaper, and will appear harsher in feeling and be even more destructive to the appearance of colors lit by them.

These deteriorations will occur in all installations of general lighting, but the idea of general lighting itself is under attack, through cost pressures, and once again we seem to be heading back to the deprived state of local lighting. When I was planning a book on library buildings, in 1978, I consulted the campus expert on lighting at the University of Colorado's College of Engineering, a college of high repute in the nation. That lighting expert is very highly regarded in his field and frequently used as a lighting consultant. He was convinced that the trend is rapidly going away from general lighting, for libraries or any other building, and recommended that I adopt the practice of encouraging the use of low-intensity general lighting in a library, about 30 footcandles, with local task lighting of various kinds to be used at reader and work stations.

I chose not to take his advice, as my chapter on lighting in that book reveals. One reason was my visit a few years earlier to the Williams College Library, whose lighting is a throwback to that former condition now heartily espoused by my engineering colleague, because of costs of electricity. It had achieved the same kind of dismal feeling, in areas where it was applied, that I had remembered from 40 years ago, and the disadvantages of the local incandescent reader lamps were compounded by equipping them with metal lampshades that functioned as effective heat radiators when the bulb was lit. We may in time get back to the cave but call it a library.

PLANNING BASES

So far, we have considered a trend back to earlier, less desirable patterns of monumental architecture, air-handling, and lighting, all of which involve design and technological problems. But overshadowing them all is a radical shift in the information bases on which libraries are planned. Keyes Metcalf began contemporary library building planning when he started to count and measure the space required by objects in existing libraries, computing how much space would be required for them in a new building and how much additional space would be required for expansion of precisely calculated increases in collection, readers, and staff. This defined basis by which informed librarians projected space replaced a vague guess-at-it method, usually in the hands of the architect.

By the 1960s, library programming was carefully based on such information as the nature of the college or university, what its academic intentions were, what it thought it would be doing a defined number of years ahead (for which the library was being planned, and how it fitted its library collection and services into its plans. These general intentions were further refined in the library by careful projections of collection growth over the defined period of the future library's life, taking into consideration the shift in curriculum expected, and changes in the number of students anticipated. The staff stations, including those for part-time and student workers, required in each library unit to handle the volume of tasks anticipated, new service points among them, were projected.

By careful stimulation, those involved in the library operation were worked up into a ferment of projecting what should happen in the new library building, in fairly precise terms. On the basis of these, an experienced librarian or library consultant would detail the furniture and equipment needed to carry out the programs in each unit, carefully estimate the space they would require in an efficient layout, and arrive at a total net square footage requirement for the new building, which was easily convertible to a gross square footage, on which the building's cost could be estimated. If it happened, as it sometimes did, that the library funding fell short of this cost, cuts could be made in the building, with sensitivity, based on very careful thinking about its projected needs.

Today, the library planning almost invariably begins with a budget figure that represents the only figure possible. It fixes the square footage before the requirements can begin to be projected or divided, and radically revises the problem of writing the program. The money available is always far too little, and the square footage it will build has to be balanced between competing elements in the library that must be carefully weighed in terms of one another and of the whole library, to achieve the best possible combination of library processes and services within the budget. This is less a process of projection and more a process of bringing the library planners into enlightened negotiations with one another. It is a far less precise, far more chancy process of planning. In a very real sense, it is a reversion to the selection of an arbitrary square footage and designing around it that we had discarded by the end of the fifties.

MICROFORMS

Though many other aspects of library planning are going back to where they were before – including shorter stack-range centers, more multiple seating, seating for a smaller percentage of student FTE, structural steel frames, less unused conduiting (the new technology being easy to accommodate) – I would like to end with a consideration of part of Ralph's Complaint that served as prologue to this article. Microforms have always been yearned for as a substitute for space. The matter of microforms is not reverting to the past, and it has never moved to the future. It is right where it was when I first encountered it, in 1938, sitting on dead center. At that time, the Yale University library, with its very strong research collection, had less than two standard microfilm cases of microform material, mostly of very rare books located in England, France, or Germany. Then, as at all times, the dedicated scholar was grateful to get in any form, including, presumably, chocolate lettering in pudding, information that he needed and could not get readily in any other form.

In the 1930s, it was Fremont Rider heralding nationally the use of microcards as the salvation of libraries, saving them in the nick of time from gobbling up preternatural portions of the globe. My generation watched with interest the general disinclination of library users to respond to microforms, but we were sure that, given time and exposure, the resistance would fade. We were wrong. Every library generation has sprouted a champion of the microforms, urged on by commercial suppliers, encouraged by grants from salvationist governments, plowing their way back and forth across the country, preaching the gospel from Chautauqua platforms called workshops, wasting ghastly sums of taxpayers' money, and all in vain.

All have been convinced that in mankind there could not dwell such profound evil as distaste for microforms, that in fact it was the fault of someone or something outside the nonuser that inhibited the true flowering of his natural bent for microforms. Most recently, the inhibitors have been the soulless library planner, lacking in true understanding of the mystical importance of microforms. The panacea is now to be the Proper Environment. Dress up the microform areas, move them out of dimmed areas that make the microforms easier to read, pretty them up, make them into rose gardens, and then just stand by and let the student addicts rush in for their daily fix of microforms.

The only thing wrong with all of this is that it leaves out of consideration the preferences of human beings. Microforms now, as always, hold an honorable if limited position in the spectrum of informs, as bearers of high bulk, low-use information. But for the general range of library uses, they are less acceptable now than in 1938, when I first began to observe their use, because reproduction in full-size paper form is so commonly obtained from the Xerox machine and its siblings. People do not like microforms now any more than they used to, because the physical factors connected with their use, almost all the physical factors, are uncongenial to most human beings – the physical feel of the materials, the sounds of the machines, the time required for adjusting the forms to the proper position – the brain-scraping blur of moving film, the upside-down wrong-side-right position of fiche – the words continually slipping out of focus, the crick-neck tilt of most screens, the intense eye-popping background lighting of positive film. In the light of all these inhibitors, it is unrealistic to believe that we will greatly increase drop-in use of microforms if we only will pretty up the area and bring it out into the open, where it will be harder to read most film.

There is a possibility for microforms in the future that I will follow with interest, as I have followed developments in microforms for more than 40 years. This possibility is inherent in the phrase in Ralph's Complaint, "a combination of computer and microfiche." It is now technically possible to combine the two, with microfiche retrieved on-call from carousels, converted from visual to digital form, transferred to a computer terminal, and reconverted to visual form or printed out on paper if so desired. This process, though limited in the amount of information it can store at present, would remove most of the factors that presently keep people away from microforms. It would make possible quick and painless location of the desired information and completely remove the necessity of handling it.

When this process becomes usable in libraries, I will observe users' response to Computerfiche to see whether it makes a great difference, because I join the stupid administrators so properly scored by Ralph in wishing that this kind of information storage were possible. If for no other reason than the fact that, with the current near-monopoly of "perfect binding" in books, and their rapid shattering in use, and the impossibility of ever being able to afford their rebinding on the scale of their disintegration, within ten years, most libraries will consist of piles of pages loosely tied together with twine. Unless we can find some substitute for them that people will actually use.

FOOTNOTES

1. This article, if you please, will be written in the rollicking style that Ralph Ellsworth would have used if he hadn't gone to Oberlin. Especially in the footnotes, which will highlight in various ways the life of Ralph Ellsworth.
2. Florida is one of the few states still expanding its system of higher education, thanks to the influx of cold Yankee bones. Moreover, Gainesville has recently bought a spectacular collection of American literature from a Boston Brahmin family, right out from under the nose of everyone, with its president acting as the main financial driver of the plot. Even more important, it is the chosen home, when he's home, of the New York-raised novelist John D. MacDonald, whose works I assiduously collect. How can you fault a state like that?
3. At 5 '6 ", Mason is no enemy of the little man. This reminds me of the time in 1971 when Ralph (6 feet tall) and I spoke at a conference at the Pennsylvania Military Academy Library, and a totally repulsive furniture salesman insisted that, despite height, all people measure the same from the waist up when sitting. We disdained his attempt to dragoon us out onto the floor to sit on a table but later tried it out in private. Of course Ralph's shoulders loomed six inches higher than mine in that position.
4. Within the brief compass of my multifarious experience, five brand-new colleges have each, sequentially and originally, invented the idea of supplying to each student a complete library on microform in a shoe box. Harvard in a hat! P.S. Not one of them ever did it. P.P.S. Three of these colleges didn't even get off the ground, indicating the level of incompetence at which this kind of idea originates.
5. Since Fyfe's report also contained some kind remarks about me, a Xerox copy of it was sent me by a friend, about eight years later, in the wondrous way that the world has of knitting itself together, given time. Ralph was the leader of that Institute, joined by Keyes Metcalf and Bill Jesse. This triumvirate, for lack of others, virtually owned the field of library-building consulting in 1964. The Institute included some remarkable experiences, such as Ruth Weinstock of EFL ripping up and totally reorganizing the schedule on the very first morning, because she did not think it intensive enough. Such as Ellsworth, Metcalf, and Jesse offering to take along any member of the gathering on their consulting assignments as observers, and none of us ever taking advantage of that remarkable opportunity.

   I think that my standing as a librarian was considerably enhanced during that Institute, when we entered the Colorado College Library (which I had left as Librarian a year before) to view its beauties, and my former circulation librarian ran out to give me a big hug and kiss. I believe it was Steve McCarthy who remarked "*Friendly* library, isn't it?" Even more intimate , my marriage to a fine librarian named Joan Shinew, which took place in the Colorado College chapel just two days after the Institute ended, was brilliantly successful, demonstrating how much one can sometimes learn at a brief Institute.

6. Among the literary giants of this century, Yeats and Joyce have been the most aware of the progressive disintegration of experience, each success incorporating seeds of its own destruction, in a cyclical manner. Passages like the following occur repeatedly throughout Yeats's later poems:

> Another Troy must rise and set,
> Another lineage feed the crow,
> Another Argo's painted prow
> Drive to a flashier bauble yet.

7. When Ralph championed the idea of a modular building, Klauder told the university Board of Regents that the concept "stifled the architect's fancy" and that if they wanted him to use it, he would resign his life contract with the University. End of dispute.

8. Ralph is the only library director I know who left a building that he planned before it got into real difficulty, then returned to reap its mature range of problems. Certain other features of Norlin Library made it the most difficult building to use I have ever seen (of more than 550 I have studied), I was charged with planning its second expansion and renovation in 1972. It was originally designed as a divisional library, a plan abandoned early in its history. Its tier-built stacks had been erected to full height in three different stages, under two managements, and the stack stairs were not coordinated. It had been added to in 1965, with a budget that required retaining the old exterior fieldstone walls. No operation in 1972 was of proper size, and it was impossible to expand through the fixed elements to make any of them the right size.

   With an 80,000-square-foot addition, designed by an ingenious architect (Ted Wofford of Murphy, Downey, Wofford & Richman, St. Louis), this was converted into a very pleasant library that is easy to use. This was achieved by making the main entrance one floor lower, on the opposite side of the building, and removing and flooring over the original tier-built stacks. This example taught me never to abandon an old library as impossible to expand, without writing a total program for the requirements of the new combined library and letting a good architect determine the possibility of adding to the old one.

9. At Krakow University, planned by Dr. Wladyslaw Piasecki, on whose piracy of the Ellsworth-Bean book on modular libraries, see Ralph E. Ellsworth, *Ellsworth on Ellsworth* [a vilely unesthetic title]. Metuchen, N.J.: Scarecrow, 1980, p. 50.
10. Donald E. Bean and Ralph E. Ellsworth, *Modular Planning for College and Small Libraries.* Iowa City: Privately printed by the authors, 1948.
11. Anthony Vaughan, "The Ideology of Flexibility: A Study of Recent British Academic Library Buildings," *Journal of Librarianship,* v. 11 (October 1979):277-293. See also the library-buildings issue of the International Association of Technological University Libraries, *Proceedings,* 11th, 1978 (Loughborough, I.A.T.U.L., 1979) to realize how unconventional open-stack libraries still are on the continent.
12. The College Library area of Norlin Library, University of Colorado, contained seats for more than double the number of occupants for which it was originally designed. Physically undesirable in almost every way, it was nicely renovated from 1970 to 1972. The two largest factors in its success were the increase in its lighting intensity and the increase of its main air-inlet ducts to more than double their original size. The effect of inadequate air turnover is a feeling of logyness, which produces inefficient study and a tendency to leave the library. Physiologically, the lowering of the oxygen content of a room results in a lessened supply to the brain of oxygen, which in ways still not well understood seems to be a critical element in fueling that complex organ.
13. I have described elsewhere the difficulties inflicted by the large west-facing windows of Sterling Memorial Library, Yale University, in "Back to the Cave, or Some Buildings I have Known," *Library Journal,* v. 94, no. 22 (December 15, 1969):4353-4357.
14. Until very recent times there was no attempt to install humidity-removal equipment in the air-tempering systems of rare-book rooms anywhere in the South. It is possible that Paul Mellon's private library, constructed in Virginia, with Paul Mellon's private resources, is the only properly atmospherically controlled library in the entire South. It is deeply distressing to anyone really concerned with rare books and fine bindings to walk into those rare-book rooms and be overwhelmed with a strong odor of mold in the air.

On Long Island, where relative humidity can reach as high as 100 percent at times and can hold at 90 percent for a week on end, the humidity in the Hofstra University Library could gradually rise until, by the middle of July, doors could not be fully closed, a condition that persisted until the heat was turned on in October.

Anyone who buys books from England and the Continent knows how much damage mold can cause in paper within a few years. Its effect in Europe has been even worse in art. The museums in Italy that house their great art collections have long ago given up any attempt to reduce humidity in their atmosphere to an acceptable level for museums. The consequent destruction to paper, cloth, pigments, canvas, and picture frames has been incalculable. It has especially damaged the paintings on the buildings themselves – walls, columns, and ceilings – which at this point in history have been retouched so many times there remains little if any of the painting made by original creative geniuses. Art history is consequently becoming more and more a fictitious field.

15. We have seen the exact counterpart to this technological decline in the field of university teaching. At the end of World War II, there was a radical surge of enrollment into colleges and universities of students financed by the G.I. bill for veterans, which for the first time in our history made higher education accessible to students from families with less than an upper-middle class income. Through a shortage of Ph.D.-educated teachers, in desperation, the universities began to use teaching assistants, graduate students on their way to getting their doctoral degrees. Although necessary if we were not to exclude from higher education vast numbers of students, this system was nevertheless clearly recognized as a highly undesirable "temporary" expedient, because teaching assistants are undereducated for the task, and their preparation time is diluted by their own collateral study and writing projects. This system has now been economically locked into university structures at the expense of the quality of education offered by the universities. There would be no glut of Ph.D.s in any academic field if high standard requirements for teachers in universities were to be re-established.

16. This same process of hiding unusual beauty under a bushel, through lack of light, was repeated some 30 years later at Yale in the Beinecke Rare Book and Manuscript Library. At the north and south ends of the mezzanine that surrounds the brilliantly lit glass-faced rare-book vault on the entrance level of that handsome building are two magnificent tables, made of Italian burl olive, which is rich in both its grain and color, a rare and extremely expensive, luxurious wood. When I first visited that building in 1963, preparing to write an article on it, the overhead lighting (incandescent spotlights, controlled by a rheostat) was turned so dim that I couldn't see the tabletops clearly until I brought a flashlight to look at them. I pointed out this obscurity in my article, which apparently was read, since the lighting was brighter and the tables more visible when I visited again some years later. But in recent years, apparently for reasons of economy, the lighting is again dim and these lovely tables again obscured.

17. A recent exception to this practice was the east-wing addition to the National Gallery of Art, Washington, D.C., financed by Paul Mellon, who seems to be creeping into this article, though I had not intended him to come in at all. Mellon insisted that no fluorescent lights be used anywhere in this addition, and since he was paying the bill for the air conditioning, and since his father had built the original art gallery and contributed a large part of its original collection, no one bothered to

argue with him. In its work areas, when I was consulting on the library portion of this addition, incandescent downlights, which I have been fighting for 20 years in library planning, were the predominant fixtures. In reading areas, they cause high reflected glare, and I recommended that they change them in the ceiling of the library reading room. But they didn't.

18. In 1939, the use of fluorescent lighting in Norlin Library, Ralph's first library building, was among its earliest uses in any public building. However, the craft of its use had not yet penetrated the skull of whomever Klauder hired as an electrical engineer. The fixtures consisted of a continuous strip of tubes completely enclosed in an architect-designed outer ornamental metal tube, consisting of a Classical-design motif used on other building ornaments. These fixture covers nearly prevented the emergence of light from the fixtures. Despite the ravages of time, a few of these fixtures were still in the building when it was renovated and completely relit, in 1976, and these covers, which were quite handsome, were snapped up by the alert when they were torn down.

19. This library also developed, in the course of its planning, a kind of dolly-jack that permits the moving of these book stacks, each detached from the others, while they are fully loaded. It is hard to see much advantage in this very expensive system of stacks. But, not to be outdone, the University of Sherbrooke library, in Quebec, proceeded to design independent stacks that could be moved separately when loaded by an *air-cushion platform*. Can't you just see the dust flying?

*G*iven the funds to do the kind of work they know they should be doing, librarians can move creatively in an environment of updating teaching methods, new learning technologies, and good academic planning—**Ralph Ellsworth.** *"The Contribution of the Library to Improving Instruction,"* Library Journal, v. 94, no. 10 (May 15, 1969):1955.

Evaluation Design:
Some Methodological Observations
and Suggestions[1]

John Lubans, Jr., Associate Director
University of Houston Libraries
Houston, Texas

Working with Ralph Ellsworth is memorable, particularly in developing new services for library users. One example: I'd struggled with the rationale of a research proposal for a day and hadn't gotten anywhere. Ralph took a look at it and put it right in a few minutes. The result was a grant to the University of Colorado from the Council on Library Resources and the National Endowment for the Humanities for a major 5-year experiment in library use instruction, the evaluation of which is briefly discussed later on in this chapter.

The combination of Ellsworth and innovative ways of creating intelligent use of libraries can be traced throughout his career. A relevant example is his chapter in a 1974 anthology, *Educating the Library User*, on the library building's contribution. Here, as elsewhere, he stresses orienting the *library*, the building and the people, to the user. This desire to see the library used and its intellectual resources *exploited* is shared by many librarians in all types of libraries working in the field of user education.

It has been remarked that "reader instruction is the most written about and least performed activity in the whole of librarianship."[2] The author might argue with such a sweeping statement but not about the *evaluation* of user education. While evaluation is endorsed as a basic principle of instructional programs, it is the least implemented.

This chapter attempts to review the state of the art in evaluation, and its purposes and benefits, particularly in the gaining of credibility for user education. In hopes of creating more awareness and triggering discussion, quite a bit of attention is paid to the problems found in evaluation efforts. Finally, the positive developments in our work and the growth this portends will be discussed.

The premises for this discussion are, first, that evaluation is in a developmental phase akin to its state of the art in other service professions and, second, that the evidence of user education's positive impact is accumulating, albeit slowly and sporadically.

THE VALUE AND PURPOSE OF EVALUATION

Perhaps it is the multipurpose aspect of evalution that causes our inertia. Five goals of evaluation come to mind. We use evaluation to

1. Assess the impact of instruction on the student
2. Modify instructional programs
3. Sell library use instruction to others
4. Upgrade methods of instruction
5. Advance educational knowledge

What may confuse this already complicated undertaking is that to achieve these goals, one may evaluate or take measurements at one or more strategic points, each one of which requires different measurements

1. The overall library system. (Circulation data; e.g., per capita and by subject, reference questions, library staff and materials budgets, other unobtrusive measures such as staffing patterns, and user traffic. More specifically, have user/nonuser attitudes changed from one "opinion" survey to the next?)
2. The instructional programs. (Questionnaire or interview data from participants, regarding their perceptions. Frequency of classes, numbers attending. Attitudinal changes toward library.)
3. The teaching methods. (Comparisons of performance between teaching methods, before and after tests of students, feedback from instructors.)
4. The students' performance after instruction. (Grades, assignments' quality, quantified use of library materials; e.g.,

per capita circulation in a target discipline, feedback from students, teachers, librarians.)

Such an array as depicted in Table 1 should emphasize the complicated undertaking that evaluation is. Failing to understand this, we may design inadequate or inappropriate evaluation strategies.

TABLE I
Relationship Between Strategy and Goal of Evaluation
in Library-use Instruction[3]

| Goals of Evaluation | Strategies of Evaluation | | | |
	A. Evaluation of overall library system	B. Evaluation of instructional program	C. Evaluation of a teaching method	D. Evaluation of impact on students' performance
I Assess impact of instruction on targeted groups		X		X
II Modify instructional efforts		X	X	X
III Sell library-use instruction to others	X			X
IV Upgrade method of instruction		X	X	
V Advance educational knowledge	X	X	X	X

Given the perspective afforded by Table I, we should have a clearer idea of the various types of evaluations. If we desire to "sell" library-use instruction to others, inside and outside the library, we will likely need to evaluate at the overall library-system level and, if feasible, even beyond that, at the society-at-large level. It is here that the lasting results of our efforts, if observable, would have the greatest impact, in showing that user education does make a difference in how libraries are used. On the other hand, if we wish to upgrade a particular method of instruction, our evaluation can take place at the method and program levels. Feedback from participants should be adequate to let us know if a method is working as expected. It should be noted that each evaluation level has different measurements. For example, at the method level, a test of retained knowledge would suffice, but at the library-wide level, we would need to use wider-ranging measures, such as usage of the library and user attitudes. Figure I depicts the systems-wide organizational setting for evaluation, and some of the research implications should be readily deductible.

CONVINCING THE UNCONVINCED

In academic libraries, user education represents an unusual phenomenon. It sprang into being at the grass-roots level and flourishes there without the usual trappings necessary for organizational existence: delegated authority from the top, budgetary recognition, and titles of office. There are exceptions to this, and of course it is changing, but its recent development is rather unique in the profession.

There are benefits to operating at the grass-roots level: the enthusiasm of the participants is certain—long hours of planning and preparation are given gladly; administrative red tape is avoided—the people directly involved not only carry out the instruction but also make decisions regarding the direction and intensity of the program; usually the program is carried out within existing budgets—no extra funds are given, nor are they asked for.

The drawback to this or any grass-roots movement is the lack of involvement by the top decision makers. Unless something is delegated and budgeted from above, it tends to lack "legitimacy," at least in the eyes of those at the top. One might contrast the administrative support enjoyed by computerization, to the minimal aid given to user education. "Legitimacy" is *not* important as long as we stay within the original boundaries. Should we wish to expand

FIGURE I
Systems View: User Education Program

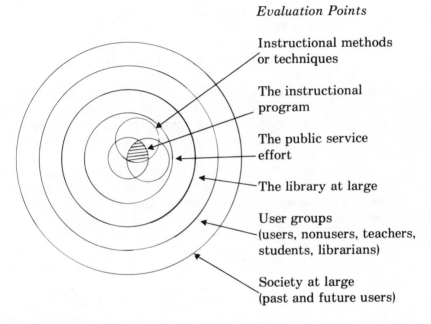

Evaluation Points

Instructional methods
or techniques

The instructional
program

The public service
effort

The library at large

User groups
(users, nonusers, teachers,
students, librarians)

Society at large
(past and future users)

Implications
1. Evaluation is multifaceted.
2. Data are needed at each point of evaluation; these may differ.
3. User-education objectives should take into account the depth of the evaluation.
4. Movement is constant if the system boundaries are porous.
5. Impact of instruction becomes harder to assess, the further one moves from the initial point of instruction.

our programs or to defend them in times of budgetary crisis, however, the commitment at the top level becomes a necessity.

One theory of how organizations or systems change suggests that change will occur only when certain conditions exist.[4] These are: a new "model," or plan; dissatisfaction, and "costs" that are lower if change occurs than if it does *not*, as depicted in the formula

$$Ch = (D \times M \times P) > C$$

Where Ch = Change
  D = Dissatisfaction with the status quo
  M = A new model for managing or organizing
  P = A planned process for managing change
  C = Cost of change to individuals and groups

Dissatisfaction with the system is only one part of the desire to change the status quo. While dissatisfaction with how libraries are used or perceived (e.g., the "storage" image popularly held by the public) may exist among practitioners, little permanent change can come about unless there is a new service model, at an acceptable "cost," and a plan for achieving the change. If one accepts this formula, it can explain why normative statements, especially popular in the library literature, rarely bring about change. All too frequently, such demands ignore the costs of change and other parts of this formula. Evaluation has a dynamic role in change, by its contribution to our understanding of the status quo, structuring the new model, and estimating the costs/benefits of the suggested change.

The problem of resistance to change is not solely limited to upper layers of the library administration; rather, it is prevalent in all of our dealings with people outside the user-education movement. If we wish to *change* the status quo of information use, we will need to gain the commitment of numerous groups and individuals outside of user education.

Keeping the systems view of Figure I in mind, one must assume that educational change at large is necessary before we are to have real change in library use. If competence in library use is to be embraced and acted upon by people outside of librarianship, then conclusive evidence of its benefits needs to be marshaled. For example, if we expect the Librarian of Congress to lend the prestige of a national library to endorse user education to the same degree that he may for literacy, we have to provide competitive ideas and evidence. Such evidence must convince this influential leader and others that user education is *not* a meaningless memorization of classification schemes, or some such nonsense, but rather an enabling component of the problem-solving process. Problem-solving, or the ability to think critically, is a process in which libraries have a major but unrealized role. We need to prove that libraries are misused, underused, and that improvements will occur through user education.

One assumption inherent in this view is that administrators in all types of libraries are not opposed to user education; rather, they are either ignorant or unconvinced of its importance amidst competing demands. Few adminstrators link instruction and the use of libraries. Similarly, all too few can visualize the potential benefits of education: it would improve the image of, and increase support for, the library. If we can substantiate the linkages, library leaders will be more willing to make the necessary investments and to take the cause beyond library walls.

Parenthetically, it will be interesting to see what changes evolve at the "graying" of the user-education movement. Will ex-library-instruction practitioners, upon donning the adminstrative mantle, be able or willing to shift budgetary emphases toward user education? Will they be more committed than their predecessors have been to bringing about change in how libraries are used?

PROBLEMS IN EVALUATION

First a disclaimer: we are not alone in experiencing the difficulties of evaluating results of our programs. Apart from the scientific laboratory, there are few endeavors that do not share in the complexities and frustrations of judging how well a particular objective has been reached within a range of possibilities. For verification, see the Porras and Berg survey in the bibliography at the end of this chapter. The ailments discussed below are not unique to user education. It may be comforting to know that they flourish in the equally fertile soil of other disciplines.

The following problems are gathered from an unscientific but, one hopes, productive dip into the user-education literature, including evaluation studies done by this author and others over the past few years.

Given that our evaluation efforts are developmental, I have chosen not to supply references for the following cases, which are used to illustrate some of the failings in those studies. Anyone wishing verification of these findings should read further in the literature.

Nonevaluation

A lengthy litany of excuses can be given for not evaluating a program's impact. They include politics, uncertainty of merit, common sense, lack of expertise, and high costs. Resistance to evaluation is a fact. As in other disciplines, what "feels good" often will gain administrative support over what doesn't feel so good. We have library-instruction practitioners who tacitly agree with this. There is a trace of smug elitism evident when people claim a successful program and allegedly have large numbers of participants yet fail to evaluate and reveal to the unenlightened at least *why* their program appears to work. This can lead to ineffective emulation.

One example is a university credit course that, owing to its unparalleled success in attracting droves of students, has served as a model user-education program. One report has it that the major reason for high enrollments is that upon successful completion of the course, the students gain a pass to the otherwise closed book stacks. Quite a carrot! If this is correct and no other evaluation is done, one would question whether this program is meeting a standard of excellence.

I interviewed a school librarian who claimed to have established a library-skills program *across* the curriculum. At first view, this did seem to be the case. Yet during the interview, something did not ring true. There was thorough documentation, contained in a fat volume, on how the program was to work in all disciplines. Yet the spacious and superbly equipped Learning Resources Center remained empty during the two hours I spent there – even though it was a school day for the one thousand or so students. One possible explanation for this incongruity might have been that the librarian's spouse happened to be the vice-superintendent for the curriculum development of this particular school district. Evaluation here would not only help outsiders better understand, but might also provide some insights for the program's designers.

Carolyn Kirkendall's LOEX data underscore this reluctance to evaluate (see reference to this author's "Assessing Library Instruction," in the bibliography). About one-half of the 830 respondents to the 1979 LOEX survey stated that they do *not* evaluate. The half that do so, use a combination of techniques such as written feedback from students and "informal" evaluation. Only 11 libraries reported using control groups.

Playing It Cozy: The Safe Hypothesis

Few will disagree that the two following statements are at different levels, requiring different strategies of evaluation. Hypothesis 1: students will be able to decipher a *Business Periodicals Index* entry. Hypothesis 2: more books will be used after instruction. For various reasons, in our research, we tend to play it safe with hypotheses closer to the first. One suspects it is because we are better able to grasp and manage the complexities of judging the former than the latter. The value of this circumscribed research is diminished, in that, while the hypothesis may be supported, it will be of little interest to people outside the actual program. On the other hand, there is embarrassment potentially involved in shooting for the moon and not lifting off the launching pad, by designing an all-too-elaborate evaluation program.

Electronic advances have decreased the complexities of proving or disproving the broader hypothesis. We are now able to do comparisons of variables in large-scale analyses that would have been depressingly tedious if done manually. Variables, both influencing and influenced by an instructional program, can be examined with an ease previously not possible. It should now be possible to include such routinely maintained baseline statistics as circulation and reference data in our analyses of user-education programs and their impact. The frequently called-for linkage of book use to teaching is now feasible.

In small-scale experiments, it is possible to use feedback from participants, concerning what influence a program has had. What we need is to develop questions to ask. And, of course, prior to this, we need to know what we want our program to do. This, by the way, is an important by-product of evaluation: the rigorous discussion involved in refining specific program goals *prior* to developing the program.

Questionable Questions

It is difficult to understand our motivations in using simplistic questions in tests. Perhaps we suffer from a statistical stupor regarding question validity or perhaps we hedge our bets on the success of a program. I refer to questions that the general public could easily puzzle out. The too-simple pretest confounds our research and confirms to some students the "Mickey Mouse" aspect of library use *and* that their library ability is already near the top.

Easy questions in one study produced mean scores of 80–92 percent for those given instruction and 80–91 percent for those who had not had it. Representative of the level of the questions asked in another study is one item which requested students to differentiate between a subject heading and a title on a catalog card. Ironically, the report of this same study reveals that the instructional program is of a high caliber, demanding concerted effort on the students' part far beyond the simplicity implied by the test. It has done itself an injustice by using questions that fail to uncover the true differences between the two groups.

Another study makes extensive use of "orientation" items. These are along the lines of "Where would you look for a *Who's Who?*" with the answer to be chosen from a list of locations. The report purports to measure the impact of an instructional effort yet actually measures only orientation.

Such questions, one suspects, are symptomatic of underlying problems: a lack of clearly stated program objectives and an unawareness of question-formulation techniques. These are controllable and easily remedied circumstances. One of the benefits of evaluation, mentioned earlier, is that it compels one to state measurable objectives. When making up the instrument that will measure the impact of the program, these objectives should be quite helpful in providing a basis for the questions. The questions should reveal if the user is able to do what he or she was not able to do before the lesson. A pilot survey, a standard routine in user surveys, should also be helpful in test formulation. Asking for a response to a draft instrument has the potential for clarifying overly complex and confusing questions as well as spotting questions that are inordinately difficult (no one gets the right answer) or too easy (everyone gets the right answer).

Making the Insignificant Significant

This situation may be found with increasing frequency as we rely solely on statistical outcomes rather than on common sense to reach conclusions about a program's value. I refer to equating "significance" with success. All statisticians will tell you significance refers to the *probability* of something happening by chance. It does not refer to importance.

One study used a multiple item pre- and post-test. Before instruction, students answered 60 percent correctly. After instruction, they were able to answer 70 percent correctly. Statistically significant, yes, but moving a student's score from certain "failure" to "near failure" does not strike me as sound evidence of a program's merit.

A second study is nearly identical. An improvement of 10 points over the pretest score of 65 percent is hailed as remarkable, considering the half hour or so spent in instruction. The content of the instruction may in fact be good, but one doubts that, given high pretest scores, the questions adequately measure the retention of the allegedly difficult concepts taught. If it turns out, however, that the questions are indeed representative of the program content and objectives, one should question the purpose of *any* instruction on the topic, since most students are already near an adequate level of understanding; i.e., two thirds of the content is known by them. After all, one purpose of the pretest is to screen out redundant instruction.

Another study is more subtle. This user education method improved student pretest scores to the point where they doubled. However, the fact that these post-test scores were still at a failing level was not elaborated upon. While the method worked exceptionally well for other generally better-educated groups, the very group of minority students for which it was originally designed, failed to perform as well as one would have wished.

We should have some cut-off point in mind, before making the study, against which to compare progress, in order to give more meaning to statistical significance.

DEVELOPMENT IN EVALUATION

More than a few published studies show progress is being made in the quality of user-education evaluation. The same studies containing the various ailments already described also demonstrate a maturing research ability on the part of the investigators.

As mentioned earlier, evaluation of library-use instruction is in a developmental phase. This is manifest in a diversity of approaches and the librarian's uncertainty of impact (not to be disparaging of their efforts). It is worth repeating that this developmental condition is shared by other library services as well as service agencies outside the library.[5] When one considers that other fields in the social sciences and management have bountiful research funds, an entrenched research network among teachers, students, and practitioners, and numerous publication opportunities, it is surprising that library-evaluation research is keeping up.

In the library literature, review articles by Harris, Crossley and Clews, Taylor, and Brewer and Hills, have increased awareness of both the problems and the complexities of evaluation. Each has constructed bridges to other disciplines' evaluation methods. This awareness of what other researchers are doing is an important aspect of growth.

STUDY DESIGN

The Campbell and Stanley models used extensively in social research appear to fit in nicely with library research. Several of the studies reviewed for this chapter refer to their work and to individuals working in the distinct field of evaluation research.

Because of this influence, librarians appear to be moving away from the simplest form of research, which is to give a program and then measure participants for any changes. This is depicted as X O in the research literature. (X is the treatment and O is the observation or test.) For example, this is the design used when screening a slide-tape program on library use and testing students on its content. One can strengthen this design by adding a control group that does not see the slide-tape program but does take the test. If there are any differences between the groups, one may ascribe them to the instructional program. Its notation is X O_1

O_2.

Confirming our growth in research capability is the frequent use of the pre- and post-test design (O_1 X O_2). Its use suggests an increased awareness of the limitations in other, simpler designs and allows one to avoid some of the common criticisms attributed to these designs. This design can also be depicted $t_2 - t_1 = \Delta$ where the measurement in "time one" subtracted from the measurement in "time two" reflects a difference, symbolized by the delta. The change, if there is one, can be attributed to the instructional program. It is possible to expand this model longitudinally over time to strengthen any conclusions reached: for example, $O_1 O_2 O_3 X O_4 O_5$ O_6 indicates user studies for three years prior to an instructional program and three years after. This design would show the long-term impact of a program rather than what could be termed just a temporary fluctuation if one used a one-time measure.

A popular design is O_1 X O_2. Several library evaluation studies
$$O_3 \quad O_4$$
have made use of it, in which both instructed and uninstructed (control) groups are given the pre- and post-test, helping us to judge better the impact of a program, since differences between O_2 and O_4 should be attributable to the instruction.

Indicative of the sophisticated designs available to librarians is the "Four Group Design" discussed by Campbell and Stanley.[6] It could be used to demonstrate conclusively the value of user-education effort, via students' work after instruction. While complicated and probably expensive to carry out, it is among the strongest designs available if one wishes to prove with a high degree of certainty that a particular method has had a desired result. The design is depicted as

R	O_1	X	O_2
R	O_3		O_4
R		X	O_5
R			O_6

It allows for two control groups and two experimental groups randomly assigned (R) in arrangements that control for outside and inside influences on results. For example, the influence of "testing" (predisposing participants with a pretest) is minimized by having a treated group, O_5, not undergo a pretest. If those results are markedly different between O_5 and O_2, then the pretest may be an influence.

The one proposed application with which this author is familiar confirms the complexity and costliness of the design. The case would test the effect of an instructional program on freshman theses. A total of eight classes would be involved, with several librarians and instructors doing the teaching. At the end of the semester, the theses would be graded, for the student's official grade, by the class instructor and then by a jury of two librarians and two faculty members. *Each* of the 160 or so papers would be examined by each jury member, using a seven-point criterion, and the collective scores computed by using analysis of variance techniques. No small amount of work! This exhaustive treatment may be why this particular design is little used. Nevertheless, it does represent a strong evaluation technique, should it be needed.

LAYING THE GROUNDWORK

Along with numerous early studies on user attitudes and library skills, there has recently been some work that should further strengthen the base for future evaluation efforts.

The University of Colorado study, using *formative* and *summative* evaluation, showed several positive outcomes of a user-education program. Questionnaires regarding attitudes of and use by students and faculty in the program revealed improvements.

For the student, the grant had these influences: economics and history students (i.e., the "treated" groups) differed significantly from the random sample of students (the "untreated" groups) in

- Asking for assistance from a librarian in the reference department (73 percent and 72 percent versus 56 percent).
- Being referred by a professor to a subject librarian (32 percent and 24 percent versus 9 percent).
- Believing their course work helps develop library research techniques (58 percent and 47 percent versus 37 percent).
- Class assignments requiring use of the library (59 percent and 48 percent versus 36 percent).
  The history and economics faculty responded even more positively.

As a direct result of the grant, they now

- Require more use of the library by students (46 percent and 50 percent).
- Believe students are better able to do research (64 percent and 90 percent).
- Believe the grant allows the librarian departmental involvement (53 percent and 50 percent).
- Would strongly support the continued allocation of department space (82 percent).

The questionnaires developed for this evaluation have been used in several other institutions, and these results could be applied in comparative studies.[7]

The University of Texas's comprehensive program of user education has gained baseline figures on attitudes from students and faculty. As evaluations are conducted, longitudinal changes should be readily observable. As well, there are possibilities for comparative studies through the use of the instruments developed at Texas.

King and Ory chose to measure an instructional program's effect through user response to general questions rather than through a skills test. They found that students with instruction claimed double the use of periodical indexes over students not instructed. Also, these students cited three periodical references, while the uninstructed group cited two articles. Considering the large numbers (65 rhetoric classes, or about 1,300 students) represented in this study, such changes are remarkable when translated into actual use of library materials.

In the school sector, with important implications for academic libraries, Anne Hyland was the first to produce a test that recognizes the difference of "product" instruction versus "process" instruction. Her work, the "Ohio School Library Media Test," measures information-finding and -using skills as part of the problem-solving thought process. Evaluation at grades 4–12 has now been facilitated. The test can also be used in public library settings where formal instruction is given to student groups. Unlike other library skills tests, with their nearly exclusive stress on specific library tools, her test covers five broad areas: *organization* of the library, *selection* of sources, *utilization* of the materials found, *comprehension* of the information given, and *production* or the presentation of the information found, to others.

VIEWPOINTS OF EVALUATION

The systems view of libraries provides a structure for evaluation as well. Figure I suggests the points at which to evaluate and should imply that the further one moves from the actual instructional method used, the more difficult becomes the ascertainment of a program's influence, because the variables begin to multiply. However, it is precisely at the outer limits that there is a need to develop research to show, for example, the influence of user instruction on the use of library resources or on the quality of research papers. To put it another way, if librarians believe instruction creates more and better use, they should be able to find it among the causes of effective use. A measure of its importance as a cause of use then could be established.

SUGGESTIONS

It is hoped that no one interprets this apparent obsession with evaluation as a desire to evaluate *all* programs. However, this author is calling for more evaluation, and evaluation beyond those studies dealing only with a particular teaching method.

Variables, such as reference and circulation data, should be studied and refined so they become sensitive indicators of library program effects.

There should be more collaboration of outside consultants and program personnel at an early point in the program. Ideally, the evaluation consultant should be called in prior to implementing the program. The involvement of such an individual can aid not only in strengthening the instructional program but also in

1. Preplanning the type and depth of the evaluation
2. Setting forth measurable objectives
3. Establishing baseline data prior to the instruction
4. Making up the time frame for the pre- and post-instruction measurements
5. Developing or adapting data-gathering instruments
6. Coordinating the evaluation
7. Analyzing and presenting the results

Practitioners are skating on ethically thin ice when they do their own evaluation. What proud parent will call his or her child ugly?

Research money should be made available for well-designed evaluations. In the U.S. alone, hundreds of thousands of dollars have been spent recently on instructional programs which have produced few evaluations, the main reason being that participants were not required to evaluate. One could venture the opinion that there are numerous programs that would opt to be evaluated, were funds made available for that special purpose.

Attention should be paid to earlier studies, for possible comparisons and baseline figures. A synthesis of what evaluation and user studies have revealed about use is probably in order.

Finally, given some standardization and linkages among libraries, it might be possible to trace the influence of user education on users as they progress through the school years to the public library.

FOOTNOTES

1. An abbreviated version of this paper was presented at the Second International Conference on User Education in Oxford, England, July 7–10, 1981.
2. John Cowley's observation, as quoted in the review by Ann Irving of *Library User Education : Are New Approaches Needed?* edited by Peter Fox, in *Infuse,* v.4 (October 1980): 13–15.
3. Adapted from M. Beer, *Organization Change and Development: A Systems View.* Santa Monica: Goodyear, 1980, p. 252.
4. *Ibid.,* p. 46.
5. An insightful discussion on the problems of evaluation can be found in Henry W. Reicken, "Memorandum on Program Evaluation," in *Organization Development,* ed. by W. French et al. Dallas: Business Publications, 1978, pp. 413–423.
6. Donald T. Campbell and Julian C. Stanley, *Experimental and Quasi-Experimental Designs for Research.* Chicago: Rand McNally, 1963, pp. 24–25.
7. For example, see Richard A. Dreifuss, "Library Instruction and Graduate Students: More Work for George" ("Library Literacy" column) RQ: (in press).

BIBLIOGRAPHY

Baldwin, Julia F. and Robert S. Rudolph. "The Comparative Effectiveness of a Slide/Tape Show and a Library Tour." *College and Research Libraries* 40 (January, 1979), pp. 31-35.

Beer, Michael. *Organization Change and Development: A Systems View,* Santa Monica, California: Goodyear Publishing Co. Inc. 1980. Especially in Chapter 14, "Evaluating and Institutionalizing Systems – Wide Change" pp. 245-253.

Brewer, J.G. and Hills, P.J. "Evaluation of Reader Instruction", *Libri* 26 (1976), pp. 55-65.

Campbell, Donald T., and Stanley, Julian C. *Experimental and Quasi-Experimental Designs for Research,* Chicago, Rand McNally, 1963.

A Comprehensive Program of User Education for the General Libraries The University of Texas at Austin (Contributions to Librarianship No. 1) Austin, Texas, The Library, 1977.

Corlett, Donna. "Library Skills, Study Habits and Attitudes and Sex as Related to Academic Achievement," *Educ. & Psych. Meas.* 34:967-969 (1974)

Crossley, Charles A. and John P. Clews. *Evaluation of the Use of Educational Technology in Information Handling Instruction: A Literature Review and Bibliography Submitted to the British Library Research and Development Department.* mimeo. no place, no publisher. 1974 47p.

Dash, Ursula. "The Self-Guided Library Tour." *Australian Academic and Research Libraries* 8 (March, 1977), pp. 33-38.

Eyman, David H. and Alven C. Nunley, Jr. *The Effectiveness of Library Science 1011 in Teaching Bibliographical Skills.* Arlington, Va: ERIC Education Document Reproduction Service, 1978. ED 150 962 30p.

Fjällbrant, Nancy. "Evaluation In a User Education Programme." *Journal of Librarianship* 9 (April, 1977), pp. 83-95

Glogoff, Stuart. "Using Statistical Tests to Evaluate Library Instruction Sessions." *Journal of Academic Librarianship* 4 (January, 1979), pp. 438-442.

Hardesty, Larry and others. "Evaluating Library-Use Instruction." *College and Research Libraries* 40 (July, 1979), pp. 309-317.

Harris, Colin. "Illuminative Evaluation of User Education Programmes." *Aslib Proceedings* 10 (October, 1977), pp. 348-362.

Hyland, Anne. "Profile of Library Skills in Ohio" *Ohio Media Spectrum* 31 (Winter, 1979) pp. 12-17.

King, David N. and John C. Ory. *Effects of Library Instruction on Student Research: A Case Study.* Urbana-Champaign, Ill.: University of Illinois. Undergraduate Library. mimeo 19 p. July 1979 Also *College and Research Libraries,* 42: 31-41 (Jan. 1981).

Lolley, John L. "Educating the Library User; the Evolution of an Individualized Library Instruction Program at Tarrant County Junior College." *Texas Library Journal* 51:30-32. (Spring, 1975).

Lubans, John, Jr. "Assessing Library Instruction: An Author's Opinion" in *Proceedings of the 10th Annual LOEX Conference.* Ann Arbor, Mich.: Pierian Press 1981 (in press)

Lubans, John, Jr. "Library Literacy." *RQ* 19 (Summer, 1980), pp. 325-328. Summary of University of Colorado Program Evaluation.

Mitchell, Rosemary. *Academic Achievement and Use of the Secondary School Library* (master's thesis) mimeo. Tasmanian College of Advanced Education, Hobart, Tasmania 1973 53 p.

Nagy, Laslo A. and Martha Lou Thomas, "An Evaluation of the Teaching Effectiveness of Two Library Instructional Videotapes." *College and Research Libraries* 42: 26-30 (Jan. 1981).

Paterson, Ellen P. "How Effective is Library Instruction?" *RQ* 18 (Summer, 1979), pp. 376-377.

Person, Roland, "Long-term Evaluation of Bibliographic Instruction: Lasting Encouragement," *College and Research Libraries* 42: 19-25 (Jan. 1981).

Phipps, Shelley and Ruth Dickstein. "The Library Skills Program at the University of Arizona: Testing, Evaluation and Critique." *Journal of Academic Librarianship* 5 (September, 1979), pp. 205-214.

Porras, Jerry I. and Berg, Per Olaf. "Evaluation Methodology in Organization Development: An Analysis and Critique", *Journal of Applied Behavioral Science.* 14: 151-173 (1978). Has extensive bibliography.

Rader, Hannelore B. *An Assessment of Ten Academic Library Instruction Programs in the United States and Canada; A Council on Library Resources Fellowship Report,* mimeo. Ypsilanti, Mich., Eastern Michigan University, 1976. 21 p. and appendices.

Reiken, Henry W. "Memorandum on Program Evaluation" in *Organization Development: Theory, Practice and Research* edited by French, Wendell L. et al. Dallas, Texas: Business Publications, Inc. 1978 pp. 413-423.

Taylor, Peter. "User Education and the Role of Evaluation." *UNESCO Bulletin for Libraries* 32 (Winter, 1978), pp. 252 - 259.

Tucker, John Mark. "An Experiment in Bibliographic Instruction at Wabash College." *College and Research Libraries* 38:203-209, (May, 1977).

*I*n spite of the fact that for more than 50 years there have been librarians who understand clearly the need for centralized cataloging, in spite of everything the Library of Congress has done, in spite of our so-called cooperative cataloging plan...we still have precious little centralized cataloging, nor is what we have extensive enough to enable libraries to reduce their cataloging costs or change their staffing patterns — **Ralph Ellsworth.** *"Another Chance for Centralized Cataloging,"* Library Journal, *v. 89, no. 15 (September 1, 1964):3104.*

Centralized Cataloging

Joseph H. Howard, Assistant Librarian
for Processing Services
Judith G. Schmidt, Technical Officer of the
Processing Services Department
Library of Congress
Washington, D.C.

The discussion of centralized versus decentralized (or cooperative) cataloging has been with librarians for many years. It is not easy to separate the two, since many practices embrace both. At least as far back as 1876, the idea of cooperation among libraries was broached. Writing in the first issue of *Library Journal,* dated September 30, 1876, and commenting on the potential role of that journal in the developing American library scene, as well as the possible role of a new national organization, subsequently to be called the American Library Association, to be formed within a matter of weeks in Philadelphia, Melvil Dewey declared that the library profession was one "within which cooperation may be made exceptionally useful. . . ." The question has been and continues to be: how to effect such cooperation? A major step forward in cooperative cataloging was taken in 1901 when the Library of Congress (LC), pressured by the American Library Association and led by a former public librarian and president of the association, Herbert Putnam, began the distribution and sale of its "card indexes," or catalog cards, as we know them. These were to a large extent to be the coin of the realm in cataloging until the advent of the cooperative *National Union Catalog* in its various forms, which came along during and after World War II.

By the time of the affluent 1960s, when federal funding for books, libraries, and education generally seemed on a never-ending upward surge, much as did the growth in the school-age population, it looked as though the Library of Congress, also young and benefitting from increased funding, would be able to provide much of the cataloging for the nation's libraries, thus more completely fulfilling the role of a centralized cataloging agency. Great strides were made, and cost savings are still being realized by many American libraries. However, it has proved difficult to meet the diverse needs of these many and varied libraries, not to mention the need for timeliness.

With increased use of computers in libraries in the 1960s, the opportunity and challenge for linking computer to computer and computer to remote terminal became real. This opportunity expressed itself in the cataloging arena, aided by the MARC format, in terms of sharing, cooperation, decentralization. But when one looks at the cataloging operations of an organization like OCLC, Inc., the sharing takes on characteristics of centralized cataloging. The catalogers are spread across the country, but the source for their work is in Columbus, Ohio.

In the shift from centralized to decentralized cataloging operations, LC's role has changed significantly. In the early Cooperative Cataloging project, LC exercised a great deal of authority over the records submitted, generally reviewing them completely. In LC's most recent cooperative venture, the Name Authority Co-op project, LC's role has changed from being largely a reviewing agency (as in previous programs) to that of being a training agency.

SHARED CATALOGING

Under Title II C of the Higher Education Act of 1965, the Library of Congress was charged with "(a) acquiring so far as possible, all library materials currently published throughout the world of value to scholarship; and (b) providing catalog information for such materials promptly after receipt. . . ."

The policy of the Library of Congress has been to use shared cataloging techniques, wherever feasible, in cooperation with national bibliography authorities. As a first step, LC entered into an experimental cooperative arrangement with the compilers of the *British National Bibliography* to use their descriptive cataloging of British books as part of the Library of Congress catalog-card data. This meant that the transcription of the title, the collation, and the imprint reflected the British practice, which was considered to be as comprehensive as current LC practice. The price of each title in English currency and the registry number in the weekly issue of the *British National Bibliography* are indicated to facilitate the ordering of books directly from the catalog-card information.

The choice and form of author entry and secondary entries, the repetition of the author statement, the subject headings, and LC and DC classification continue to follow current Library of Congress practice.

On the international level, LC's shared cataloging program is a cooperative decentralized venture. However, on the national level, it provides cataloging data for foreign publications as a centralized cataloging program, with the cataloging provided by LC to the American library community.

This program was expanded and LC offices were established in many other Western European countries. While some of these offices have been closed, the closings do not have a measurable impact on LC's cataloging or acquisitions from these countries.

The future of this international shared cataloging program will include the continued exchange of MARC tapes among the countries producing them. While these tapes are presently available, LC has not yet utilized the tapes of other countries. The capacity of LC to load foreign tapes into their systems will be crucial to LC's continued role as a centralized cataloging agency for foreign imprints.

This matter, of course, is a high priority in automation planning at the Library of Congress. It affects not only the loading of foreign tapes, but also the loading of tapes from American sources, which will be important to the successful automation of the *National Union Catalog*.

BIBLIOGRAPHIC UTILITIES

The major bibliographic utilities have created a revolutionary environment where the potential for cooperation is seemingly limitless. Many libraries, including the smaller libraries, can bypass manual operations by utilizing the systems provided by such utilities as OCLC, Inc., Research Libraries Information Network (RLIN), and Washington Library Network (WLN).

While the potential for cooperation is great, there is no single set of quality controls over the records put into these systems. The question has been and will continue to be: can or should these systems be linked into one nationwide data base with LC?

RLIN and WLN agreed in 1979 to take initial steps toward cooperation. More recently, the two have been working together with LC in the Council on Library Resources' Bibliographic Service Development Program, Linked Authority Systems Project. The goal of this program is the linking of systems to share authority data so as to develop effective, consistent authority files in each of the systems.

CONSER

With plans to utilize the OCLC, Inc., system for data-base building, the CONSER (Conversion of Serials) project got underway with a meeting held at York University in 1973. In late 1974, contractual arrangements were finally made, and the project became operational in November 1975. Presently, there are 19 participants, including the Library of Congress and the National Library of Canada.

The objective of the project is to build and maintain a quality U.S.-Canadian data base of active serial titles. To achieve this objective, the "center of responsibility" concept was established as the foundation for the project. The Library of Congress and the National Library of Canada certify data content and content designation of the full record or portions for their respective areas of responsibility, which are based on imprint.

As both a center of responsibility and an active participant in this program, the Library of Congress has reviewed and modified many of its serial cataloging policies and procedures in order to benefit more effectively from data contributed by other participants. For the participating institutions, training sessions were conducted at the beginning of the project, to allow for uniform interpretation and implementation of accepted cataloging rules, the MARC-Serials format, and the CONSER bibliographic conventions. In addition, methods for timely updating of documentation on cataloging and editing practices have been devised, in order to inform participants more promptly of new developments. Periodic meetings convened by OCLC, Inc., of both the administrative representatives and the operational staff of CONSER institutions have also contributed to improved uniformity of data supplied by the participants as well as adherence to national cataloging practices.

LC's commitment to this shared data-base-building activity was reflected early in the project by a decision to accept bibliographic information contributed by the participants for the Library's own serial cataloging operations. Twenty-five percent of the serials newly received and cataloged by the Library are represented by existing records on the CONSER data base that have been contributed by member institutions – thereby eliminating the need for the Library to perform original descriptive cataloging for one-fourth of its current serial cataloging. Serial catalogers accept this information as provided by the CONSER participants unless it is obviously in violation of accepted cataloging rules. Additional data or updated information may also be added to these CONSER records if available at the time of cataloging.

Upon authentication, these records are subsequently made available via the MARC Serials Distribution Service and, for LC's cataloging only, via printed cards. The authenticated records reflect the equivalent of national bibliographic records rather than records uniquely representative of Library of Congress holdings and could only be produced through a cooperative mechanism like the CONSER Project. The timeliness and reliability of the cataloging information provided by other institutions is therefore having a significant beneficial impact upon the Library's own serial-processing activities. And as the CONSER Project develops further, the benefits to all participants can be expected to continue and increase.

LC's participation in this cooperative CONSER project reflected more trust, a moderate change in philosophy. In the past, LC carried the burden of complete revision of the full cataloging record in the Cooperative Cataloging program. This new and more limited role was to become a trend in the direction of more and greater cooperation, in the sense that LC received, accepted, and provided access to cataloging data from other institutions.

Name Authority Cooperation

In recent years, many of those persons who have been involved in establishing pieces of the projected nationwide data base for libraries have become convinced that an important, indeed critical, component will be an integrated, consistent authority file. An authority file contains the words, terms, and cross references – the access points – that impose consistency on files of bibliographic data. Consistent files with clearly established access points are, of course, much easier for users to search. The authority file that these planners have in mind would contain records contributed by a variety of institutions and created in accordance with established rules and procedures. It would be available for use nationwide. Building such a file would reduce the aggregate costs of authority work by the sharing of authority records; in addition, it would assist in the creation of more consistent bibliographic records, which in itself would improve current cooperative cataloging efforts.

Authority work is the most costly part of the cataloging process. While much cataloging information is now successfully shared, the means for sharing the most expensive product, the authority work, has not been so well established.

With these factors in mind, as well as the need to reduce duplication of effort, the Library of Congress began its cooperative efforts in name-authority work, basing its program on training and trust. In 1977, the Name Authority Co-op (NACO) was established in the Descriptive Cataloging Division, and the first participant was the U.S. Government Printing Office (GPO) Library.

At that time, a cataloger from the U.S. Government Printing Office Library was given intensive training in LC's current cataloging practices in general and in the use of LC's automated name-authority system. The GPO catalogers complete a name-authority worksheet for each new heading needed. It is reveiwed by the GPO coordinator and forwarded to LC, where it is compared with LC's manual name-authority data base. A 3 x 5 copy of the final heading is returned to GPO for use in its files until the printed authority card and cross references are available (usually within 6–12 weeks). From NACO, the worksheet is forwarded for keying into machine-readable form. From the machine-readable record are produced the printing cards, magnetic tapes for the distribution service, and *Name Authorities,* cumulative microform edition, all of which are made available through the Cataloging Distribution Service.

Initially, the project was confined to corporate headings. In December 1978, GPO felt that it had enough experience with the system to expand the project to include personal names. This greatly increased the magnitude of the project.

Since January of 1979, all GPO headings have been coded for the AACR 2 form of the heading. LC provided training in AACR 2 to the GPO catalogers in August 1979, and the AACR 2 coding has been added to the name-authority records at GPO since that time.

Another aspect of LC's cataloging cooperation with GPO has been the negotiation between LC and GPO in order to arrive at a common interpretation of the cataloging rules. The two agencies meet

regularly. In addition to the GPO and LC participants, a representative from the Federal Library Committee and representatives
from the ALA Government Documents Round Table's Cataloging
Manual Committee (for AACR 2) have been invited to attend these
meetings. Agreement has been reached between LC and GPO
regarding the choice of options, the use of alternative rules, and rule
interpretations under AACR 2.

The latest development in LC-GPO cooperation is that the
Library of Congress and the Government Printing Office informed
OCLC, Inc., that GPO would become the center of responsibility for
descriptive cataloging of monographic U.S. Federal government
documents, effective October 20, 1980, the date that GPO implemented AACR 2. GPO modifies and enhances all OCLC records
it utilizes, to create the *Monthly Catalog.* The Library of Congress
obtains the descriptive cataloging from the OCLC system for the
government documents it adds to its files after January 1, 1981. For
these documents, LC continues to add subject headings, LC
classification, and Dewey Decimal numbers. LC also continues to
work with GPO to ensure the quality of the cataloging. This project
culminates an intensive effort over several years to harmonize LC
and GPO cataloging practices and to reduce the duplication of effort
in the cataloging of government publications.

The original agreement between the Library of Congress and
Texas State Library called for a six-month project for cooperation in
the area of Texas State governmental corporate names. That agreement expired in August 1979. Negotiations were completed to extend the agreement for another 12 months and to expand the scope
of the project. The new agreement included all corporate headings
that represented Texas bodies, public or private. The third agreement, which began in August 1980, again enlarged the scope of the
project to include personal names used in the cataloging of Texas
documents. All headings in this project have been coded for
AACR 2.

With a view toward the decentralization of cataloging responsibility and toward cooperation, LC has increased the number of
projects in which it is involved, basing the agreements on the experience with GPO and following similar methods of training. Two
new ventures began in January 1980, with the libraries at the
University of Wisconsin-Madison and the University of Texas at
Austin. The University of Wisconsin-Madison is submitting
headings in the following languages: French, Italian, German,

Slavic, Scandinavian, and Japanese. The University of Texas at Austin is now contributing a substantial number of Latin American headings for both corporate and personal names.

Later in 1980, Northwestern University Library formalized its participation in the NACO project, as an outgrowth of a previous cooperative effort involving bibliographic records for the *Joint Acquisition List of Africana* (JALA). The Minnesota Historical Society, which functions as a state library and is a quasi-governmental agency, entered the program in March 1980. Under the agreement, headings for Minnesota state agencies are submitted.

Further expansion has taken place to include four major research libraries and two additional state libraries. The University of California at Berkeley Library submits both personal and corporate headings which require cross references. Princeton University Library contributes personal and corporate headings in Hebrew and in the general area of social sciences. The University of Michigan Library is contributing personal and corporate headings in Arabic, Persian, and Turkish; and Yale University Library specializes in Slavic headings. In October 1980, staff members from the New York State Library and the Montana State Library were at LC for training. They will be submitting headings related to publications by or about their respective states.

In an effort to create an atmosphere to encourage maximum nationwide cooperation, the Library of Congress offered to provide training to personnel from the major bibliographic utilities. It is hoped that such training will lead to an increased understanding of how LC operates and what goes into the creation of the MARC tapes. Under this program, a representative from Washington Library Network (WLN) did receive training.

All of the aforementioned agreements, projects, and efforts are initial stages in what LC hopes to be a comprehensive cooperative name-authority data-base-building effort. It is hoped, as staffing and budgets permit, that each participant will contribute all name authorities established as part of their routine cataloging.

STANDARDIZATION

For many years, the Library of Congress has assumed the responsibility for developing and maintaining standards for bibliographic records which would promote consistency in cooperative input to a national bibliographic data base. Such decisions as the standards to be required for the format of the record, as well as the content of the record, must be made. The former has been addressed through the MARC formats, and the latter will be addressed with the series of documents entitled *National Level Bibliographic Record (NLBR)*.

Libraries acknowledged the importance of standardization long ago. Machine systems, however, showed the need for an extra measure of conformity over what had been apparent in the past. What appears in the printed record is readable by humans, not bit configurations representing characters or codes or explicitly identifying content data. Variations in the placement or format of words, paragraphs, numbers in the printed record are not too damaging to the initiated, but can be intolerable to efficient machine processing. The interest of libraries in the computer for library operations was increasing in the 1960s. The availability of cataloging data in machine-readable form supplied by LC, the need to input cataloging data locally, the possibility of sharing these locally generated records, the potential for using computer programs across organizations to reduce the high cost of designing and writing software, and the need for hardware capable of handling large character sets were all factors that put increased emphasis on the establishment and conformity to standards.

It was in the 1960s that the Library of Congress developed the standard bibliographic format for machine-readable cataloging records. The Machine-Readable Cataloging (MARC) format permits the exchange of machine-readable cataloging information from library to library. This sharing is now done via magnetic tapes.

The philosophy behind MARC is the design of one format structure (the physical representation on a machine-readable medium) capable of containing bibliographic information for all forms of material (books, serials, maps, music, journal articles, and so on) and related records (e.g., name and subject reference records). The *structure* (or empty container), the content designators (tags, indicators, and subfield codes) used to explicitly identify or to additionally characterize the data elements, and the *content*, the data themselves (author names, titles, and so forth) are the three components of the format. It was recognized that under ideal conditions, the universe of material to be encoded would be studied at one time for a more coordinated approach to the assignment of content designators. However, those responsible knew the magnitude of such a task, the time required, and the need for specialists to be involved. Consequently, it was decided to handle one form of material at a time, beginning with books.

In accordance with the original plans to specify MARC formats for forms of material other than books, LC has published formats for serials, maps, films, manuscripts, and music. These several formats were published in combination by cooperative effort between the Research Libraries Information Network and LC in 1980, under the title *MARC Formats for Bibliographic Data.* There are also MARC formats for authorities and technical reports.

The impetus given to standardization by LC/MARC is doubtless one of its most important results. The establishment of bibliographic standards did not happen chronologically, but in many instances overlapped. Some of these standards include the *International Standard for Bibliographic Description* and the *Anglo-American Cataloguing Rules,* second edition (AACR 2).

Another significant outcome of the MARC efforts was the design of an extended character set for roman-alphabet languages. At the onset of MARC, a character set was specified, based on the work in progress by the Library Typewriter Keyboard Committee of the Resources and Technical Services Division of the American Library Association. Later, LC, in consultation with the National Agricultural Library and the National Library of Medicine, turned its attention to the development of an extended character set to cover all the major roman-alphabet languages as well as the romanized forms of nonroman-alphabet languages.

Although the primary advantage of the MARC records and the MARC distribution service is considered to be the cost savings resulting from centralized cataloging and from centralized editing and transcription of machine-readable records, another by-product of MARC is often overlooked. It is impossible to estimate the resources (people and time) saved through the use of MARC publications by national and international organizations while implementing local automated systems. LC language and country codes and character sets have been widely adopted and various MARC manuals adapted to local needs.

With MARC established as the means for standardizing the format of a record, attention could be turned to the content of the record. It seemed useful for the Library of Congress to try to develop an explicit statement of what should be required in a machine-readable record for that record to be considered full level or minimal level for purposes of a nationwide data base, so that potential contributors to such a data base could plan for future requirements or could begin to create such records in the expectation of contributing them to a nationwide data base in the future.

The *National Level Bibliographic Record* documents contain specifications for the data elements that should be included by an organization creating cataloging records for materials in machine-readable form for the aforementioned purpose. The intent of these documents is to define the required and optional content of such machine-readable cataloging records (both variable field data and coded data fields). It should be noted that these specifications are designed only for records to be contributed to a nationwide data base, not necessarily for records for local use.

Two of these documents have been published by the Library of Congress: *NLBR-Books* and *NLBR-Films*. Several others are in various stages of preparation as of this writing: maps, music, and serials, as well as the *National Level Authority Record*, preliminary edition.

The *NLBR-Books* provides the standard for putting in cataloging records for books according to the MARC formats standards, which are published in a companion publication, *MARC Formats for Bibliographic Data*. Emphasis is on the choice of data elements to be included in a record rather than on content designation. Because content and content designation cannot be separated in machine-readable records, however, the NLBRs are based on the MARC formats.

The information, effective as of 1981, with the adoption of AACR 2, is presented in tabular form and includes the name of each element defined for each type of material (as presented in the *MARC Formats for Bibliographic Data*) as well as some local elements, an indication of whether or not the designator is used in MARC records created and distributed by the Library of Congress (as presented in the *MARC Formats for Bibliographic Data*), and the data-element requirements based on the AACR 2 cataloging rules for both full- and minimal-level records, reflecting original cataloging by organizations in the United States, including the three national libraries.

One of the most significant benefits of the publication of the *NLBRs* is that they spell out the requirements for minimal-level cataloging (MLC) records. These records are significantly less expensive to prepare and, when put into a cooperative data base, could be upgraded by any library. MLC affords LC and other libraries the opportunity to catalog materials that might otherwise go uncataloged, in addition to making time available to give full-level cataloging to government documents, analytics, and so forth.

CHALLENGES FOR THE FUTURE

The general issues facing libraries today and for the near term include the expansion of networking and national and international standardization and cooperation, and cooperation in subject cataloging and classification. One way in which the Library of Congress is tackling the issue of national cooperation is through improvements in and enhancements to the *National Union Catalog* (NUC). The new NUC will be machine-produced and subsequently published in a register/index format.

Since many libraries still do not benefit from the programs of the Library of Congress or of private bibliographic agencies, because location and subject information available from these sources is either too costly or is inaccessible for another reason, it is imperative that LC revise its publishing program. The coverage of the present NUC will be expanded to include in a more detailed manner many of LC's other existing book catalogs, such as the *Chinese Cooperative Catalog, Monthly Checklist of State Publications, New Serial Titles,* and the *National Register of Microform Masters,* and to fill the current language gaps.

The improvement in coverage for Chinese, Japanese, Korean, Arabic, Persian, Hebrew, and Yiddish will involve the use of multiple LC systems, which will include the capability to process Library of Congress, as well as outside library, reports. The NUC register portion will have the potential to carry records in both romanized machine form and vernacular manual form.

LC has not, until recently, had machine access to bibliographic records in Japanese, Arabic, Chinese, Korean, Persian, Hebrew, or Yiddish (JACKPHY). The Library of Congress is changing this situation and continuing to produce non-MARC vernacular printed cards as well. The Library's automated in-process file (APIF), which contains brief (preliminary) cataloging records, does not have the capability for handling vernacular scripts. The input of records in romanized form to APIF for titles in all nonroman languages, including JACKPHY, has begun. Thus, for inprocess purposes only, the Library has a machine-readable brief romanized record for these languages. This record initially contains, among other fields, the main entry, description, and call number, but no notes or subject headings. The Library will continue to print cards for the complete record, as it has in the past, in the vernacular, with certain portions romanized.

These machine-readable records can be used to make brief entry indexes to JACKPHY records, thus making it possible to expand the NUC to include JACKPHY. Additional information such as subject headings, however, will have to be added to the APIF record.

The register portion of the NUC will contain a separate set of manually mounted printed cards in the vernacular for titles in JACKPHY. The indexes will be produced, however, by machine-utilizing the data captured in APIF.

Obviously, in order to make this portion of NUC a true union catalog, the Library will need reports from other libraries. The Library of Congress is considering the expansion of NUC to include JACKPHY records from other libraries for prospective imprints. Those that are duplicates would be listed in the *Register of Additional Locations* (LC/NUC card number index). For original vernacular records, the Library would key the romanized access points, which would permit the creation of the indexes to the NUC. The full vernacular record would be included in the manually produced register with all of the Library's records. For original romanized records, the entire record would be keyed and used in the machine-produced romanized register and indexes.

Better utilization of LC's automated systems will require that LC be able to process tapes for all types of cataloging records from non-LC sources, for inclusion in the NUC. As in the Shared Cataloging program, this tape-processing capability is crucial.

The advantages of the proposed register/index system include multiple access points to all NUC entries, broader coverage, and more prompt publication (assuming that the form of publication is computer output microform). At the same time, when such bases of information as state documents are added (in lieu of the *Monthly Checklist of State Publications*), the user will find that additional locations are available. The same will apply to maps and atlases. A third advantage will be timely-subject search capability.

While LC has expanded its acceptance of non-LC cataloging to CONSER records and to GPO descriptive cataloging, as well as the name-authority work done for NACO, there needs to be a major effort toward cooperation in subject cataloging and the assignment of classification numbers. To date, little has been accomplished in this area.

As in the NACO project, LC could turn its efforts to training catalogers from other institutions in LC practices. These catalogers could, in turn, train their colleagues, cooperative arrangements with LC could be established, and the records generated could be put into

LC's data base. Only then will there be standardized and fully cooperative cataloging with no need for LC review.

The potential for international cooperation and the sharing of cataloging data has been enhanced by recent developments in international cataloging codes. The *International Standard for Bibliographic Description* (ISBD) sets forth the rules to describe materials. The recently-published AACR 2 incorporates the ISBD and is used in all English-speaking countries, Scandinavia, Africa, Asia, and South America. Many countries are now using the Dewey Decimal classification system, which will also facilitate the exchange of data.

The use of MARC-compatible formats for machine-readable cataloging data is widespread throughout the world. Loading these tapes of bibliographic records, specifically from national libraries, into LC's automated data base is a high priority.

The UNIMARC format has been developed as the communications format that will facilitate the translation of these locally generated MARC formats, one to another. Implementation of the UNIMARC format has not been fully realized and remains a challenge for the future, for international cooperation and networking.

CONCLUSION

Although the Ellsworth statement that introduces this essay remains essentially true, and although the trend is toward cooperative cataloging, LC has made strides in centralized cataloging for foreign imprints.

The bibliographic utilities represent a blend of the two concepts of centralized and cooperative cataloging. Some of the earlier experiments in cooperative cataloging in the United States were somewhat less than highly successful, because most of them depended either upon one centralized agency, usually the Library of Congress, to do most of the cataloging, or each institution involved in the cataloging insisted upon redoing or rechecking the bibliographic data provided by another institution so the record would conform to local standards or practices. Participants in the CONSER project, for example, have recognized that insistence on local methods is costly and tends to defeat the purpose of cooperation. With clearly written guidelines agreed upon by all, each institution is able to use and contribute to records prepared by another institution, and amendments or changes for local needs are kept to a minimum.

Until a few years ago, it was unheard of for the Library of Congress to accept, without further checking and consideration, bibliographic data prepared by another agency. With both the CONSER project and, to a greater degree, with the NACO project, LC is changing that.

As the challenges of the future are met — with greater national and international cooperation — it may be possible to continue to reduce cataloging costs, as Ellsworth suggested almost 20 years ago. With the reduced cataloging costs, staffing patterns could be shifted toward increased emphasis on public service.

The journey undertaken more than 100 years ago has not been a particularly easy one, nor has it easily lent itself to completion. However, the prospects are good and the challenges are welcomed.

*T*he complexity of the storage problem . . . leads clearly to the awareness that each institution will have to weigh carefully a number of factors and arrive at a conclusion that may be quite different from those found on another campus — **Ralph Ellsworth**. The Economics of Book Storage in College and University Libraries. *Metuchen, N.J.: Scarecrow Press, 1969, p. 21.*

Interlibrary Cooperation

*Joe A. Hewitt, Associate University Librarian
for Technical Services
University of North Carolina
Chapel Hill, North Caroliona*

"Interlibrary cooperation" is a topic which affords the opportunity
to write an essay with a truly Ellsworthian approach. Given the im-
mensity of the literature on cooperation, and the space constraints
of this *Festschrift,* the only choice is to attempt to discover the
critical theme of the issue and to deal with it as succinctly as
possible.

Throughout his career, it was Ralph Ellsworth's style to find the
core of a problem, fix on it stubbornly, and to refuse to allow
himself, or others, to be led astray by the errant detail. Since that is
a particular hazard with a topic as vast, diverse, and ultimately as
intractable as interlibrary cooperation, there is a special comfort in
finding it appropriate to adopt the Ellsworthian approach.

The central theme of this chapter is that bibliographic communication is the critical component of all interlibrary cooperation.
A revolution in the technology of bibliographic communication,
such as the development of online networks and interactive online
catalogs, will also revolutionize the cooperative environment of
academic libraries. A history of library cooperation written at the
close of the 20th century will reveal, in all probability, a distinct and
fundamental shift in the scope and nature of interlibrary cooperation after the advent of online networks in the 1970s. This chapter
will speculate on the nature and the effects of this shift, perhaps in a
vein similar to Ellsworth's own speculations on centralized cataloging, in the *Colorado Academic Library* in 1963.[1] Ellsworth's ad-

vocacy of centralized cataloging, his role in establishing the Midwest Interlibrary Center (now the Center for Research Libraries), and his service on the ARL-ALA Committee on the National Union Catalog place him at the heart of the major cooperative developments which predate online bibliographic networks. The appropriateness of focusing on the transition occasioned by online networks is perhaps best emphasized by the fact that the publication of the pre-1956 segment of the National Union Catalog, with which Ellsworth was closely involved, has been characterized as the monumental achievement of its kind and the signal of the end of an era in bibliographic communication.[2]

BIBLIOGRAPHIC NETWORKS

It is hardly necessary to trace the development of the bibliographic networks – OCLC, RLIN, WLN, and UTLAS. These organizations and their services are familiar facts of life for most academic librarians, and network-based cataloging systems can now be considered the operational norm for academic libraries in the United States. The networks represent a considerable cooperative as well as technical achievement. Their origins are based for the most part on a concern for the traditional preoccupations of interlibrary cooperation – shared cataloging, resource sharing, and cost effectiveness of library operations – and their early success was due in each case to a fortunate combination of leadership, available technology, and a substantial commitment to cooperation on the part of a group of libraries. Over time, however, the cooperative thrust that was so vital in the early stages of network development has become less critical to the survival of the network, which are now fused with their participants in a mutually dependent operational and economic relationship that transcends the mere inclination of libraries to cooperate. Barring national economic castastrophe, both the survival of the networks and the continued refinement and expansion of network services are assured by the operational dependency of their memberships. Migration between the networks may continue, but the pattern of dependency is established by the fact that total network membership continues to increase and very few libraries withdraw from network participation in spite of frequent complaints about network performance.

The gradual evolution of a system that might reasonably be called a national bibliographic network will continue through forces already in motion. The course of this development will not always be smooth, straightforward, or logical, but neither will it be subject to the disastrous setbacks that have traditionally plagued projects which rely solely on the willingness of libraries to place a high priority on cooperative activity. The same cannot be said, however, of programs such as coordinated collection development, coordinated cataloging, and cooperative preservation and conservation, which have become practicable through the success of the bibliographic networks. These programs must still face the imposing obstacles that have always confronted interlibrary cooperation. As Weber points out:

> When one remembers that almost any two institutions are disparate in program, financial support, and a host of other variables, one may wonder whether any cooperation can be effective and lasting. The challenges, the opportunities, and the problems do not seem to change fundamentally with the passing of time.[3]

The underlying question with respect to the prospects for interlibrary cooperation in the next decade is whether the age-old problems and challenges of interlibrary cooperation have finally been mitigated by the existence of bibliographic networks. If bibliographic communication is indeed the critical element of all interlibrary cooperation, then it might be safe to speculate that these conditions are in fact undergoing a process of fundamental change.

From its inception, the Research Libraries Group, Inc. (RLG) has been dedicated to a cooperative approach to a broad range of problems facing research libraries. In addition to the goal of improved bibliographic control and access, RLG has adopted the goals of coordinated collection development, cooperative programs of conservation and preservation, and the improvement in physical access to research library collections.[4] More recently, the Online Computer Library Center, Inc., (OCLC) has begun to give attention to these same problems, and may develop similar programs through its Research Libraries Advisory Committee.[5] Such programs, however, have traditionally been the domain of local and regional consortia. *The Directory of Academic Library Consortia* includes 125 academic library consortia active in the United States in 1970.[6] A large number of the activities of these organizations are focused on improving physical access through reciprocal borrowing privileges, expanded interlibrary loan services, delivery services, and reciprocal photocopy agreements. A second area of high activity is coordination of collection development through mutual notification of purchase, assigned areas of specialization, and joint purchase of materials. The only area of cooperative activity not reported by the Cuadra survey is cooperative preservation and conservation, if it can be assumed that cooperative storage centers are not operated principally for the purpose of preservation. The idea of cooperative preservation and conservation as a network function seems to have gained its major impetus from RLG.

Programs such as these will continue to test the cooperative spirit of academic librarians. Coordinated collection development, increased dependence on resource sharing, and cooperative conservation and preservation must still overcome such traditional roadblocks to interlibrary cooperation as the preeminence of local priorities and the hostility of faculty, which are still sometimes abetted and magnified by the attitudes of librarians.

The situation is not without historical precedent. In a comprehensive inventory of cooperative projects in 1945, Downs describes the relative success of bibliographical projects – union lists, union catalogs, and bibliographical centers such as the Bibliographical Center for Research, Rocky Mountain Region.[7] At the same time, programs of collection specialization or division of fields were much less successful, and Downs made note of the considerable skepticism about "the practicality of agreements for dividing collecting interests among libraries."[8] Thus it seems that cooperatively developed bibliographic systems have always outdistanced the abilities of libraries to capitalize on them, and the distrust of coordinated acquisitions has for many years coexisted comfortably, if illogically, with the knowledge that even the largest libraries can acquire no more than a fraction of the world's published literature. All of the successful coordinated collection-development programs noted by Downs were local in scope, such as that in Chicago among the John Crerar, the University of Chicago, the Newberry, and the Chicago Public Library, an observation which also may be relevant to the current situation.

Have the online bibliographic networks finally created an environment in which more difficult programs of interlibrary cooperation can flourish? The answer is yes. But problems remain to be solved which will demand a sustained effort beyond that required to continue the development of the bibliographic support services of the networks. Whether the academic library community is prepared to dedicate the necessary energy to these arenas of cooperation remains to be seen, and is perhaps questionable for the immediate future, since considerable staff and financial resources must still be dedicated to technological development for authority control systems, linking of the networks, and local online catalogs.

The remainder of this chapter examines in a somewhat speculative vein the prospects for several areas of interlibrary cooperation which could be facilitated by the bibliographic networks – coordinated cataloging, cooperative preservation, and coordinated collection development and resource sharing. The first two are dealt with rather briefly; coordinated collection development and resource sharing are given fuller treatment, for it is here that the break with the past will be most dramatic and the philosophical clash most intense. In short, it will be a battle that will delight Ralph Ellsworth, and in which he may even be tempted to join.

COORDINATED CATALOGING

In 1963, Ellsworth described his vision of a national cataloging center in Washington, D.C., to which expert catalogers from throughout the country would migrate, leaving only skeletal professional cataloging staffs in the nation's libraries.[9] Online networks have now made it possible to achieve an effect similar to that sought by Ellsworth, without the disruption of library organizations and personal careers entailed by his proposal. The networks are powerful tools for sharing bibliographic data. They have vastly extended the range of cataloging data available to libraries and immeasurably improved the accessibility and convenience of use of shared cataloging information. But the network data bases continue to represent haphazard accumulations of records rather than the product of a concerted effort to provide coordinated coverage of the world's literature. Coordination of this cataloging effort, as an extension of the shared cataloging capabilities of the networks, would result in a benefit to libraries that could approach Ralph's vision.

CONSER (Conversion of Serials project) is a major example of cooperative input of bibliographic data into machine-readable form, but with its focus on the conversion of records rather than ongoing cataloging, CONSER hardly serves as a suitable example for all types of coordinated cataloging. Other projects may be more instructive for describing the possibilities of cooperative cataloging with divisions along subject or geographic lines. A little-publicized project of the Seminar on the Acquisitions of Latin American

Library Materials (SALALM) is perhaps a relevant example of both the goals and the problems of coordinated cataloging, and might well be considered a forerunner of more formal programs to be organized by the networks in the future.

SALALM's Cooperative Cataloging Project, initially proposed by Cornell University, is conceived as a means of supplementing the cataloging of Latin American materials by the Library of Congress, through the efforts of an informal consortium of OCLC members with strong Latin American interests. The purpose of the project is stated thus:

> ...to have this cataloging data in the data base, and ready for use, as soon after the publication of the materials as is reasonably possible. Libraries cooperating in this effort have voluntarily committed themselves to give high cataloging priority to materials published in pre-selected Latin American countries. Each cooperating library has accepted priority cataloging responsibilities for the new publications of one or more Latin American countries, including those of the Caribbean area. When these responsibilities are viewed collectively, all countries will be covered by at least one library.[10]

Participants in the project agree to maintain blanket order plans for newly published materials from the Latin American country or countries for which they have accepted responsibility. They also are to perform original cataloging and to put these records immediately into OCLC if a Library of Congress record is not available when the material is received. It is an admirable concept, and one which in some respects has worked well, but the project has been beset from the beginning with the problems inherent in voluntary cooperation. These problems should be documented appropriately by the individuals most closely involved, or by an independent investigation, for the purpose of gaining an understanding of SALALM's experience as the basis for planning similar programs of coordinated cataloging, but there are tentative signs that erratic financial commitment, the inability of participants to maintain priorities in the face of competing local priorities, and the varying levels of staff and financial resources among the participants have all been factors that have had an effect on the SALALM project. In spite of these problems, the SALALM project has survived and enjoys a modest degree of success.

Perhaps the major blow to the SALALM Cooperative Cataloging Project was the migration of several of the original members from OCLC to RLIN, which suggests an issue of some concern with respect to the immediate future of interlibrary cooperation. The Council on Library Resources (CLR) is attempting to promote the linking of OCLC, RLG, and WLN (the Washington Library Network) so that members of one network will have access to the data bases of the other networks. This goal will be costly, particularly if the most attractive technical options are chosen. It also faces severe political hurdles and carries the burden of association with a study of questionable research value. But this particular version of the linking problem may be minor in comparison with the broader issue of *program* linking. As OCLC, through its Research Libraries Advisory Committee, moves into areas already addressed by RLG (coordinated cataloging, coordinated collection development, and cooperative preservation of materials), there will be an urgent need for firm and effective program coordination. It would represent a massive duplication of effort if both national networks were to maintain programs of coordinated cataloging of Latin American materials, for example, with each aimed at comprehensive coverage and with each involving a complex system of assignments to cataloging centers. When one considers the large number of subject, geographic, and format categories for which coordinated cataloging is conceivably appropriate, the possibility of two organizations operating parallel programs on each front is as preposterous as the conditions that inspired Ellsworth's vision of a national cataloging center.

Another example of a promising area for coordinated cataloging is microforms. The need for improved bibliographic control of microforms has long been recognized, and there have been a number of background studies and proposals of a variety of courses of action, yet most libraries continue, out of financial necessity, to catalog massive microform sets under collective entries, thus denying users access to separate bibliographic units through analytics, considerably diminishing the value of these materials for research-library collections. In spite of the long history of concern for bibliographic access to microforms, it is difficult to disagree with Myrick's assessment of progress to date:

> The need for bibliographic control of microforms is generally recognized. Obviously, the technology for establishing such control exists. Just as obviously, efforts so far towards achieving this end have been uncoordinated, poorly supported, and generally unsuccessful.[11]

A similar area of great potential is music cataloging. Although there is an impressive tradition of cooperation among music librarians, coordinated cataloging through the networks has been thwarted by the lack of a MARC format for music scores and sound recordings. In anticipation of the implementation of these formats, the music libraries contributing to *Music, Books on Music,* and *Sound Recordings* and participating in the OCLC Musical Recordings Analytics Consortium (OMRAC), have proposed a project aimed at cooperatively building a music data-base and perhaps creating the foundation for an ongoing program of coordinated cataloging of music scores and sound recordings.[12]

Latin American materials, microforms, and music scores and sound recordings represent promising areas for programs of cooperative cataloging which illustrate a need for three somewhat different approaches to coordination. Together these examples illustrate the types of programs which could come to dominate cooperative cataloging practice over the next decade. The SALALM Cooperative Cataloging Project could well become a prototype for coordinated cataloging programs divided along geographic lines to supplement LC's effort to provide timely, high-quality bibliographic coverage for current publications from throughout the world, a goal which takes on special significance in light of the dismal prospects for LC's operating budget. Other areas of the world with characteristics similar to Latin America in terms of the acquisitions and cataloging problems they present to U.S. libraries include Eastern Europe, Africa, East Asia, and the Near East. Finely tuned coordination of the collective effort dedicated to cataloging materials from these areas of the world could result in considerable savings to research libraries supporting area studies and language programs at the research level. The same concept might well be applied to subject divisions for materials in English and Western European languages, although it is likely that subject programs will be more difficult to define and administer than those based on the clearer distinction of country of origin.

Coordination of microform cataloging involves another set of factors altogether. In contrast to the SALALM project, a cooperative project to create analytical records for microform sets would be aimed at extending access to a class of materials now receiving only minimal coverage, rather than improving the timeliness and quality of coverage for materials which in all probability would be cataloged in any case. Few libraries currently dedicate substantial staff resources to the creation of original analytics for microforms, and libraries which assume responsibility for the original cataloging of microforms will face significantly increased commitments. Unlike the SALALM project, which involves only the focusing of existing efforts, cooperative cataloging of microforms will increase the total cost of cataloging in academic libraries, because it will provide a service that is not now provided on a broad scale. Even libraries participating only to the extent of making use of the greater number of microform analytics available in network data bases will experience increased costs for copy cataloging staff, FTU charges, catalog maintenance, and/or local processing and storage of machine-readable records. Because the number of discrete bibliographic units extant in microformat is so great, cost of catalog with copy will be considerable in libraries with extensive microform holdings, and many libraries may not have the resources to make full use of the records made available through the cooperative program.

The goals of the proposed music cataloging project are similar to those of the SALALM cooperative cataloging project in that the former is concerned with disseminating records for materials for which bibliographic control is customarily provided. The motivation for coordination of music cataloging, however, also involves an element of similarity with cooperative microform cataloging. Music librarians have for years expressed a need for deeper indexing of sound recordings, and the resources of music libraries have been strained to provide the intensive analysis these materials are thought to require. Coordinated cataloging of sound recordings will attempt to combine the goals of increasing the availability of shared cataloging copy and providing deeper analysis of each item cataloged.

Although coordinated efforts to establish comprehensive bibliographic control over microforms and to provide more intensive analysis of other types of materials could result in vastly improved services to library users, it must be recognized that new services are not free even when delivered through cooperative means. It may be necessary to make a distinction between programs aimed at improving the cost effectiveness of traditional services and those which deliver new or expanded services. It may be useful to recognize three rather distinct orientations for programs of coordinated cataloging through the bibliographic networks, for purposes of assessing their prospects for the immediate future: (1) providing a greater number of shared cataloging records on a more timely basis for monographs and serials from throughout the world, (2) extending coverage of materials for which bibliographic control has been inadequate or non-existent, and (3) providing more intensive analysis for special materials.

Low-cost extensions of the shared cataloging capabilities of the networks such as the SALALM cooperative cataloging project are long overdue. They have great potential payoff in terms of improved cost-effectiveness, because they are based on existing resources in network libraries and need not involve high administrative overhead. Forceful planning initiatives by the networks and formal recognition and commitment on the part of participating libraries will be the principal ingredients for the success of those programs.

Subject-oriented groups may play important roles in defining the scope and nature of these projects, but it is not likely that any program of coordinated cataloging can be successful in the long range if operated by an informal consortium of subject catalogers and bibliographers. Formal institutional commitment is required if coordinated cataloging is to avoid becoming a casualty of the ebb and flow of resources and the instability of priorities at the local level. Although the erratic willingness of libraries to maintain cooperative commitments in the face of changing local priorities is still the key to the success of coordinated cataloging, the SALALM experience has demonstrated that such commitments can be fairly well matched to existing institutional programs and need not involve increased costs on a significant scale. If coordinated cataloging programs of this type receive the attention they deserve from the networks and other organizations such as CLR and ARL, they could become commonplace by the mid-80s—a result that could be achieved merely by taking the initiative to capitalize on the improved bibliographic communication allowed by the networks, without competing with other program areas for scarce resources.

The same cannot be said, however, of microform cataloging. It is difficult to visualize a comprehensive program of coordinated cataloging of microforms without a national agency acting as a clearinghouse and representing libraries to the microform publishing industry. Some form of compensation may be necessary to induce libraries to take on cataloging responsibility for massive sets. Since many sets cross subject, language, and period boundaries, it will be more difficult to find single libraries with staff resources matched to the content of specific sets. Full-time coordination would be required to assign projects and to negotiate with libraries serving as cataloging agencies, in contrast to the permanent assignments possible in programs based on language, subject, or country of origin. In short, coordinated cataloging of microforms represents a major new enterprise, and must compete for resources with other local projects such as retrospective conversion, as well as with other cooperative programs such as coordinated preservation of collections.

Because interlibrary cooperation is the only realistic approach to establishing bibliographic control over microforms, the failure to date to make progress in this area is sometimes viewed as a failure of cooperation. This is only partially accurate. Any new project, cooperative or otherwise, must compete for limited resources both with established services, whose costs are constantly rising through inflation, and with other prospective programs. Perhaps a more substantive cause for the lack of comprehensive bibliographic control over microforms is the possibility that this lack is not widely perceived as an urgent problem. Although this observation should not be taken as a reflection on the microform issue, it is necessary to make the point that cooperative programs are not inherently more deserving than locally oriented priorities, and it is not always a lack of vision or cooperative spirit that leads library administrators to neglect a cooperative activity.

Thus, the prospects for coordinated cataloging programs depend to some degree on the extent to which they are perceived as urgently needed by the library community. As staff costs continue to climb and increased pressure is brought to bear on libraries to moderate the rise of operating costs, it can be expected that the need for programs of coordinated cataloging will soon be perceived as powerfully urgent, particularly in areas in which libraries are already heavily committed in terms of providing bibliographic access. Programs representing increased services and commitments will materialize more slowly, and in the worst case may be delayed until there is a general upswing in funding for library services. In any case, the very fact that these cooperative options can be realistically considered at all results from the technological revolution in bibliographic communication represented by the online networks.

COOPERATIVE PRESERVATION OF MATERIALS

Perhaps the most disturbing problem facing research libraries today is the physical deterioration of their collections. The magnitude and significance of this deterioration has been described many times, and the increased awareness of the scope of the problem has led to the widespread conviction that it can be solved only through collective action.

With minor enhancements, the bibliographic networks could serve as mechanisms for disseminating information on the existence of master preservation copies in network libraries, and thus provide a basis for coordinating preservation activities. The development of a data base of master copies may well follow a course similar to the development of the bibliographic data bases themselves. The tool will be provided by the networks for the sharing of information on microform masters and treated copies, followed by a period of independent and somewhat haphazard preservation activity and conversion of associated records into the data base. At some point, however, these activities will have to come under programmatic control if they are to have a significant impact on the national preservation problem. As with other cooperative programs, the tool for coordination is likely to exist for some time before libraries begin to use it with skill and effect.

A number of developments will need to take place before there can be a systematic cooperative preservation program on a national scale. Existing preservation master copies must be recorded in the network data bases, and steps must be taken to enter records for titles being processed by currently active projects. It must become standard practice for all preservation projects to include a bibliographic dissemination component, a requirement which should be established by NEH, HEA Title II-C, and foundation funding of preservation activities. The dissemination of copy-specific information will be an essential step to avoid expensive duplication of effort by independent preservation projects occurring prior to the establishment of a national program. Means must be found to deploy preservation technology and trained manpower in research libraries throughout the country. Standards for the creation of preservation master copies and their storage under archival conditions must be adopted in order to qualify participants in the program. At some point, national priorities will have to be determined, and the segments of the total program assigned to participating libraries.

To this point, libraries have achieved very little in terms of cooperative preservation of collections. Gwinn points out:

> Although a lack of fiscal resources and technical procedures, along with a lack of trained manpower, has adversely affected development of a national strategy for preservation, the current lack of leadership and the failure by librarians to assume responsibility are perhaps the most serious impediments to progress. Plainly speaking, academic and research libraries, whose collections comprise the cultural record and which therefore are the most threatened, have historically shown little capacity for collective action.[13]

It is necessary to take issue with the foregoing assessment to some extent, because factors at work with respect to cooperative approaches to preservation are similar to those involved with microform cataloging. The main obstacle, once again, is the inability of research libraries to redirect resources on a large scale to an expensive *new* enterprise. When a significant number of libraries begin making a serious commitment to the preservation of their collections, these efforts will no doubt be viewed collectively and, in time, be coordinated on a national scale.

A coordinated program of preservation will be costly and technically demanding, and will require such massive shifts in resource allocation, that it could well become the major issue in interlibrary cooperation during the remainder of this century, and the supreme test of research libraries effectively to pursue collective action.

COORDINATED COLLECTION DEVELOPMENT AND RESOURCE SHARING

The belief that resource self-sufficiency is an impossible goal for libraries has been stated so often that it has become a truism, accepted both by active proponents of resource sharing and those who continue to view increased reliance on resource sharing with caution. When such an assertion achieves such widespread acceptance that it is never questioned, it tends to obscure some of the finer points of an issue, especially when the assertion is used in a sledgehammerlike manner in debate. It would serve no useful purpose to question the position that library self-sufficiency is a myth, but it is an issue that requires expansion and reexamination before it can serve as a useful starting point for a discussion of resource sharing.

It is doubtful that research libraries have ever operated under the assumption that self-sufficiency is an attainable goal, and it is impossible to win converts to resource sharing by attacking unrealistic goals if there are no adherents of such goals. The traditionally heavy emphasis on collection building is based instead on the more defensible assumption that the larger the collections to which scholars and students have direct physical access, the more useful these collections are to their work. Resource-sharing activists have produced no evidence to refute this position.

The emphasis on the impossibility of self-sufficiency also obscures the point that, while no library can expect to meet all of the demands of its primary user group, research libraries come rather close to doing so on some measures. A comparison of the interlibrary-loan-borrowing statistics of research libraries with circulation data and measures of in-house use reveals the overwhelming preeminence of local collections in meeting the needs of research library clienteles. The fact that a single library collection, a small subset of the published literature, can fulfill such a high proportion of user demand in most research libraries is due mainly to two factors. First, collections are selected to meet institutional program requirements and specific individual needs. Second, demand is to some extent defined, shaped, and at times unduly narrowed by limitations in the range and depth of the resources in local collections.

The latter factor in particular underscores the special significance that materials in local collections have for users, as compared to materials available only through resource sharing. There are critical differences in terms of use between materials available on site and those which must be provided through interlibrary loan, however bibliographically accessible these may be. Materials available only from remote sites cannot be used for current awareness, browsing, and screening large amounts of material for relevance to a given need. Above all, they are not available on a timely basis when needed, and frequently cannot be retained for the period of time required to use them productively. An attitude toward resource sharing which is typical of a great number of faculty users of research libraries is expressed with some feeling in the University of Pittsburgh's Senate Library Committee (SLC) report, prepared in response to the Kent Study (KS).

> KS is a clear threat and a present danger. The curtailment of library acquisitions which KS is an attempt to justify must push us, willy-nilly, into ever heavier dependence upon materials sharing (interlibrary loan, in oldspeak). Researchers can manage when the percentage of materials which must be obtained by interlibrary loan or from storage is small. As the percentage grows, research soon becomes impossible. The developers may do grave damage to our research libraries by their insistent promotional activities on behalf of materials sharing. They simply do not begin to explain what might be the consequences, the social costs, of the shifts they recommend. The natural consequence of the impairment of our library environment will be the impairment of our research and teaching.[14]

Regardless of who is right in the debate occasioned by the Kent

Study, the fact that an attempt to promote resource sharing is capable of arousing such an outraged response from faculty should be taken as a warning by librarians who are convinced that increased reliance on resource sharing is inevitable. The Pittsburgh incident must be taken as instructive with respect to the manner in which research librarians promote resource-sharing programs to their constituencies. Although the following points are not intended to imply that the Kent Study embodies these errors in judgment, they do speak to practices widely evident in the literature of resource sharing.

Use of rhetorical arguments based on the impossibility of self-sufficiency should be avoided as essentially irrelevant to serious, practical discussions of resource sharing, since generalizations of this order tend to undermine the focus on constructive issues. Sharing of materials cannot be presented as an alternative which is equal to providing materials on site, in terms of service to users. The preeminence of local collections in meeting the needs of users must be acknowledged, and the view that increased dependence on resource sharing represents a deterioration in service must be accepted as a valid position which deserves honest examination. Enthusiasm for new technology must not blind librarians to the fact that electronic networks linking library collections throughout the world does not represent utopia to users, as it does to some librarians, but an inferior substitute for housing all needed materials in one's own library. It is both a tactical blunder and an unsound position to present programs of resource sharing as inherently in conflict with the traditional emphasis on local collection development.

On the other hand, sensitivity to the perceived needs of users must not restrain librarians from continuing to develop the mechanisms of resource sharing to meet the severe economic realities faced by research libraries. This is a classic double bind, and one which must be solved if resource sharing is to assume its appropriate role in the delivery of library services. One apparent solution lies in the combination of resource sharing and coordinated collection development, a combination which will be necessary if programs of materials sharing are to be devised which address the concerns of faculty as expressed in the SLC response to the Kent Study.

Coordinated collection development among research libraries is based on the assumption that each library acquires the materials to support its programs of instruction and research at a reasonably adequate level. There is a rather large and increasingly expensive body of library materials which must be purchased each year by an institution with a comprehensive range of programs, to support its instructional and research activities at a basic level. Beyond that, most research libraries aspire to collect in some fields in great depth, perhaps even exhaustively, to support particularly distinguished or active departments and individual scholars, or to maintain traditionally strong areas of the collections. Many research libraries are currently overextended in the number of areas to which they are committed to collect to substantial depth, some dangerously so. The goal of coordinated development of collections is to allow libraries to restrict the number of specialities in which they collect esoteric and little-used materials, while assuring that users will have access to materials consciously excluded from their collections, through systematic arrangements with other libraries.

Coordinated collection development is necessary for an intentional transition to greater dependency on resource sharing, for several reasons. The Pittsburgh Senate Library Committee report shows concern for "willy-nilly" approaches to resource sharing, a concern which is justified if a shift toward resource sharing is not accompanied by plans to coordinate acquisitions with other libraries. An attempt should be made to identify reliable alternative sources for materials no longer to be collected, perhaps with associated arrangements for priority handling of requests and extended loan periods. These arrangements serve to reduce to some degree the gap in service between owning materials and depending on the resources of other libraries. More important, however, the scrutiny of collections and collection-development policies involved in developing such agreements insures an orderly and systematic transition to greater dependence on resource sharing, and specific resource-sharing arrangements can become operable factors in selection decisions. A relevant example of such a factor already at work in some libraries is the adjustment of collection-development policies resulting from membership in the Center for Research Libraries.[15]

As already noted, a shift toward coordinated collection development and planned resource sharing must not be allowed to displace the emphasis on local collections. Indeed, the primacy of the local collections should be reaffirmed as part of the basic philosophy of these programs. If the acquisition patterns of research libraries are observed closely, one is likely to discover that the exhaustive collections in some fields have been built at the expense of others which are only minimally supported, in spite of being active areas of instruction and research. Added copies to improve access to high-use materials are likely to be neglected. It is also not unlikely that areas of traditional strength have been inconsistently supported in recent years, though not by conscious choice, with the effect that a number of subject areas show uneven depth. The justification will still be strong for maintaining support for local collections within the context of resource sharing in order to maintain basic coverage at an adequate level. The image of the library as a "bottomless pit," which is said to be held by some institutional administrators and funding bodies, can only be improved by purposeful attempts to restrict the range of areas in which a library attempts to collect exhaustively. Decisions to reduce the level of acquisitions in certain fields can be used to highlight the necessity of maintaining consistent support for those that remain as areas of concentration. It can also be demonstrated that collection-development agreements magnify the effects of funds spent for library acquisitions, and that a failure to meet commitments under these agreements, endangers programs which allow users priority access to the holdings of other libraries on which they are dependent by design.

Research libraries thus have valid incentives both to seek increased support for their collections and to develop programs of resource sharing. Although the opposing pressures bearing on library administrators, from faculty, for improved collections and services, on the one hand, and from institutional administrators, to reduce costs, on the other, will never be totally relieved, programs of coordinated acquisitions and resource sharing offer the opportunity to make constructive simultaneous efforts in both directions. Ultimately, there must be a common understanding of the problems facing research libraries among adminstrators, librarians, and scholars, which implies the need to involve faculty and administrators in the development of programs of interlibrary cooperation. This need has been recognized by the Association of American Universities, which commissioned an important position paper addressing this issue.[16]

In spite of the clear logic and urgent need for well-planned programs of cooperative acquisitions and resource sharing, their success in the immediate future is not assured. It was noted earlier that the bibliographic networks are no longer subject to the insecurities of projects based on voluntary cooperation, because of the economic and operational dependency of their memberships. Programs of resource sharing will not achieve a similar stability until participants feel the same degree of dependence, a development which may not be as soon in coming as conditions appear to demand.

One behavioral factor that may inhibit the realization of this dependency is the tendency of users to concentrate their demands on the local collection. The need for an exhaustive discovery of the literature in scholarship and research is perhaps overrated by librarians, and is an exercise only rarely undertaken even by advanced scholars and researchers. A large proportion of the most relevant and significant literature is likely to be available in most research libraries as a result of the processes of selection by which the collections are built. Beyond that, users habitually substitute sources when possible and appropriate, and rely on nonlibrary channels for acquiring printed information, such as informal networks among colleagues for distributing offprints and preliminary reports. Research projects, particularly those of students, may be intentionally restricted to areas for which the local collections are capable of providing primary support. In short, users of research libraries appear inclined to use off-site materials only when these materials are of unquestioned relevance and high presumed need. Thus, an operationally critical level of dependency on materials sharing may not come about until one of the following events occurs: there is a disastrous decline in materials budgets which leaves research-library collections inadequate to provide basic support to their primary clienteles; or bibliographic apparatus and systems of transmission become capable of providing a remote interaction between users and materials more nearly comparable to direct inspection of text. Without either of these events, resource sharing will remain an increasingly significant, but supplemental, service.

The coordinated acquisitions programs offering the best prospects for assuming critical roles for users are those between libraries in close geographic proximity. The collections of neighboring institutions to which users have direct access and special borrowing privileges, and which may be connected by daily delivery services, can play a role similar to the collections of the home library. With close coordination of acquisitions, neighboring research libraries can develop complementary resources with respect to research-level collections, and thereby vastly extend the range of materials conveniently available to users of both institutions. An example of this type of coordination is the long-standing collection development agreements between Duke University and the University of North Carolina at Chapel Hill.[17] The only obstacle to developing and using these collections as a unified resource is the lack of remote bibliographic access, a problem that in all probability will be solved in the 1980s, through the development of interactive online catalogs.

Coordinated collection development on a broader geographic base, such as the programs of RLG and those which may be mounted under the auspices of OCLC's Research Libraries Advisory Committee, will meet greater obstacles to becoming viable forces in the lives of the users of participating libraries and will be more vulnerable to criticisms such as those directed at the Kent Study. Until delivery systems are greatly improved or text transmission systems are affordable, such programs of collection coordination among distant libraries are likely to play distinctly secondary roles for the majority of users.

On the other hand, programs of coordinated acquisitions at the network level offer the most promising means of insuring the availability of all published materials of any potential research value, which suggests a possibly useful hierarchical distinction between the goals of various levels of cooperative acquisitions. In time, research libraries might reasonably expect to be party to a series of cooperative agreements – with neighboring libraries, with libraries in the state and region, and with coparticipants in national networks. The institutional collections and those of near neighbors will continue to fulfill most user needs, but the total program will allow each library to contribute to, and to reap the benefits of, a national effort to collect and preserve the cultural record. Such a program would hardly deserve the ire of the University of Pittsburgh Senate Library Committee.

CONCLUSION

Coordinated collection development and resource sharing have been presented as a single category of interlibrary cooperation because, from an ideal perspective, they are inseparable, and together they constitute the critical core of advanced cooperative programs made possible by online bibliographic communication. The separation of interlibrary cooperation, for purposes of discussion, into coordinated cataloging, cooperative preservation, and coordinated collection development and resource sharing, tends to create artificial divisions. Effective cooperative programs in each of these areas will in fact depend upon some level of interprogram coordination, so that a library's cooperative responsibilities for acquiring, cataloging, and preserving defined catagories of materials are roughly congruent. A library serving as a cataloging center for materials from a given Latin American country, for example, should also be expected to serve as a major resource center for these same materials. Filming of endangered materials will of necessity be based on the strengths of retrospective and current collections. As programs of various types are established, they must in turn evolve in the direction of total program integration, with coordinated collection development and truly serviceable means of sharing resources serving as the central programs round which the others evolve.

This discussion began by posing the question of whether electronic bibliographic communication had so altered the cooperative environment that traditionally difficult programs of interlibrary cooperation are now feasible. The online networks do without question provide the technical means to deliver cooperative programs which in the past were envisioned by forward-looking librarians like Ralph Ellsworth, but which could not overcome the perplexing combination of technical and political hurdles. Librarians and funding agencies are still to a large extent preoccupied with the technical development and performance of the networks. A shift in focus will be necessary before the potential of interlibary cooperation in the network environment can be fully tested, but this shift will come as a greater number of librarians begin to reflect, as did Ellsworth, on the ends of interlibrary cooperation as well as the means.

FOOTNOTES

1. Ralph E. Ellsworth, "Another Chance for Centralized Cataloging," *The Colorado Academic Library,* 1, no. 1 (Fall 1963).
2. "The National Union Catalog: Pre-1956 Imprints: A Celebration of its Completion," *LC Information Bulletin* (February 20, 1981): 65–68.
3. David C. Weber, "A Century of Cooperative Programs Among Academic Libraries," *College & Research Libraries,* 37, no. 3 (May 1976):213.
4. The Research Libraries Group, Inc. *A Plan for the Development of a Research Libraries Network,* RLG, 1979.
5. Harold W. Billings, "Research Libraries Advisory Committee to OCLC Established," *Research Libraries in OCLC: A Quarterly,* 1, no. 1(January 1981):1-2.

6. Carlos A. Cuadra and Ruth J. Patrick, "Survey of Academic Library Consortia in the U.S.," *College & Research Libraries*, 33, no. 4(July 1972):271-283.
7. Robert B. Downs, "American Library Cooperation in Review," *College & Research Libraries*, 6, no. 4(September 1945):407-415. 1945):407-415.
8. *Ibid.*, p. 411.
9. Ellsworth, *op. cit.*
10. Seminar on the Acquisition of Latin American Library Materials, Ad Hoc Committee on Cooperative Cataloging, *Statement of Purpose* (unpublished).
11. William J. Myrick, "Access to Microforms: A Survey of Failed Efforts," *Library Journal*, v. 103, no. 20(November 15, 1978):2304.
12. Music OCLC Users Group, The Committee for REMUS, *Preliminary Proposal for REMUS (Retrospective Music)*. (Unpublished) 1981.
13. Nancy E. Gwinn, "CLR and Preservation," *College & Research Libraries*, 42, no. 2(March, 1981):118.
14. University of Pittsburgh, Senate Library Committee, *Report on the Study of Library Use at Pitt by Professor Allen Kent et al: a Pittsburgh Reply*. ERIC E9D 178 100, pp. 46-47. Quoted from Casimir Borkowski, "A Reply to the Kent Study," *Library Journal*, v. 106, no. 7 (April 1, 1981):713.
15. John Shipman, "Signifying Renewal As Well As Change: One Library's Experience with the Center for Research Libraries," *Library Acquisitions: Practice and Theory*, 1, (1978):243-248.
16. Barbara Turlington, *Research Libraries*. Association of American Universities, 1981. (Unpublished)
17. Jerrold Orne and B. E. Powell, "The Libraries of the University of North Carolina and of Duke University," *Library Trends*, v. 15, no. 2 (October 1966):223-247.

*W*e cannot or will not agree among ourselves in the large
libraries on a division of collecting policies, because at heart
we are all bibliographic empire builders. — Ralph Ellsworth.
"*Midwest Reaches for the Stars,*" College and Research Libraries, v.
9, no. 3 (April 1948):137.

Collection Development

Dale M. Bentz, University Librarian
Frank Hanlin, Bibliographer
University of Iowa
Iowa City, Iowa

It is the authors' intent to review Ellsworth's 50-year career as it relates to collection development and attempt to convey some of his thoughts on, and contributions to, this very important part of librarianship. We recognize that his greatest expertise did not lie in this area, and he is probably best known for his work in library-building planning, and internationally, as a building consultant. However, his creation of the Committee on Resources when President of the Association of College and Research Libraries; his influence in the establishment of the Midwest Inter-Library Center, now the Center for Research Libraries; his Chairmanship of the ARL Committee on the Microfilming of Doctoral Dissertations; and his work on the joint ARL-ALA Committee on the National Union Catalog are a few obvious examples in which his career clearly can be identified with the development and sharing of resources in academic research libraries.

In addition to discussing these major developments during his professional career, we also plan to consider some of the current issues in collection development and to speculate about what the next 50 years will bring librarians in terms of this subject – something Ralph enjoyed doing on all levels of library administration.

Ralph Ellsworth's career began in 1931, as Librarian of Adams State College, in Alamosa, Colorado, where, under primitive conditions and circumstances, he began to develop the collections of the college library. In his words, "There were fewer than 6,000 books in the library at Adams State, and my first year we had a book fund of less than $100.00. The College boasted of one special collection, consisting of a hundred or so out-of-date medical books donated from the estate of a local doctor." That first year, he acquired as a gift from Colorado College an attic full of unbound volumes of 19th-century general magazines.[1] He not only began to develop the collection but also started his own preservation program.

RIGHT-WING LITERATURE

To say that Ellsworth had no interest in collection development would be a serious misstatement of fact. In 1946, while at the University of Iowa, he single-handedly began collecting ephemeral material which he felt not only affected public opinion but also reflected the important current social, political, and religious issues of our times. Ellsworth's intent was to build as complete a collection as possible of those publications of right-wing organizations and of individuals who are characteristically opposed to centralized government as well as to any foreign entanglements. He wanted to be certain that future historians would have at their disposal the necessary resources to enable them to evaluate properly the beliefs and activities of these groups.

Ralph explained,

> I started the "Tensions File" to correct an error most of us University Librarians have always made. By this I mean that while we collect and preserve the printed books of our time, we fail to collect the pamphlets, bulletins, leaflets, etc., of groups that are worried about events and are trying to influence political action. Our "Tensions File" includes material on all the observable points in the United States today – on over 100 subjects, ranging from the Alaska Mental Health Law to the St. Lawrence Seaway problem.

> One of the most important tension points is the clash between the Left and Right, between Communism and Free Enterprise. I know that the FBI and several right-wing organizations are collecting the writings of the Communists, but who is collecting the publications of the rightist groups? I believe that our library is the only place doing the job thoroughly. We have been able to do this only because practically all rightist groups have been willing to give us their serial publications. This enabled us to use our limited funds to organize the material, to write letters to new organizations, and to buy the rightist books which could be secured only by purchase. Until October 1956, these limited funds came entirely from the regular library budget.[2]

The Collection is a large assemblage of materials published by right-wing, conservative, and libertarian organizations and contains periodicals, newsletters, pamphlets, correspondence, brochures, booklets, handbills illustrated with photographs, flyers, cartoons, drawings, bumper stickers, broadsides, house organs of innumerable businesses and industries, serious studies of current legislation of the time, published broadcasts of radio commentators, writings of newspaper columnists, and the writings of many, many individuals who release mimeograph accounts of their considered opinions.

Ellsworth was relentless in his efforts, and with the help of three different and very able assistants he was successful in soliciting as gifts much valuable material. One very significant donor presented his entire collection of papers, letters and articles, contained in some 35 boxes. The donor had corresponded with many people in the so-called "right-wing" movement for 20 years, had collected their published materials, and was himself active in many related political and social-action groups and organizations. This unique gift in itself was expected to support some very significant studies.

Having received a small grant from The Fund for the Republic, Inc., Ellsworth and one of his assistants prepared a complete bibliographic description and an impartial analysis of the collection, and this was eventually published under the title, *The American Right Wing; a Report to the Fund for the Republic.*[3]

One reason for wanting to publish the foregoing report was the hope that it might attract competent scholars to Iowa, to conduct research in this field. The Fund for the Republic obviously agreed, as indicated in a letter of September 2, 1958, to Ellsworth. "Historians at some point in the future are going to be grateful to you, as you have known all along, for your able efforts to put together and make sense of an enormous and ephemeral literature. The Fund, right now, is grateful to you. Your report more than justifies our modest grant.[4]

The Report does give a sampling of the abundance and variety of the right-wing literature available from more than 1000 organizations and groups of various kinds. The Tensions File still thrives at the University of Iowa but is now known as the Social Documents Collection, the name given to it in the summer of 1958. Today there are more than 3000 organizations represented in the files, and the University of Iowa Libraries regularly receive more than 250 periodicals for the collection. The researcher will find material from every geographic region of the United States on such topics as integration, taxation, states' rights, fluoridation, socialized medicine, and the United Nations. As the material is acquired, it is divided into serial and nonserial publications and is cataloged under author or title. Cross references are used frequently, but there is no descriptive cataloging of materials. A separate card catalog for the Collection is in the Special Collections Department, where the materials are housed in a controlled stack area in 584 boxes and 21 file drawers for serial publications and 31 file drawers for nonserial publications.

The conception and the beginning of this remarkable collection were truly tremendous efforts on the part of Ralph Ellsworth, and if for no other reason than that, he may be considered an important contributor to the field of collection development in academic research libraries. This very valuable and useful resource has been made available to the world of scholarship at large, through the Microfilming Corporation of America.

MICROPUBLISHING

One of the greatest innovations affecting collection development in libraries more than 40 years ago was the microfilming of some back files of the *New York Times*. Obvious advantages were the reduction of the need for a large storage space, the preservation of decaying newspapers, and the availability for a modest price of resources which otherwise might not have been available to the research-library community.

In his book *Photographic Reproduction for Libraries,*[5] Fussler lists four areas in which microfilming would be useful in libraries: condensation, preservation, acquisition, and dissemination. Although each of these uses relates to the development of library resources in institutions of higher education, we are concerned here with the acquisition and dissemination of library materials referred to in this chapter. Fussler termed these two inseparable, because information cannot be used or loaned before it is acquired.

Since the first use of film, microforms have become necessities in building library research collections, and valuable holdings exist in microcard, microprint, and microfiche, as well as in microfilm. Also, access to collections through the use of computer-output microfilm (COM) is a decided advantage.

All of us are familiar with some of the valuable resources in microformat existing in our collections. For example, in microprint, we have the *English and American Drama of the Nineteenth Cen-*

tury (1801-1900); the *Early American Imprints (Evans Bibliography, 1639-1800)* and the subsequent Shaw-Shoemaker bibliography, covering the years 1801-1819; *Three Centuries of English and American Plays, 1500-1800;* and the *British Sessional Papers.* In microcard, there are the Lost Cause Press publications, such as Coulter's *Travels in the Confederate States;* the *Early English Text Society Publications,* and the ACRL Microcard Series. In microfiche, we have the ERIC microfiche series, the *American Statistics Index* and the *Statistical Reference Index,* and the *Congressional Hearings,* published by the Congressional Information Service. Finally, in microfilm, there is the Short Title Catalog series, consisting of books listed in Pollard and Redgrave as well as those from the Wing catalog for the period 1641-1700.

Apart from user resistance and lack of access through improper or nonexistent indexes, many of our universities, which had phenomenal growth in their library holdings during the late fifties and early sixties, built their collections through acquiring microforms. Micropublishing answered the needs of many research libraries, and great numbers of important monographs, journals, government publications, manuscripts, and archives which were previously unavailable in original formats became widely accessible.

One needs only to examine the ARL Statistics for the past dozen years to ascertain the great volume of microforms being added to our library collections. Southern Illinois University is an example. From the *Library Progress; a Report on Developments in the Libraries of Southern Illinois University at Carbondale,* comes the following statement: "Since the SIU Library has grown into maturity as a research institution during a period when microtext was the only source for many of the older scholarly works, we have made extensive use of these forms."[6]

Thirty years ago, one of the serious gaps in the dissemination of information pertained to the proper distribution of the research being performed by doctoral students in research institutions. By this time, most American universities were no longer requiring the publication of doctoral theses, and as a result, much worthwhile information was not easily obtainable except through interlibrary loan.

As the first Chairman of the ARL Committee on the Microfilming of Doctoral Dissertations, Ralph Ellsworth was most influential in the development of this program, with Eugene Power, then President of University Microfilms, Inc. He accomplished this task at the risk of antagonizing many of his good friends in the Association.

At that time, microfilming was becoming a "way of life" in our society, and University Microfilms, Inc. was already publishing *Microfilm Abstracts,* which consisted of the abstracts of theses and dissertations. UM was in the business of making positives of these abstracts for sale upon demand. It was Ellsworth's contention that this program could be expanded at the national and international levels and that University Microfilms, already in business, would be the logical agent to microfilm the dissertations of those institutions which wanted to participate. These universities would then ship the original copy, before binding, to University Microfilms for microfilming, so that positive prints could be made available for purchase by scholars and institutions throughout the world. One great advantage of this proposal was that the microfilm copy could be purchased for less than the cost of mailing the original hardbound copy back and forth through interlibrary loan, and further, the borrowing institution would then own the copy. The negative, or archival, copy would be retained in the vaults of University Microfilms, Inc.

Ellsworth was successful in pushing this program through ARL after much debate on the legality of the venture and on the willingness of the member institutions to place this responsibility with a commercial enterprise rather than the Library of Congress or some member university. Ellsworth, always persuasive, convinced his colleagues, and the idea was adopted, without a dissenting vote, at the annual meeting of ARL, in Iowa City, Iowa, on January 26, 1952.[7]

NATIONAL UNION CATALOG

As early as 1904, Ernest Cushing Richardson, Librarian of Princeton University, in a speech at the ALA Conference, in St. Louis, remarked that "every librarian very soon finds the limitations of his own library at a thousand points, and the practical need of referring readers to books that one does not have in one's own library . . . "[8] This statement, made more than three-quarters of a century ago, suggested a need which may be even more relevant today. A system which makes the important resources of a large number of libraries available to the scholarly community led to the creation of the *National Union Catalog (NUC).* This great bibliographic record provides libraries with a listing, by main entry, of published works held in the major institutions around the country and enables them to use it as a book-selection tool. Such use could eliminate needless duplication of acquisitions.

In 1954, the American Library Association's Board on Resources of American Libraries appointed a new subcommittee on the National Union Catalog. Ralph Ellsworth was a member of this initial committee, which met frequently during the fifties, and the work of that committee ultimately led to the publication in book form of the *National Union Catalog.* This massive undertaking resulted in a listing of the titles and holdings of books with imprints from 1956 on which were reported by other North American libraries to the Library of Congress, in addition to those books previously covered by the publication of the Library of Congress printed cards. This most welcome development in achieving some bibliographical control of library resources encouraged the NUC subcommittee to continue its work, and a supplement in 30 volumes was later published to include the 1952-1955 imprints.

Although Ralph Ellsworth initially questioned the feasibility of publication, he was interested in improved interlibrary cooperation and worked diligently to achieve the desired results. He even proposed a system whereby a library contributing to the NUC could provide its own personnel to help record the holdings of the respective institutions and to assist in eliminating the 2,000,000 cards which constituted an impossible backlog at the Library of Congress.[9] His proposal was never adopted, but the first phase was completed during his membership on the subcommittee. During this period, Ellsworth also served as Chairman of the ALA Resources and Technical Services Division's Committee on Resources of American Libraries. In the words of the Committee under his chairmanship,

This expansion constitutes a major step toward providing a guide to the library resources of the United States and toward making generally available in book form information previously found only in the card catalog in the Library of Congress hitherto known as the National Union Catalog. It is expected that the value of this expanded work, for research use and for library planning, will be felt immediately and will increase greatly in the years to come.[10]

The success of its previous venture convinced the subcommittee that every effort should be made to publish the older portion of the National Union Catalog and to incorporate in it the 1952-1955 supplement. This led to the publication in book form of the *National*

Union Catalog: Pre-1956 Imprints by Mansell Information/ Publishing Ltd., and resulted in the largest bibliographic project ever contemplated or completed. This bibliographical treasure has been published over a period of years and makes available in book form the total National Union Catalog maintained on cards by the Library of Congress since 1901.

At the time this is being written, the Library of Congress is celebrating the completion of the 755-volume *National Union Catalog: Pre-1956 Imprints,* described as "a monumental 14-year publishing project of great importance for libraries and the world of scholarship. Completion of this unique, cooperative publishing and bibliographical venture also marks, in many ways, the close of the era of non-automated bibliographical control."[11]

The conception, planning, and completion of this bibliographical resource represent yet another instance of Ellsworth's untiring efforts and influence on a project of major importance.

FARMINGTON PLAN

Another important event which affected collection development in the major university research libraries during the active career of Ralph Ellsworth was the conception of the Farmington Plan. The Librarian of Congress initiated a meeting on October 9, 1942 at Farmington, Connecticut, at which time a discussion was held concerning specialization among research libraries and a sharing of the responsibility in book collecting. As stated by Edwin E. Williams in his *Farmington Plan Handbook,*

> The Farmington Plan is a voluntary agreement under which some sixty American libraries, as a means of increasing the nation's total resources for research, have accepted special responsibility for collecting. Ideally, if the plan could be extended to all countries and all types of publications and if it could be made fully effective, it would make sure that one copy at least of each new foreign publication that might reasonably be expected to interest a research worker in the United States would be acquired by an American library, promptly listed in the *National Union Catalog,* and made available by interlibrary loan or photographic reproduction.[12]

Obviously, the original concept of this plan was to obtain for this country and to record centrally one copy of each book of research importance, thus making it possible for university libraries to act with greater selectivity in their book-selection responsibilities.

Until this time, much had been accomplished in making resources accessible, but little had been done to develop collections through cooperative acquisition.

As a result of that first meeting at Farmington, a special committee was appointed to advise the Librarian of Congress on cooperation among research libraries, in an effort to achieve the results previously discussed. That committee's report, "Proposal for a Division of Responsibility among American Libraries in the Acquisition and Recording of Library Materials," was subsequently approved by the American Library Association, the Association of Research Libraries, the Council of National Library Associations, and the American Council of Learned Societies.

Much discussion ensued at each semiannual ARL meeting, and a special two-day session of the Association was held in March of 1947, after which the Plan was launched. Immediate steps were taken to secure funding to make the idea succeed.

Although Ralph Ellsworth was never a member of any of the ARL Farmington Plan Committees, he was very much a part of the spirited debate which often took place at the ARL meetings. At one point, when it seemed that the discussions were being bogged down by details, Ralph remarked that "he thought the Farmington Plan had originated as a major project designed to achieve something of major importance and it appeared to have degenerated to such a point that we were spending our time talking about cataloging troubles, etc., which may be involved."[13] Ellsworth always seemed to be a catalyst, and if the discussion became sidetracked for any reason, he spoke his piece. Sometimes his impatience irritated some of his colleagues, but his heart was always on the side of progress.

At the ARL meeting, in Chicago, in January of 1959, a conference on the Farmington Plan was held prior to the regular meeting of the Association. At that time, there was discussion concerning the responsibility within the profession for the development and coordination of major scholarly acquisitions programs. The suggestion was made that perhaps the ALA RTSD Committee on Resources should assume this responsibility. Ellsworth, as chairman of this committee, felt strongly that there was considerable difficulty in working within the bureaucracy of the ALA organization, and that the job of coordination of major cooperative acquisitions programs should not be attempted through the Committee on Resources. He preferred to see the responsibility remain with ARL. Later during the same conference, when the question of duplicate copies of Farmington Plan publications was raised, Ellsworth reminded the membership that earlier, it had been proposed that all Farmington Plan acquisitions be placed in the Library of Congress and paid for by libraries on a graduated fee basis. His view was that this proposal was still relevant and it might be wise to have such a national acquisitions plan in order to provide an insurance copy, allowing each university or research library to determine its own need for additional copies.

The Farmington Plan was successful from the beginning, and foreign publications came into those participating libraries according to country and subject responsibilities as previously divided. During 1951, some 17,000 books were received, and it was estimated that at least half of them would have been otherwise unobtainable. By the end of 10 years, some 150,000 volumes had been purchased, at a cost of approximately $275,000. Robert Vosper, then University Librarian at Kansas, was asked by the ARL to conduct a survey of the Farmington Plan. This he did, with the assistance of Robert L. Talmadge, his associate director. Talmadge later commented on the success of the Plan as follows: "Ever since it got underway, the Farmington Plan has been regarded . . . as one of the most important, most enlightened, and most hopeful instances of interlibrary cooperation in the history of American libraries." He further stated, "It has brought our major libraries to the recognition of their collective responsibility for covering the world's publications in the national interest."[14]

This program continued actively for almost a quarter of a century, until its demise, in December 1972, 30 years following the first discussions which led to its beginning.

MIDWEST INTER-LIBRARY CENTER

Perhaps because of the miniscule collection in his charge at Adams State, Ellsworth may have realized, from his earliest days as a librarian, the necessity and value of sharing resources, and was willing to encourage new and untried methods to accomplish this. While Director of Libraries at the University of Iowa, the opportunity arose for a cooperative enterprise to improve the library resources of the Midwest. In 1947, the Carnegie Corporation of New York made a grant of $5000 to study the feasibility and ramifications of a cooperative library project among midwestern libraries. Under the chairmanship of President E. C. Colwell, of the University of Minnesota, there was formed an organizing committee consisting of President H. B. Wells, of Indiana University; E. W. McDiarmid, University Librarian at the University of Minnesota and also President of the American Library Association; President E. B. Fred, of the University of Wisconsin; and Ellsworth. By January 1949, the boards of trustees of 10 midwestern universities had approved in principle a program which would furnish central housing and the means for servicing littleused research materials to be deposited by the participating libraries, in recognition of the severe space shortage being experienced by many of those institutions. In addition, there was envisioned a joint acquisitions plan whereby cooperative purchase of little-used materials would be made by the central organization for the use of all member libraries. In the spring of 1949, the Midwest Inter-Library Corporation was incorporated under the laws of the state of Illinois and a $1,000,000 capital fund was made available by the Carnegie Corporation and the Rockefeller Foundation. The 10 libraries were immediately joined by three others, and a board of directors was named, including a representative from each of the participating institutions. The University of Chicago donated land on its campus for the site of a building, construction of which began in July 1950. Thus, the Midwest Inter-Library Center (MILC) came into being.

At the MILC dedication ceremony, held on October 5, 1951, Ellsworth presented a paper in which he showed he was already reaching beyond the immediate goal of storage of little-used materials, by stating: "Cooperative storage of publications is not the main purpose of this association. Cooperative acquisition and planning are."[15] And beyond these needs he saw an urgent need to solve the "problems involved in getting . . . to where we can use the Library of Congress printed catalogs . . . in an economical relationship to our local records."[16] But he recognized even these problems and solutions to be "transitional" and said that "shortly it will be clear to all that these rather minor matters will be overshadowed by other parts of the country and between all the centers and the Library of Congress."[17] Lest it can be thought that his stargazing was limited to regional or national boundaries, he concluded his remarks by saying that "each [problem] must be evaluated in its national as well as its regional setting," but "I am aware that, once we have solved our local, regional, and national problems, we shall merely have laid the groundwork for the international ones that lie ahead."[18]

Although the activities of MILC during its first few years

centered primarily on accepting, cataloging, and shelving the thousands of deposits received from member libraries, it also gave almost immediate attention to the purchase of library materials for the use of all member libraries. In the First Annual Report, following the close of the first fiscal year, on June 30, 1950, Director Ralph T. Esterquest noted that a five-man committee had been appointed to formulate an acquisitions policy for the Center, "with a view to rendering service to participating institutions" by the "purchase of books, periodicals, and other library materials from its own funds for the joint use and service to its member libraries and their users."[19] By the time of the Second Annual Report, a firm policy had been established and the first large-scale program – the Foreign Newspapers on Microfilm project – had begun; and in the Third Annual Report, a number of such direct acquisitions was reported. By 1956, the Foreign Language Newspapers on Microfilm had been taken over by the Association of Research Libraries so that a much-expanded list of newspapers would be available to a larger constituency, but the administration and housing of the project were maintained by MILC.

Almost from the beginning, too, were hints from some member libraries that if MILC were to pick up subscriptions to certain little-used periodicals, the participating libraries would cancel their own subscriptions. By 1956, these more or less haphazard quid pro quo ventures into periodical subscriptions reached much larger proportions when a grant was made by the National Science Foundation (NSF) to survey the members of MILC as to their current subscriptions to serials listed in *Chemical Abstracts,* with a view to comprehensiveness by MILC subscribing to those not held by any member, and asking those members with the only subscriptions to a journal to maintain their subscriptions. Within another six months, an additional grant was received from NSF to cover journals listed in *Biological Abstracts,* in the same manner.

Some 16 years later, in 1972, when the growing problems of inflation and relatively smaller acquisitions allocations had made serious inroads upon the collection-development programs of the member libraries, the Carnegie Corporation made a grant to the renamed and greatly expanded Center for Research Libraries (CRL) to make a more thorough search for little-used titles to which subscriptions might be dropped by member libraries and be picked up by the Center. This program, however, met with only limited success, perhaps because the initiative was mostly left up to the individual libraries to survey their entire subscription lists rather than upon the use of such standard guides as *Chemical Abstracts* and *Biological Abstracts;* perhaps because the provision of some of the periodicals was to be by the British Library Lending Division at Boston Spa; but perhaps also because some of the members could not yet give an affirmative answer to Ralph Ellsworth's question of 1947: "Are we prepared to discard our inherited philosophy of trying to make each of our libraries as large and inclusive as possible in favor of a philosophy of building the contents of each of our libraries in relation to the inclusive contents of a group of homogeneous libraries?"[20] For whatever reasons, the range of participation varied widely.

There is not space to chronicle here all, or even a small portion, of the acquisitions activities and projects engaged in by CRL, but it must suffice to mention that they involve many microform and reprint projects, collection of state and foreign documents, college catalogs, foreign dissertations, and elementary and secondary-school textbooks – some by direct purchase, some by deposit, others by gift or exchange. From the beginning, the interest in the aspect of the Center as a storage facility for little-used research materials was evidenced by the fact that many libraries from all over the country and a number from abroad, as well as such organizations as the Midwest Stock Exchange, American Medical Association, federal and state courts, and many others, sent quantities of materials.

In 1960, R. B. Downs, then Chairman of the Board of Directors of MILC and Director of the University of Illinois Libraries, used his report to the membership to note the trend of MILC "towards its becoming a national rather than a strictly regional organization" and that "within certain well-defined fields . . . MILC has become and should be regarded as a national library and ought to be supported as such." He then followed this remark with several suggestions for the future development of MILC. Among them was that MILC "should open membership to any research library in the United States which would find our collections useful, and is in general sympathy with our objectives."[21] The University of Toronto became the twenty-first member, in 1963, and in 1965, MILC formally changed its name to the Center for Research Libraries and opened its membership to all research libraries.

This brief and very incomplete recounting of MILC/CRL perhaps only hints at the great revolution that had occurred in collections development within the space of a few years. Its impact and the changes which it brought about in the collecting policies of not only member libraries, but nearly all U. S. research libraries, are probably not felt by the newer generations of librarians, who have "grown up," so to speak, with the Center and its various programs at their beck and call.

But in moving on to another of collection development, we will again call on Messrs. Ellsworth and Downs as spokesmen for MILC/CRL. As we noted earlier, very early in the planning and opening of MILC, Ellsworth called for collection development beyond the mere storage of little-used materials by member libraries. A number of the ideas presented in his papers on MILC came to fruition over the course of several years. But implicit in his remarks was the notion that each library needed to analyze its collections to ascertain its strengths and weaknesses, then build upon its strengths and rely upon other cooperating libraries and the Center to fortify against its weaknesses. In Ellsworth's speech at the dedication of MILC, he suggested that "we should begin at once to survey the special collection resources of the region and to strengthen each existing collection . . . to make a single strong research resource."[22]

Nine years later, in his report as Chairman of the Board of Directors of MILC, R. B. Downs suggested there be made

> . . . a sharper definition of MILC's collecting responsibilities . . . and . . . that the Center should expand the plan to assign responsibility to its member libraries for materials falling within their special spheres of interest . . . We need more detailed information about the resources of libraries in the Midwest, particularly specialized collections of a scholarly and research nature . . . Any intelligent program of cooperation and coordination must be based upon exact knowledge of where we stand and in what directions we are going. For this purpose, full descriptions or guides to existing resouces of the region would be valuable, and in fact almost indispensable.[23]

While sporadic attempts had been made to analyze research library collections and to relate them to cooperation with other libraries, these were principally arrangements between or among a small number of libraries in generally close geographic proximity—perhaps within the same city or state or small region.

APPROVAL PLANS

Approval plans were another innovation during the five decades of the Ellsworth career, and they became very important acquisition tools for many libraries. They also undoubtedly affected collection development on many campuses. These plans may have been an outgrowth of what have commonly been known as standing orders, or in some cases, blanket orders, from designated publishers. When these programs, although still in use, proved to have some limits, a system was developed whereby subject-area interests were defined and profiles were established so that the libraries would promptly receive those titles necessary to round out their collections. One of the great advantages of these plans was the freedom to return books, if so desired, upon review by both librarians and faculty.

Much has been written in recent years on the pros and cons of approval plans, and most objections have centered on the theme that acquisitions personnel and/or collection-development officers have abdicated their responsibility for book selection and given it to the library vendors. The advantages of this system of book procurement seem to outweigh the disadvantages, and most librarians participating in such programs agree that much time is saved in the book-selection process and that approval-plan books generally are received before many of the orders could have been otherwise generated.

The intent here is not to evaluate these plans or to discuss again the details of their operation, but merely to include the subject as one of the issues in librarianship as it relates to collection development in our libraries.

Ralph Ellsworth, appearing in a symposium in celebration of the 200th anniversary of the establishment of the University of Pennsylvania Library, presented a paper entitled, "The Balance of Conflicting Interests in the Building of Collections: Comprehensiveness versus Selectivity."[24] The title of that paper suggests at least a debate within the profession concerning many of those problems or questions currently relating to approval-plan purchasing—years before such plans as we know them today were in existence.

In that paper, Ellsworth states:

Prior to World War II the debates on "comprehensive versus selectivity" were almost always exhortative, abstract, and always ending in platitudes about numbers of dollars available. On the surface, I think this is still true, for how can most of us with book budgets in the one to two hundred thousand dollar range—and largely tied up in journal subscriptions (and those predominantly for the sciences)—and with constantly rising binding costs for those journals, pretend that we can do anything more than buy a fair share of the new press releases and now and then engage in a little retrospective gap filling?[25]

Ellsworth's thesis simply was that librarians must spend their book dollars selectively and learn to depend on regional centers for less-used materials as well as for those specialized resources in microformat which may be easily transportable. His argument that we must "pool our buying" is just as relevant today, with book budgets in the million-dollar range, as it was 30 years ago. Aren't we talking about resource sharing today more than ever before? Ellsworth concludes by saying that

> The age-old debate on the question of "completeness versus selectivity" is largely a sterile exercise in verbal virtuosity unless it is considered in the light of such contemporary concepts as the increasing massiveness of literature, the development of a biblio-technology and the proper balancing of the use of the national and regional unit for bibliographic control and for book handling.[26]

An approval-plan program is useful in collection development in academic libraries, and particularly for the systematic purchase of current titles, regardless of one's theory of book selection. Even though the use of such plans as a book-selection tool may remain controversial, librarians continue to use them to advantage.

COLLECTION ANALYSIS PROJECT AND RESEARCH LIBRARIES GROUP

As libraries encountered the problems of inflation, relatively smaller acquisitions budgets, and increasingly specialized fields of teaching and research, it became more and more clear that something beyond just a subjective analysis of collections was needed, not merely to relate acquisitions funds as closely as possible to the purchase of materials reflecting institutional priorities, but also as a means of enhancing interlibrary cooperation and resource sharing. It was with these objectives in mind that, in 1977, the Office of University Management Studies of the Association of Research Libraries, with the support of a grant from the Andrew Mellon Foundation, developed a procedure known as the Collection Analysis Project (CAP), "which university research libraries can use to analyze collection, acquisition, retention, resource-sharing and preservation practices."[27]

The procedures developed for CAP require that the team charged with carrying out the CAP at a particular institution come face to face with the historical development of the collection, the library's goals and objectives, and local factors affecting collection development, followed by a close analysis of operating practices, collection assessment, resource sharing, and preservation. The end result of the study, wherever conducted, should be "a series of specific, recommended actions for a new and improved approach to operating the library's collection development program."[28]

The CAP was undertaken as a pilot test by the libraries of Massachusetts Institute of Technology, Arizona State University, and the University of California at Berkeley. Other libraries followed after revisions and refinements had been made as a result of the pilot tests.

We turn now to an aspect of the CAP which has been picked up by another group of libraries, the Research Libraries Group (RLG), and which is even more closely aligned to the implicit statements of Ralph Ellsworth and the more explicit ones of R. B. Downs. This recently formed group, consisting at this writing of 23 rather widely-scattered research libraries, is undertaking a closely detailed assessment of present collections and collecting activities, with the purpose of determining strengths and weaknesses among the group and eventually seeking volunteers from the group to agree to continue comprehensive or even exhaustive collections in those areas in which they may already have such collections, so that other libraries in RLG may perhaps decrease their coverage of those areas and rely upon their stronger partner. Already some agreements have been reached for comprehensive coverage in selected areas, and more generous lending privileges have been agreed upon. In addition, an information network has been established by the group to keep members informed of serial publications being considered by, subscribed to, or canceled, and to announce the planned or actual purchase of expensive items which can be made available to other members.

It is perhaps ironic that these excursions into cooperation and coordination, suggested by Ellsworth for MILC's consideration some 30 years earlier, should now be picked up with fervor by another group, all of whose members are also members of MILC's enlarged group, CRL. Rumination upon this fact may suggest that the present size of CRL might have an inhibiting effect upon such a detailed and exhaustive program which requires close attention by the member libraries and by the headquarters staff.

NATIONAL PERIODICALS CENTER

We turn now to yet another multi-library project, which as yet is only in its proposal stages, but which is in some ways an outgrowth of ideas and activities of CRL from its earliest years. This is the proposal for a National Periodicals Center "prepared by the Council on Library Resources (CLR) at the request of the Library of Congress," which "continues a series of steps initiated by the National Commission on Libraries and Information Science (NCLIS),"[29] which culminated in the latter's 1977 document, *Effective Access to Periodical Literature.* The NCLIS recommended that "the Library of Congress assume responsibility for developing, managing, and operating the center. . . . The goal of the National Periodicals Center is to improve access to periodical literature for libraries and thus to individuals using libraries."[30] Details of the proposal will not be gone into here, as they may be readily surveyed in CLR's document, but in the authors' opinion, the NPC, in its proposed and realized form, would probably have the most important impact upon the collections development program of research libraries since the foundation of MILC and its expansion into CRL. It should be remarked, of course, that the natural predecessors of the NPC were, in many ways, the three editions of the *Union List of Serials* and its foster-child, *New Serial Titles,* which in themselves have contributed to collection-development policies of large and small libraries throughout the United States and Canada.

Although funding for the proposed NPC seems doubtful at present, there should be hope that the proposal itself, at least in a modified form, will continue to be referred to as a means of serving research libraries and scholarship even better but more economically than now.

OTHER PROGRAMS

Space does not permit us to attempt any further recounting of other collection-development programs involving specific libraries, groups of libraries, or libraries generally. They would include such diverse programs as the Latin American Cooperative Acquisitions Project and other similar cooperative programs, PL480 and its successor, the federal funding for library projects under Titles II A and II C, the various regional bibliographical and storage centers, the recent White House Conference, with its statements regarding resource development and preservation, and a host of other programs, plans, and proposals relating to collection development.

Ralph Ellsworth would have agreed with some of these programs and would probably have opposed others, either in some detail or in toto. But there seems little question that, in general, the gradual inching forward of cooperative and coordinated collection-development policies and procedures must bring a sense of satisfaction to Ralph Ellsworth. In addition, we can recognize echoes of his earlier exhortations, pleadings, chastisements, and pronouncements in many of our collection-development activities of today. Some of his suggestions of 25 or 30 years ago have not yet been realized — and it must be admitted that some of them may never be realized, because they were impractical to begin with, or because more modern technology that even he couldn't foresee, has simply made them obsolete and passed them by.

THE NEXT FIFTY YEARS

Much has been written in recent years about the forthcoming paperless society and an age in which we will have information systems available through computers and controlled by brokers. In a meeting held prior to the ALA Conference in New York City, in 1980, Newton Minow, Chair of the meeting entitled "An Information Agenda for the 1980's," declared, "The Information Age is about to transform all of our lives."[31]

If we believe these statements, then libraries as we know them today will undergo a radical change. That change will obviously necessitate a rethinking of our book-collecting habits, and all of our theories pertaining to collection development will have to be either discarded or altered, to meet these changing demands of our clientele.

This is not to imply that in 50 years, there may be no books or journals or libraries as we know them today, because nothing is going to surpass the joy of reading a book for the mere pleasure of it. Serving the informational needs of society by electronic means is one thing, but satisfying the cultural and recreational needs through books is another. Then, too, there are the bits and pieces of factual information which will always be available in books and which would be impractical to store and access electronically.

It is true, however, that developments which have taken place during the last 20 years may well change our traditional concepts of collection development in university research libraries. Witness the appearance of machine-readable data bases used for computerized literature searching for both retrospective and current information. There are more than 500 of these data bases at our disposal, and most of them have been developed by private industry. We are familiar with the products provided by Bibliographical Retrieval Services, Lockheed Information Systems, and the System Development Corporation. We have access to source material in most disciplines, such as INFORM (Business), Compendex and NTIS (Engineering), ERIC (Education), INSPEC (Physics, Electronics, Computer Sciences), MEDLINE (Medicine), LEXIS (Law), and Psychological Abstracts (Psychology). When one realizes that there are more than 360,000 records in the post-1967 Psychological Abstracts data base alone, and that approximately 95 percent of the contents covers periodical articles, one can readily appreciate the consequences this has for library use, and the effect it will ultimately have on journal subscriptions. As the use of computers becomes more economical and these data bases can be accessed in the office or from the home, then the user will become less directly dependent on our library collections.

In recent months, Dow Jones & Co. announced plans for using cablevision as a means of distributing information to subscribers, and that company's entry into the personal computer markets calls for a News/Retrieval Service which will provide the only source for the full text of the *Wall Street Journal*.[32]

During the decades of the sixties and seventies, a very dramatic decrease in the cost of searching these data bases increased their use through online searching. It seems reasonable to assume that within the next 50 years, access to information by the computer process may be cheaper than purchasing and storing the information in paper format and may help to reduce the need for personnel to retrieve the desired information.

If we can believe the projections of F. W. Lancaster and his colleagues, we can expect that printed journals will disappear, owing to the high cost of print on paper. Even today, many of the scientific journals are being priced above the ability of many libraries to pay. This does require greater resource sharing among libraries and a willingness to rely on other sources of information. When this happens, and it is beginning now, collection-development policies and programs in most libraries, and particularly in the large research libraries, will have to change.

Lancaster goes so far as to say that

The implications of this for libraries are obviously of the greatest significance. The library problem will no longer be one of inadequate space. It may not even be one of inadequate financial resources. Rather, it is likely to be one of justification for existence and simple survival. Will libraries be needed in an electronic world in which documents exist in machine-readable rather than printed form and any such document can be accessed by an individual who can reach a terminal wherever that document happens to be stored?[33]

The following is from an editorial entitled, "Academic Libraries in the Computer Age."

What will academic libraries and higher education be like 10 or 50 years hence? Consider the following scenario culled from the predictions of selected futurists listed in *The Book of Predictions* by David Wallechinsky, Amy Wallace, and Irving Wallace (Morrow, 1980):

1985-1990 – Pocket-sized electronic books will be produced which consist of mini-cassettes that are either inserted into calculator-sized terminals for text display or hooked up to domestic computer systems for print-outs of typeset quality or read-outs by voice synthesizer.

Twenty thousand pages of text can be transmitted by computer in one second and stored on two square inches of film, glass, or other surface and read by a computer looking for specific concepts at one thousand pages per second.

1991-2030 – The price/performance ratio of computers will be reduced to one-sixteenth its current value, and hardware costs will become nominal.

Online link-ups to large research libraries in home, school, and office will cause a decline in published reference books, newspapers, and magazines.

A Universal Information System will be in operation, giving access "at any given moment to the contents of any book that has ever been published or any magazine or any fact." Printing-on-demand modules in both urban and rural locations will permit hard copy reproduction of any material required – granting, of course, that the copyright laws have changed by then.[34]

Ellsworth was asked to comment on some of these predictions concerning the future of libraries and library service. He responded as follows:

At any one time, there must be millions of people using data, information, knowledge and wisdom (in the form of books, etc.). The printing press makes this possible because it is economical to make multiple copies so that each person, within reason, can have his own viewer. But in the electronic world, each person would need a screen or a terminal, and all have to be connected by wires to sources of power and information. But people aren't always tied by the umbilical cord to these wires as they work and plan and learn. Engineers are out in the field, so are geologists and so are learners that like to learn sitting under a tree, or lying in the bathtub, or in bed. And the cost of all those screens and terminals would be pretty high. My guess is that when we strike a balance between cost, convenience, and need, we may find that we will use the computer for some things and the printed books for others. Only time can enable us to strike the balance. We can't force it. When you look at all the printed material that comes into a library from all over the world, I don't see how the issuance of this could be regimented enough to get it on the computer. Would the writers of all those letters, memos, pamphlets, etc. in the Tensions File[35] have been willing to issue their ideas on the computer? And think what that kind of world would do to freedom of expression. The present situation is fairly decentralized and many people, singly or in groups, can get their messages into the stream of persuasion without being censored by anybody with absolute control of the publishing outlet. But in the paperless world, there would have to be a much narrower point of issuance. I can see that it is easy to put the current input of our books on a national or regional computer system, as we are doing, but there are so many local needs that would be too costly and cumbersome on the big system. We might overload the system to the point of absurdity.

And then, there is the question of the relationship between information and the other kinds of human communication we use. As we say, man doesn't live by communication alone. I am now reading two novels currently. I pick up one and read it one night and the other the next night. I see no way in which the electronic world could meet my needs in fact or in cost. Also, I use information and other kinds of records differently. I may need to study, carefully and painfully, an article or chapter, and when I do I may need to study several hours, and to repeat and review. Can you visualize how learning from a screen or terminal could meet my needs? I assume that we may still continue to have children, maybe several of them in a single family. Will each one need his or her terminal in his or her room, and can everyone afford this or have the space? Think of the poor people in our inner cities. I also wonder about the effect on the consumption of energy, which I assume will be in short supply in the future. It's possible that by doing everything electronically instead of heating, lighting, air conditioning, and transporting all the people involved in the print world, we might use less energy. I don't know but I am skeptical.

So, all in all, there are deep philosophical, economic, human nature, and other elements involved in the evolution of the electronic age of communication. Up to this time in human history, technology has always won, but it doesn't follow that it will always win in the future because there are new elements involved: supply of energy, numbers of people, a highly organized community organization, etc. How will the issues be resolved? I don't know but I suspect by the slow, painful trial and error methods.[36]

Critical times are facing librarians in the years ahead. Public funding at all levels will be in short supply, and this, coupled with the information explosion and technological revolution, both of which have become parts of our workaday world, will require the greatest ingenuity of all of us. We will need the vision, the versatility, the wisdom, and the nerve of a Ralph Ellsworth to help us plan and direct the course of our actions during the next 50 years.

FOOTNOTES

1. Ralph E. Ellsworth, *Ellsworth on Ellsworth.* Metuchen, N.J.: Scarecrow, 1980, p. 7.
2. Letter from Ralph E. Ellsworth to Bradford Martin, Editor, *Right,* 28 February 1957.
3. Ralph E. Ellsworth and Sarah M. Harris, *The American Right Wing; a Report to the Fund for the Republic, Inc.* Washington, D.C.: Public Affairs Press, 1962.
4. Letter from the Fund for the Republic, Inc., to Ralph E. Ellsworth, 2 September 1958.
5. Herman H. Fussler, *Photographic Reproduction for Libraries.* Chicago: University of Chicago Press, 1942, p. 11.
6. *Library Progress; a Report on Developments in the libraries of Southern Illinois University at Carbondale* (February 1973): 3.
7. Association of Research Libraries (ARL), *Minutes of the Thirty-eighth Meeting* (Iowa City, Iowa, 26 January 1952), p. 20.
8. Ernest Cushing Richardson, "International Bibliography," *Library Journal* v. 29, no. 2 (February 1904): 94.
9. Ellsworth Correspondence in the Archives of the University of Iowa Libraries.
10. *The National Union Catalog* (Ann Arbor: Edwards, 1958), 1(1953-57): iii.
11. "Library of Congress Information Bulletin," 40(1981): [61].
12. Edwin E. Williams, *Farmington Plan Handbook,* rev. to 1961 and abridged [Ithaca, N.Y.]: Association of Research Libraries, 1961, p. 9.
13. ARL, *op. cit.,* p. 8.
14. Robert L. Talmadge, "The Farmington Plan Survey: an Interim Report," *College & Research Libraries,* v. 19, no. 5 (September 1958): 375, 383.
15. Ralph E. Ellsworth, "Tasks of the Immediate Future," *Library Quarterly* v. 22, no. 1 (January 1952): 19.
16. *Ibid.*
17. *Ibid.*

18. *Ibid.*, p. 20.
19. Midwest Inter-Library Corporation and the Midwest Inter-Library Center (MILC), *First Annual Report.* Chicago: [1950], p. 10.
20. Ralph E. Ellsworth and Norman L. Kilpatrick, "Midwest Reaches for the Stars," *College and Research Libraries,* v. 9 (April 1948): 137.
21. Midwest Inter-Library Corporation and the Midwest Inter-Library Center, *Eleventh Annual Report.* Chicago: [1960], p. 3.
22. Ellsworth, "Tasks of the Immediate Future," p. 19.
23. MILC, *Eleventh Annual Report,* pp. 3-4.
24. Ralph E. Ellsworth, "The Balance of Conflicting Interests in the Building of Collections: Comprehensiveness versus Selectivity," in *Changing Patterns of Scholarship and the Future of Research Libraries.* Philadelphia: University of Pennsylvania Press, 1951.
25. *Ibid.*, p. 73.
26. *Ibid.*, p. 79.
27. Duane E. Webster, preface to *Collection Analysis in Research Libraries.* Washington, D.C.: Association of Research Libraries, 1978, p. i.
28. *Ibid.*, pp. 8-9
29. Council on Library Resources, *A National Periodicals Center: Technical Development Plan.* N.p.: Council on Library Resources, 1978, p. [vii].
30. *Ibid.*, p. [ix].
31. Lois R. Pearson, "Think Tank Tackles Knotty Questions of Information Blitz in the '80s," *American Libraries,* v. 11, no. 7 (July/August 1980): 406.
32. "Advanced Technology Libraries," v. 10 (1981): 3.
33. F. Wilfrid Lancaster, "Whither Libraries? or, Wither Libraries," *College & Research Libraries,* v. 39, no. 5 (September 1978): 346.
34. "Academic Libraries in the Computer Age," *College & Research Libraries News* 42(1981): [29]-30.
35. Discussed earlier in this chapter.
36. Letter from Ralph E. Ellsworth to Dale M. Bentz, 13 February 1981.

If the so-called conservative point of view . . . prevails and grows and if we find ourselves really coming to grips with some of the problems of the Post-Industrial Revolution — such as human genetics, population control, racial equality, abortion, right to live, energy, etc. — I would expect . . . libraries to encounter more difficulty in . . . censorship of books whose contents are offensive to certain groups in the communities. — **Ralph Ellsworth.** *"Second 200 Years: the Peaceful Revolution," Illinois Libraries, v. 58, no. 5 (May 1976): 349.*

The Pendulum Swings to the Right: Censorship in the Eighties

Abigail Dahl-Hansen Studdiford, Executive Director
New Jersey Library Association
Passaic, New Jersey

GET RID OF THAT BOOK! came the howl of an outraged library trustee of the 3000-volume subscription library in a small farming town in the South. The time was the summer of 1958, in Denmark, South Carolina; the summer librarian, a high school senior; the book, George Orwell's *1984*. My first encounter with the heavy hand of censorship left me with a skeptic's view of where the final authority in book selection lies, as well as with a paperback copy of *1984*, paid for out of my own pocket. Never mind the fact that the senior class of that town had been required to read the volume that spring as a class project.

The purpose of this chapter is to review the significant trends of selection and censorship of library materials and then to look ahead with the aid of an Ellsworthian crystal ball. I must admit a bias; my professional experience has been concentrated in large university libraries, thus limiting first-hand experience with school and public libraries. I have tried to overcome the limitation by extensive reading and discussion with those knowledgeable about this murky topic. The most helpful interpretive commentary for my review came from a little article by Lester Asheim, "Not Censorship But Selection" (Wilson Library Bulletin, September 1953); from Eli Oboler's collected articles, *Defending Intellectual Freedom*, (Greenwood Press, 1980); from the comprehensive *Censorship Landmarks*, by Edward De Grazia (R.R. Bowker, 1969); from two issues of

Library Trends: July 1970, *Intellectual Freedom* and Winter 1979, *Libraries and Society: Research and Thought;* and from Robert Downs, *The First Freedom* (ALA, 1960).

The issues which march through the literature of censorship, selection, and intellectual freedom ebb and flow with the tides of permissiveness and reactionism. In 1934, the courts decreed that James Joyce's *Ulysses* was not obscene within Section 305 (a) of the Tariff Act of 1930, thus permitting its legal sale and distribution in this country. In his opinion, Augustus N. Hand wrote, "we think that *Ulysses* is a book of originality and sincerity of treatment and that it has not the effect of promoting lust. Accordingly it does not fall within the statute, even though it justly may offend many."[1] The decision for *Ulysses* provided a precedent for subsequent literary works, where "standard works of literature are not banned merely because they contained some obscene passages" and where "confiscation for such a reason would destroy much that is precious in order to benefit a few."[2]

OBSCENITY

The Free Speech Movement of the sixties introduced the curious notion that it is OK for me to have my say on my cause but it is not OK for you to have an equal opportunity to have your say, especially if I disagree with your philosophy. As a young adult in the sixties, I could espouse many of the issues of the day, until it came to quashing the advocate of an opposing view. In the decades following World War II, American society has become more complex; values and attitudes toward religion, government, schools, minority groups, women, and sex have undergone radical revision. Visual and written expressions once looked upon as vulgar are now commonplace. As a result of the liberations of the sixties and seventies, book protests are flaring up; school curricula on controversial subjects such as sex education and the theory of evolution are being criticized and taken to court; stricter controls of pornographic bookstores and theaters are demanded; and some parents' groups aligned with the antisecular humanism movement of 1981 are calling for literature that avoids divorce, suicide, abortion, drug addiction, teenage pregnancy, homosexuality, and other harsh realities of life. *The New York Times* of Sunday, May 17, 1981, describes the proponents of the current swing of the pendulum of intellectual freedom as being "armed with sophisticated lobbying techniques and backed by such national organizations as the Moral Majority, the Eagle Forum and the Christian Broadcasting Network." *Brave New World* and *Catcher in the Rye* have once again been dropped from classes in literature, and birth-control information has been removed from the high-school guidance office (in Onida, South Dakota). We can only speculate that *Show Me* is permanently absent from the library shelves as well, while the test-tube baby of *1984* is a reality.

In 1973, Eli Oboler suggested that "the librarian is, ideally considered, the chief modern promulgator of knowledge; there is just too much to know and learn for any one . . . to be able to serve as the conveyor of knowledge . . ." Thus, "the burden of storing and arranging and making available what there was and is to know is carried by the librarian."[3] The dichotomy which we face—as chief disseminators of recorded information—is the right of the individual to have access to information, on the one hand, and the right of the individual not to be offended, whether the issue is theory of algebra, Lucy and the origins of man, or disparate political systems.

At the center of the censorship controversy, past and present, lies the question of what constitutes obscenity and pornography. The courts have moved in curious circles, trying to define these terms, which in fact are so ambiguous as to defy that single definition which will satisfy social change from one decade to the next, or current standards from one community to the next. Of equal importance to the library community is intellectual freedom, where the question is one of obligation to have available various sides of issues of concern, both in anticipation of need and in response to demand. It may be that the academic library and the special library, which each exist in a research setting, experience greater tolerance for collecting the Other Side of the story than do the public and school libraries, which exist in settings reflective of the real-life mores of that community. But let us take a brief look at the history of intellectual freedom and the etymology of censorship in the U.S. court system, to identify the issues as they constrain librarians today.

In 1711, the Colony of Massachusetts established the first American law on pornography and obscenity. This law reads, "Evil communications, wicked, profane, impure, filthy and obscene songs, composures, writing or prints do corrupt the mind and are incentives to all manners of impieties and debaucheries . . . ."[3] Oboler notes that it was not until 1821 that there was a prosecution under this statute, when the "first American publisher of *Fanny Hill* was tried and convicted."[5] Although the first federal obscenity statute was passed in 1842, barring importation of "indecent and obscene prints, paintings, lithographs, engravings, and transparencies," it was the Comstock Act of 1873 which prohibited sending a comparable list of indecent and obscene items through the U.S. mails.

Notwithstanding the 1934 decision on *Ulysses*, which allowed importation of that title, the Supreme Court, in 1957, in *Roth v. United States*, finally dealt with the basic constitutionality of obscenity laws. In upholding a lower-court decision to convict Samuel Roth, a publisher, of using the mails for obscene materials, the Supreme Court ruled for the first time that obscenity does not fall under the protection of the First Amendment, although the opinion noted, for the record, that "this court has always assumed that obscenity is not protected by the freedoms of speech and press."[6] In *Roth*, Justice William T. Brennan wrote: "All ideas having even the slightest redeeming social importance – unorthodox ideas, controversial ideas, even ideas hateful to the prevailing climate of opinion – have the full protection of the guarantees. . . . But implicit in the history of the First Amendment is the rejection of obscenity as utterly without redeeming social importance." The Court continued: "Sex and obscenity are not synonymous"; "the portrayal of sex, e.g., in art, literature and scientific works, is not itself sufficient reason to deny material the constitutional protection of freedom of speech and press"; and that "sex . . . is one of the vital problems of human interest and public concern." Brennan, quoting *Thornhill v. Alabama*, 310 U.S. 88, 101-102, continued the majority opinion:

> The freedom of speech and of press guaranteed by the Constitution embraces at least the liberty to discuss publicly and truthfully all matters of public concern without previous restraint or fear of subsequent punishment. . . . Freedom of discussion, if it would fulfill its historic function in this nation, must embrace all issues about which information is needed or appropriate to enable the members of society to cope with the exigencies of their period.

Here Justice Brennan provides the subtle but elusive link between obscenity on the one hand and protection of controversial ideas and intellectual freedom on the other. Unfortunately, while the guidelines from *Roth v. United States* establish precedent for works of art, literature, and scientific works, which can be interpreted outside the courts, there is not an equally clear path for decisions on sex education in schools or for public library material on the social manifestations of the 1980s adolescent.

Shortly after *Roth v. United States,* a U.S. District Court ruled that the unexpurgated version of *Lady Chatterley's Lover* "was not obscene and could not be banned from the U.S. mails." Judge Frederick vanPelt Bryan stated in the 1959 ruling that "There have been enormous shifts in the standards of sexual mores;" furthermore, "what may be offensive to residents of a small rural community would be not at all offensive to the more sophisticated residents of a larger city."[7] This decision rests squarely on the shoulders of the definitions asserted in *Roth,* that material could be judged obscene if it:

a) appealed to prurient interest.
b) was patently offensive under current community standards.
c) was utterly without any redeeming social value.[8]

The next plateau was reached in 1973 when the Supreme Court rendered a series of decisions which set up national standards for obscenity:

1. Whether the average person applying contemporary community standards, would find that the work, taken as a whole, appeals to the prurient interest;
2. Whether the work depicts or describes, in a patently offensive way, sexual conduct, specifically defined by the applicable state law;
3. Whether the work, taken as a whole, lacks serious literary, artistic, political or scientific value.[9]

It is now clear, from the cases which have followed, that this standard is confusing and ambiguous and that the Supreme Court passed the hot potato to the communities, leaving them to decide for themselves.

OTHER CENSORSHIP ISSUES

Thus far, we have dealt with definitions of obscenity and censorship regarding materials of appeal to the adult. But what are the rights of the child and the adolescent, adult in all respects but chronological age? Some wag has observed that male and female of the human species reach a prime reproductive stage far earlier than the law allows; thus, to disallow information at the age of adolescence is to deprive nature herself. In the 1980s, the adolescent has a far more diverse menu of information needs than sex education alone. The legally underage—indeed, even the grammar-school student—needs to know about drugs, alcohol, abortion, and a long list of other forbidden fruit. As Alex Allain observed in the July 1970 issue of *Library Trends,* "the usual fear expressed is that material thought to be obscene might fall into the hands of young adults and encourage them to delinquency or sexual experimentation."[10] While earlier studies held there was little proof that reading "questionable" material led to acts of passion,[11] there is a growing body of concern and evidence that visual presentations have influenced acts of violence in imitation of the dramatic. The lower courts have now begun to try juveniles as adults for certain crimes, and to recommend punishment previously reserved for the adult offender. It is the classic hen-and-egg situation, in which resolution might lead to a wider range of books available to the person under 18 or might lead to a general purge of "questionable" items from the library, the school curriculum, and, do we dare suggest, even from the newsstand and the corner grocery store.

John J. Farley wrote that "the attempts to censor young people's reading seem principally to have centered upon the subjects of sex and politics."[12] While that may sound a bit too pat for today's audience, Farley also presents us with the heart of the matter: "The complexity of the censorship question in schools" and, by extension, in public libraries,

> is indicated by the apparent incompatibility of two ideas:
>
> 1. adolescents must gradually be led to the appreciation of mature, adult literature, and to the development of their critical faculties by exposure to controversy; and
> 2. the school's curriculum and the reading provided under the school's auspices must reflect in some way the values of the adult society.[13]

Looking ahead in 1970, Farley suggested that the Free Speech Movement on American college campuses during the late sixties might have an impact on the demand for freedom and self-determination among the emerging crop of adolescents. Time has borne out his predictions with the Me-First generation of the seventies. It is my observation that the parents, school boards, and library trustees of the eighties are going to push the pendulum hard, toward the control side of the spectrum, perhaps because of their own Dr. Spock-permissive upbringing; perhaps because they are honestly outraged by the content of today's art and literary works; and perhaps because they are being exhorted by certain elements of the clergy to return to traditional values, whatever they were.

It was Farley who observed that the librarian who deals with the adolescent must, of necessity, work "in close proximity to the adult community which controls the schools and libraries, and as long as schools and libraries exist, will evidently continue to live with the tension between the adolescent and his elders."[14] The question for the eighties is: to what extent will the adult community be successful in removing material of "potential harm" from use by other members of the community? After the hard-fought battles of the 1950s, it is a bitter and redundant pill for the professional librarian to swallow. Given these predictions, I would urge the leading jurists to dust off the case law on First-and Fourteenth-Amendment decisions and prepare to do battle.

Numerous attempts have been made to categorize censorship; the most familiar groupings are political, religious, social, and pornographic. So far, we have dealt with the most blatant, those of social and pornographic censorship, especially as it impinges on our rights to a published copy of a literary work, scientific tract, or art form, and as it affects the rights of children to receive information. Whether or not a particular item is available in a library collection is another matter.

The initial attempts of the colonies to control printing and freedom of the press were shortly put to the test, first in the case of Pennsylvania's first printer, William Bradford, who, in 1683, "had his press seized by the government, was charged with seditious libel, and spent more than a year in prison for printing a pamphlet entitled the *Frame of Government*, which was a copy of the colony's charter."[15] In 1735, John Peter Zenger was acquitted of libel arising from his newspaper publication of satirical ballads about Governor William Cosby and his Council. The Zenger case paved the way for acceptance of the principle of a free press in this country.

At the turn of the 19th century, Thomas Jefferson stated his concern for intellectual freedom, in his first inaugural address, on March 4, 1801, noting that he hoped those who "would wish to dissolve this union or to change its republican form" should be "let [to] stand undisturbed as monuments of the safety with which error of opinion may be tolerated where reason is left free to combat it." However, it is John Stuart Mill's ideas on intellectual freedom, expressed in *On Liberty*, that have been absorbed into our cultural consciousness, with the notions that (1) suppression of opinion may blot out the truth; (2) even though an opinion is false, truth is served by refuting error; and (3) an unconventional opinion may be useful, because it contains some particle of truth.[16]

The 20th century seems to be contributing more than its share of notable examples of successful censorship attempts, if one chronicles the raids on various ethnic groups suspected of Communist sympathies in the 1920s and the McCarthy witch hunts of the 1950s designed to flush supposed Communist agents from the federal government. We have only to look to the daily newspaper to see fresh examples of political censorship in the form of neo-Nazism and Klan rallies.

While attacks on intellectual freedom are much more likely to relate to political opinion than to religious belief or heresy, one can only speculate what may happen as conservative church groups build momentum.

Looking ahead in 1976, Ralph Ellsworth applied a degree of Alvin Toffler's *Future Shock,* with the observation that

> if the conservative point of view . . . prevails and grows, and if we find ourselves really coming to grips with some of the problems of the Post-Industrial Revolution—such as human genetics, population control, racial equality, abortion, right to live, energy, etc.—I would expect school libraries to encounter much more difficulty in textbook selection and censorship of books whose contents are offensive to certain groups in the community.[17]

As if on cue, the Moral Majority is here today, bringing the suggestion that one group wishes to restrict or suppress certain beliefs, ideas, and thoughts of others. Such actions would deny a person constitutional and civil rights to which he or she is entitled. There is a further ingredient to be added to the stew of national consciousness—the threat of external aggression and war. As we enter the eighties, the Executive branch of the federal government is prepared to shift spending from social programs, including libraries, to national defense and armaments. It was not so long ago that all manner of things were done, at a hotel named Watergate, in the name of national security, which leads to the concern that the current climate in Washington may "confuse our vigilance on matters of personal liberties and rights . . ."[18] Not being noted for my theories of doom and gloom, I am somewhat surprised to see where the evidence is leading; namely, into a decade of repressive policies for intellectual freedom, true to the 30-year cycle of such things.

The inherent danger of putting the issues of censorship into neat categories and reviewing pertinent case history in light of the issues of the day is to view the study of intellectual freedom from the narrow right-to-read perspective and to treat censorship as an external phenomenon. The threads of all the social, political, religious, and pornographic themes must come together as in a finely woven Indian blanket, in the work of a library-materials selector.

COLLECTION DEVELOPMENT

Mythology has it that research libraries once had a mission to collect, house, and make available all of man's recorded knowledge. Nonsense. Perhaps the library at Alexandria had that objective, but evidence to support the notion is long gone. Conventional wisdom holds that libraries should collect to support current programs and anticipated trends, all within their budget, thus requiring skillful selection and rejection on the part of the person responsible for collection. The librarian in an academic library has the responsibility to understand the instructional program of the university as well as its research programs, anticipating need, responding to changes in the academic program and the discipline itself, and balancing conflicting, divergent theories on a topic. The objective is to achieve a collection which will meet the needs of the students and faculty of the institution at that time. It is my observation that, of all librarians, the one in an academic setting has the greatest flexibility to merge the tenets of intellectual freedom and selection of material, without the constraints of censorship. Obviously, budget, space, and the responsibility to provide designated services are common constraints in all types of libraries, imposing restrictions and guidelines in each library that in turn affect what is actually selected. And just as obviously, the school librarian and the public librarian must understand the information needs and socio-ethnic composition of the community or school system; the difference lies in the more formal role a public-library board or school board has in the administration of the library, as compared to practice in the academic community.

Lester Asheim's article "Not Censorship But Selection" identifies the three states of censorship: the patron who cannot get a title from the library because

1. it has been banned from sale and distribution in the United States;

2. the librarian decided not to buy it;
3. a local pressure group forced its removal from the shelves.[19]

In each of Asheim's situations, the person "is deprived of access" to the information. Asheim continues with a lively set of questions about why situations 1 and 3 can be defined as censorship and 2 described as selection. I subscribe to the nuances among the three.

The responsibility to make the buy/not buy, select/reject decision has been delegated to the librarian, by definition and by tradition. As we seek to maximize the titles available to library patrons in the eighties, a variety of options is available. The decision not to buy may imply a cooperative direct-borrowing agreement, a link with a regional or national interlibrary loan or document-delivery system, an assessment of low use which could be satisfied by a remote storage center, or knowledge that the content of the item is available through a public cable network. A decision not to buy may also imply that the item is not suitable, because of quality, level, or subject matter, for inclusion in the collection. The format of an item exerts its own subtle brand of censorship; for years, libraries were slow to purchase titles in microform, and even slower to make their existence known through the public catalog, because microform, after all, was not the real thing and should thus not be given the status of a book, which full cataloging implies. Either decision deprived the patron of access to information. The sheer impossibility of handling each physical item in a way unique to each library lies in the dust of Library of Congress printed cards, replaced by documents and reports produced exclusively in microformat or in an electronic medium. The librarian selecting for scope of coverage, quality, and reliability must now also be concerned with quality control of the content of an item. In electronic publishing, who referees? Who publishes? What copyright guidelines apply?

I am not so troubled by the sale of bits of data, bibliographic citations, and abstracts as I am by the concern that librarians are not moving into the leadership roles for needs assessment and design of the information industry. If we visualize the librarian as the facilitator in an information exchange, as the provider of facts, data, stories, poems, novels, biography, and formulae, not merely as the storekeeper of the containers of all these things, then we could visualize libraries as a Public Information Utility. As such, libraries could manage cable TV and interactive information banks such as those tested in Ohio. Many libraries conduct search services into remote conglomerate data files such as SDC, Lockheed, and BRS.

The individual data bases are usually regular products of publishing ventures such as *Chemical Abstracts, Psychological Abstracts,* and *Dissertation Abstracts,* reference services generally purchased by larger libraries. There seem to be trends which suggest that some libraries are willing to give up the hard-copy version of certain abstracting and indexing services in favor of the speed and convenience of an online search, despite the cost factor. As costs drop for home computing, and computing expertise becomes common, individuals are now contracting directly with the conglomerate for their information needs, rather than using an intermediary in the library. It seems a logical extension of a public-information utility to include management of these data files within the region, accessible with local-rate interactive computing. Educational computing networks maintain electronic mailboxes and bulletin boards; popular subject headings are chess and recipes. The Public Information Utility has a role here!

CONCLUSION

The library community can make significant contributions to the design of information packaging, its distribution, and accessibility; the effort might preempt going the way of the California Condor. Information systems – books, telecommunications, interactive three-dimensional graphic consoles, video-disk storage and retrieval – can be designed which might promote exchange of ideas and reading, not inhibit it; might multiply the points of view which will find expression, not limit them; and might be a channel for communication, not a bar to it.[20] In other words, the librarian must assert a leadership role in the information industry in the next two decades, to assure a broad base for the principles of intellectual freedom, which includes the right to reject physical possession of an item for a library collection in lieu of other options.

FOOTNOTES

1. *United States v. One Book Entitled "Ulysses,"* 72 F. 2d 705 (1934).
2. *Ibid.*
3. Eli M. Oboler, *Defending Intellectual Freedom.* Westport, Conn.: Greenwood Press, 1980, p. 95.
4. *Ibid.,* p. 130

5. *Ibid.*
6. *Roth v. United States,* 354 U.S. 476 (1957).
7. Gerald S. Snyder, *The Right To Be Informed: Censorship in the United States,* New York: Julian Messner, 1976, pp. 39-40.
8. *Ibid.,* pp. 42-43.
9. Oboler, *op. cit.,* p. 135.
10. Alex P. Allain, "Public Library Governing Bodies and Intellectual Freedom," *Library Trends,* v. 19, no. 1 (July 1970): 61.
11. A 1958 study by Brown University psychologists, cited in Allain, *op. cit.,* p. 61.
12. John J. Farley, "The Reading of Young People," *Library Trends,* v. 19, no. 1 (July 1970): 85.
13. *Ibid.*
14. *Ibid.,* p. 87.
15. Robert B. Downs, "Freedom of Speech and Press: Development of a Concept," *Library Trends,* v. 19, no. 1 (July 1970): 11.
16. David K. Berninghausen, *The Flight From Reason.* Chicago: American Library Association, 1975, p. 2.
17. Ralph E. Ellsworth, "The Second 200 Years; The Peaceful Revolution," *Illinois Libraries,* v. 58, no. 5 (May 1976): 349.
18. *Ibid.,* p. 351.
19. Lester Asheim, "Not Censorship But Selection," *Wilson Library Bulletin,* v. 28, no. 1 (September 1953): 63.
20. *Ibid.,* p. 67.

*O*ur generation has won considerable recognition in many colleges and universities, not just as good librarians but as good academicians. — **Ralph Ellsworth.** The Library's Life Style: A Review of the Last 35 Years," Michigan Librarian, v. 36, no. 3 (Autumn 1970):30.

Librarians as Scholars

Le Moyne W. Anderson, Director of Libraries
Colorado State University
Fort Collins, Colorado

If one accepts the definition of a scholar as a learned person or one trained in a special branch of learning, then it naturally follows almost syllogistically that a librarian – any librarian – is a scholar. If one adheres to the definition of the adjective "scholarly" as "having or showing much knowledge, accuracy, and critical ability, or one who is studious and devoted to learning,"[1] then it does not logically extend in thought, even remotely, that any librarian is necessarily scholarly.

Grappling with definitions is a tricky business, and establishing the librarian/scholar relationship is no exception. Alas, one must stipulate at the outset of any discourse, the definition of terms. For the purposes of discussion, a *librarian* is a person holding the minimum credentials of an accredited graduate library-school degree. The 1970 *ALA Policy Statement on Library Education and Personnel Utilization* states that "a good liberal education plus graduate-level study in the field of specialization (either in librarianship or in a relevant field) are seen as the minimum preparation" for the first professional category.[2] Let us accept the proposition, furthermore, that a *scholar* is one who contributes to the extension of knowledge in some meaningful and identifiable way.

Given these definitions, then, one is able to attempt to measure scholarship, or even infer that specific contributions are indeed the result of scholarship. This thought process leads gradually to the realization that one must ultimately quantify the results. If research is the other name of the game of scholarship, then an inventory of such activities must be made, through the dissemination and reporting of the results. This measure of research, and therefore scholarship, is next related directly to the publications appearing in the various media.

Proceeding from this base, several assumptions can be stated. Scholarship is a desirable product of academic librarianship. Scholars are valuable members of library faculties in both the national and international scene. The results of the research, investigations, or studies by scholars are of benefit to academic librarianship. The need to report the results of these scholarly efforts in such forms as journal articles, monographs, chapters of books, sections in compendia, or numerous other packages of information, is adequately met by the various outlets of the publishing community.

Having agreed upon the definition of a scholar and delineated certain assumptions about it, the next phase of the encounter with the librarian/scholar condition is to determine the magnitude of its existence. A first approach, of course, is to rely upon one's impressions or vague notions and feelings. One impressionist may be older than another, thus gaining more credence, by virtue of the added years of experience, than the young novice scarcely out of graduate school. The judging and assessing of a situation based solely upon impressionistic thinking, however, is fraught with uncertainty.

A review of the literature is in order. It is essential to peruse the publications on a subject, inasmuch as all efforts must be made to be exhaustive during a scholarly study or an investigation worthy of the name. The shaky premise in such an exercise, of course, is that we are dealing with a subject about which something has been written. In the event that no information or data are uncovered, however, it may be necessary for the investigator to conduct a bit of original research in order to establish certain facts.

LITERATURE REVIEW

Having come this far in considering the processes of analytical thinking as well as the subsequent applications to the study of a topic, how do we proceed? Let us start with a search through the professional literature. We soon find that, on the basis of the comments of colleagues in print, the role of the librarian as a scholar has been treated very sparingly and even superficially. Those who have cited the librarian as a contributing scholar do so with a decided lack of detail and persuasion.

During a convocation at Dartmouth College recently, Gordon Ray stated that "American librarians no longer need to be burdened with a sense of inferiority. Not only do they manage our large and complex libraries with competence, they also include in their ranks many persons who are scholars in their own right, and not merely in the field of bibliography."[3]

In a discussion of the topic "on the preparation of library directors," David Kaser referred to the several leading librarians of the 1960s holding the highest academic degree (Ph.D.) as follows: "All of the directors had been in their doctoral experience imbued with the rigor of scholarly methods, yet it is interesting and perhaps meaningful to note that with the exception of one or two, none of them pursued scholarly research in their late lives."[4]

A few years ago, during an intensive period of advocacy by librarians for faculty status, numerous views were advanced supporting this posture. It was generally agreed, within the professional associations, that an academic librarian's work was akin to the teaching faculty in terms of intellectual content and value, as Beverly Lynch forthrightly notes.[5] The "Joint Statement on Faculty Status of College and University Librarians," furthermore, states: "Librarians perform a teaching and research role. . . . Librarians are also themselves involved in the research function; many conduct research in their own professional interests and in the discharge of their duties."[6] One can infer from such a professional stance that librarians and scholars are one and the same.

Perhaps the great Louis Round Wilson spent as much time as any library educator in attempting to inculcate the need for scholarship and research activity in academic-library leaders. Yet, he concedes that the separation of librarianship and scholarship is inevitable, for the following somewhat contradictory reasons:

> The director of the large American library is usually so pressed with details of administration that he does not become a productive scholar in the sense that directors of many European libraries do. Nevertheless, the names of librarians like those of Winsor and Gilman . . . find their places in the list of American scholars; and American librarians had, and are having, a direct and important part in the promotion of scholarship.[7]

It is interesting to note that the premier international society in librarianship, Beta Phi Mu, has as a motto, "Scholarship and Service." In reference to this declaration, a former dean of the Columbia School of Library Service, Jack Dalton, has stated: "We have always been long on one and short on the other. We have never had, and we do not have today, our share of young scholars and the need for sound scholarship has never been greater."[8]

Well, are librarians scholars or aren't they? A simplistic response would reveal that some are and some are not, of course. It is this author's contention, however, that a more thorough and exhaustive review of the literature will reveal nothing more or less than what has already been noted in the foregoing sample of references.

THE STUDY

We say we are librarians and scholars, and yet the observations of a few notable figures regarding this issue do not concur – in every detail, at least. This is hardly enough evidence upon which to base sound conclusions. This suggests that some sort of empirical study should be designed and implemented, in the hope of discovering situations that would establish more positively that librarians are, or are not, scholars.

The previously cited opinions of experts and the accumulated years of professional experience ultimately led this author to design a mini-study. Its intent was to test the hypothesis that the higher the post in the library organization, the more likely will be the incidence of research and scholarship among academic librarians.

The study's primary objective was to evaluate the activity of research in order to determine levels and rates of contributions. At the outset, it was conjectured that if the study's hypothesis is generally true, it should apply to an academic librarian at any institution of higher learning in the United States. The study tested the logical consequence of the general statement, "Given a selected group of academic librarians at a medium-sized university who have had varying educational backgrounds and professional experiences, the academic librarians with the higher positions within the organization will produce significantly more research than those without these duties, all other things being equal, because, as the level of duties increases, so does the librarian's responsibility to the larger community of librarianship, through sharing the results of research."

In this study, certain assumptions were also made. Academic librarians share the same educational background required to conduct research and report the results. Academic librarians understand equally the value and importance of scholarship in the field of librarianship. All academic librarians have equal time and access to resources in order to conduct studies and report the results. The final assumption was that the same motivating factors to do research exist for all academic librarians, such as rewards of tenure, promotion, and/or salary adjustments.

The different procedures whose effects are to be measured and compared are described under the general term "observations." Several accommodations were considered at one point or another and eventually rejected. It was decided ultimately to observe the following conditions: (1) the status of the librarian, (2) the background of the librarian, (3) the amount of research and scholarly activity engaged in by the librarian, and (4) the types of publications produced.

The Design

This author attempted to make the study simple, knowing that it would increase the likelihood of accuracy. No complicated techniques were used, particularly in those areas of tabulating the results of the observations.

The choice of the unit of study was of primary importance. In planning the project, it was decided to concentrate upon the academic librarian—that is, the professional staff member. These persons were easily identified and were used as the subjects. No further selection was made regarding composition of the study unit.

The site at which the study was conducted is the land-grant Colorado State University. The fundamental consideration was to have a place where the investigator had access to an academic library and where he could obtain maximum accuracy in return for a reasonable expenditure of time and labor.

The library facilities for patrons at this university are similar to others throughout the land. The library system is primarily an instrument of research and teaching. The professional staff, the administrative organization, and the physical facilities are so planned as to implement teaching, learning, and research, by the use of all library materials. The professional staff is composed, therefore, of educators who teach and do research, not necessarily in the classrooms and laboratories, but by mobilizing the resources of the libraries according to a well-defined program.

The Methodology

The initial design of the study included a plan for the selection of the subjects, the observation of the records, and the collection and tabulation of the resultant data. The study units had to be selected from the finite population representing all academic librarians on the staff of this institution.

In each of the 43 observations, the data regarding every academic librarian were studied carefully. They were transferred subsequently to a final summary-tabulation sheet. All percentage rates of observation were calculated for each observant. Given the observation group with an N of 43, and 34 indicators of research activity, this would be included, finally, in an appropriately constructed matrix.

The Causation

Among the first points, in this mini-study, to be considered after the observance of the incidence of publication was to ask the question, "Why publish?" The quest for an explanation is always foremost in the list of priorities in completing such an analysis of data.

The method of analysis of the data was important, in order to determine not only how things were, but how they work, ultimately enabling the cause-and-effect relationship to be understood. It was decided that if the study's hypothesis was supported by the results, a final consideration would be to determine whether the postulated causal element had been operating.

It was not possible, unfortunately, to gather additional data directly from the academic librarians in the study. The causal element of the hypothesis was based, therefore, upon implications from the literature and the current observations of the other academic librarians, as well as the personal experiences of the author.

It was the purpose of this phase of the survey to ascertain the reasons for an academic librarian to publish. It was also thought desirable to determine if suggestions might be discovered of other ways by which an academic librarian could participate in research efforts.

It has been said that "there are only three methods of obtaining data in social research: one can ask people questions; one can observe the behavior of the persons, groups, or organizations, and their products or outcomes; or one can utilize existing records of data already gathered for purposes other than one's own research."[9] The principle objective of an analysis of the survey data, then, was to identify causation by the method of inference from the literature and general observations by the investigator.

The Findings

Basic to the analysis of the results of this study is an ordering among the observations made. The hypothesis states that the higher a position is in a library organization, the greater will be the incidence of research effort.

In the investigation at hand, 43 subjects were chosen from the professional staff of a university library. They were subsequently arrayed by their rank in the staff hierarchy. The number of publications per subject were then tallied according to the predetermined packages of information. All of these data were entered into a matrix, which was constructed to include the subjects on the vertical, and the publications on the horizontal, axes.

The definition of "publications" in these instances includes those published in legitimate (nonvanity) outlets. Publications therefore include journal articles, monographs, sections or chapters of books, bibliographies, book reviews, and technical reports, as well as complete books. They include no in-house reports, papers, or position statements. Neither do they include papers delivered at professional meetings unless they were ultimately published in a proceedings volume or one of the other conventional vehicles of dissemination.

The final results are shown in Table I. Each cell represents the largest number of all types of publications observed for each of the seven categories.

Out of this survey of 43 personnel records, it was found that 34 librarians (79.1%) have made a contribution of 335 items to the professional literature. Of the 34 writers, editors, bibliographers, and/or compilers, three persons (8.8%) provided 146 items, or 43.6 percent of the total output. The number of items contributed per librarian range from zero to 49. The three top contributors, who offered the 146 items, clustered at a per-person rate of 49, 49, and 48 respectively (see Table I).

In relation to the staff hierarchy, (positions #1 through #43) the three heaviest contributors represent positions #1, #4, and #13. Of the lowest six contributors – that is, only one item each – the positions identified are #5, #20, #23, #26, #34, and #36. Of the nine noncontributors, the represented positions are #18, #21, #28, #37, #38, #39, #40, #42, and #43.

Of the 43 subjects, 2 are full professors (4.7%), 16 associate pro-

TABLE I

A Composite of the Number of Observations of Items Published by Librarians

Items by Type of Publication

Rank	Librarian Title	Sex	A Journal Article	B Bibliog.	C Book (Chap/Sec)	D Review	E Tech. Report	F Mono-graph	G Other	Totals
#1	Professor	M	26	1	6	7	4	3	1	48
#2	Assoc. Prof.	M	1	0	0	0	0	2	1	4
#3	"	F	5	0	0	0	1	0	1	7
#4	Professor	M	15	1	4	6	13	0	10	49
#5	Assoc. Prof.	M	1	0	0	0	0	0	0	1
#6	"	M	0	2	0	0	0	2	0	4
#7	"	M	19	1	0	0	0	5	0	25
#8	"	F	1	4	0	0	0	1	2	8
#9	Asst. Prof.	M	0	0	0	3	0	3	0	6
#10	Assoc. Prof.	M	9	3	0	3	0	2	10	27
#11	"	M	3	1	3	0	1	1	0	9
#12	"	F	0	0	0	3	0	0	0	3
#13	"	M	19	8	0	1	0	13	8	49
#14	"	M	0	0	0	0	0	3	0	3
#15	"	M	4	6	0	0	5	1	0	16
#16	"	F	2	0	0	0	1	4	1	8
#17	"	F	0	4	0	0	1	2	1	8

	Rank	Sex								
#18	Asst. Prof.	F	0	0	0	0	0	0	0	0
#19	"	F	2	0	0	0	0	0	1	3
#20	Assoc. Prof.	F	0	0	0	0	1	0	0	1
#21	Asst. Prof.	M	0	0	0	0	0	4	0	0
#22	Assoc. Prof.	M	2	0	0	0	1	1	0	7
#23	Asst. Prof.	M	0	0	1	0	0	2	0	1
#24	"	M	2	0	0	0	0	1	0	5
#25	"	F	0	4	0	0	1	1	0	2
#26	"	F	0	0	0	0	0	2	0	1
#27	"	M	1	0	0	0	1	0	0	8
#28	Instructor	M	0	0	0	0	0	0	0	0
#29	Asst. Prof.	F	0	1	2	3	0	1	2	3
#30	"	F	0	0	0	5	0	0	1	10
#31	"	F	1	0	0	0	0	1	1	3
#32	"	F	0	0	0	0	4	0	0	6
#33	"	F	1	0	0	3	0	0	0	4
#34	"	F	1	0	0	0	0	1	0	1
#35	"	M	1	0	0	0	0	0	0	2
#36	"	F	1	0	0	0	0	0	0	1
#37	"	F	0	0	0	0	0	0	0	0
#38	"	F	0	0	0	0	0	0	0	0
#39	Instructor	F	0	0	0	0	0	0	0	0
#40	"	F	0	1	0	0	0	0	0	0
#41	"	F	1	0	0	0	0	0	0	2
#42	"	F	0	0	0	0	0	0	0	0
#43	"	F	0	0	0	0	0	0	0	0
Totals			118	34	16	31	34	56	40	335

fessors (37.2 %), 19 assistant professors (44.2 %), and 6 instructors (13.9 %). Of the 3 highest contributors, 2 are full professors and 1 is an associate professor. Of the 6 lowest contributors, 2 are associate professors and 4 are assistant professors. Of the 9 noncontributors, 4 are assistant professors and 5 are instructors. In the composite of professors, it is apparent that the librarians holding the higher professorial title contribute the greatest number of items to the literature. In this case, nearly one-third of the output (29.0 %), or 97 items, come from the full professors, who represent only 4.5 percent of the total staff. The next highest level, the associate professors, representing 37 percent of the staff, contribute 53.7 percent of the publications. The assistant professors include 44 percent of the staff and have published 16.7 percent of the total output. At the lowest end of the scale, the instructors, who number 14 percent of the staff, contributed only 0.6 percent of the items to the professional literature (see Table II).

TABLE II
A Composite of the Observations
of Published Items, by Professorial Levels

		Titles			
	Professor	Associate Professor	Assistant Professor	Instructor	Totals
Staff	2 (4.6 %)	16 (37.2 %)	19 (44.2 %)	6 (14.0 %)	43 (100 %)
Items	97 (29.0 %)	180 (53.7 %)	56 (16.7 %)	2 (0.6 %)	335 (100 %)

Out of the 34 contributors, 16 (45.5 %) were women and 18 (54.5 %) were men. Eight (88.8 %) of the noncontributors were women, and there was one (11.2 %) man. This distribution is based upon a total of 43 subjects, with a ratio of 24 women (56 %) and 19 men (44 %) (see Table III).

As has been noted previously, out of a total staff of 43 persons, there were 335 items of professional literature contributed by 34 librarians. Out of the ranks of the 24 women (55.8 %), 72 items were contributed, or 21.5 percent. In the case of the 19 men on the staff, 263 items were offered, or 78.5 percent of all publications (see Table IV).

TABLE III
A Composite of the Contributors/Noncontributors
of Published Items, by Sex

	Contributors	Noncontributors	Totals
Women	16 (45.5%)	8 (88.8%)	24 (56%)
Men	18 (54.5%)	1 (11.2%)	19 (44%)
	34 (100.0%)	9 (100.0%)	43 (100%)

TABLE IV
A Composite of the Observations
of Published Items, by Sex

	Women	Men	Totals
Staff	24 (55.8%)	19 (44.2%)	43 (100%)
Items	72 (21.5%)	263 (78.5%)	335 (100%)

Of the 43 librarians, five (11.6%) were in the administrative special services division of the library organization. There were 21 librarians (48.8%) in the public services, 17 (39.6%) staff members in the technical-services units (see Table V). There appears to be a positive correlation, furthermore, between the distribution of assignments and the numbers of contributors and noncontributors. For example, the greatest percentage of staff contributing to the professional literature was in the public-services division, as was the greatest percentage of those who did not contribute. In descending order, the same situation is observed for the technical services and administrative/special services divisions respectively.

It is noted, furthermore, that the division of administrative/ special services has only five staff members (11.6%) and it produced

100 publications, or nearly 30 percent of the total output. The 21 librarians in the public-services division (48.8%) produced 139 items, or 41.5 percent of the total. In the area of technical services, the 17 staff members (39.6%) published 96 items, or 28.7 percent of the 335 items (see Table VI).

TABLE V
A Composite of the Contributors/Noncontributors
of Published Items, by Library Function

	Contributors	Noncontributors	Totals
Administrative/Special Services	4 (11.8%)	1 (11.2%)	5 (11.6%)
Public Services	16 (47.1%)	5 (55.5%)	21 (48.8%)
Technical Services	14 (41.1%)	3 (33.3%)	17 (39.6%)
	34 (100.0%)	9 (100.0%)	43 (100.0%)

TABLE VI
A Composite of the Observations
of Published Items, by Library Function

	Administrative/ Special Services	Public Services	Technical Services	Totals
Staff	5 (11.6%)	21 (48.8%)	17 (39.6%)	43 (100%)
Items	100 (29.8%)	139 (41.5%)	96 (28.7%)	335 (100%)

A construct of the staffing pattern into three separate groups of near-equal numbers was developed. The high group (A) consists of the top 14 positions within the library hierarchy, the next 16 positions comprise the middle group (B), and the last 13 positions are included in the low group (C). The preponderance of publications, 243 out of 335, or 72.5 percent, are contributed by librarians in the A group. The B group offered 73 items, or 21.8 percent of the total output. Out of the publication mass, the C group contributed nineteen items, or 5.7 percent (see Table VII).

TABLE VII
A Composite of the Observations
of Published Items, by Ranking of Libraries

	High	*Middle*	*Low*	*Totals*
Group	A	B	C	
Items	243 (72.5%)	73 (21.8%)	19 (5.7%)	335 (100%)

The findings of this mini-study were determined in two important categories of effects and causes, as follows:

1. There is a relationship between the rank of the position which a person holds on the library staff and his/her rate of publication.

2. There is a pronounced number of items contributed in the top one-third of the staffing pattern, a lesser number noted in the middle one-third, and the fewest number of items in the bottom one-third group.

3. There is a significantly greater rate of publication among the full professors of the library faculty than among that of the descending ranks of associate professors, assistant professors, or instructors.

4. There is an interrelationship of items contributed among the various assignments of the library staff that indicates the management-oriented administrative/special group produces the greatest number of publications per librarian, compared to public and technical services personnel.

5. There are data which correlate the male librarian and the greater amount of research conducted per capita as reflected in publication output.

The Limitations

Only after limitations implicit in the design and method of the mini-study have been made explicit, should conclusions be drawn and generalizations made, based upon these findings. Those which are important to the report are listed as follows:

1. The librarian was studied only at a medium-sized land-grant institution. No librarians and scholars at small or very large academic institutions were considered.

2. Inasmuch as the librarians under observation had conducted research and/or published the results at one type of library primarily, the findings would be applicable to librarians at other types of libraries only to the extent that their working conditions and personnel situations were similar to those in the test library.

3. The generalization that scholarly work is conducted by librarians in academic libraries rests upon the assumption that the education and experience of each librarian and the obligation to participate in scholarly pursuits are recognized equally by all participants.

The Conclusions

Based upon the findings in the investigation, and within the limitations of the study, several conclusions are drawn.

1. The effort put forth by librarians in scholarly activities is effective. The number of publications would likely be fewer without the general awareness to do research and engage in scholarly pursuits.

2. The higher the rank in the academic library staffing pattern, the more fully the librarian tends to participate in research. These greater job responsibilities suggest in the minds of librarians a sense of concern and consequently stimulate them to participate in scholarly activities.

3. There is little doubt that as a librarian assumes more responsible duties, he or she also senses the need for others to con-

tribute to the wider dimensions of librarianship. All efforts to aid the lower-ranking librarian to contribute to the profession as a whole seem to be worthwhile.

4. This study tends to support the contention that the librarian assigned to administrative or special duties is more likely to participate in scholarly work, too. There is less difference in this regard, however, when comparing public- and technical-service personnel's output.

5. This study tends to refute the notion that men and women participate more or less equally in scholarly activities. There is a difference, and librarians may want to further study the phenomenon of sex as a meaningful indicator of the extent and level of participation in publishing the results of scholarship.

In the classic relationship between tasks of the job and work in the realm of scholarship and research, the challenge of scholarly productivity falls on the individual librarian himself or herself. It is particularly important for a library staff to have available the widest range of opportunities to do research. The librarian often fails to utilize the resources available, and as a result frequently does not reach full potential. An apparently insignificant problem, therefore, becomes one of great importance, particularly as the numbers of academic librarians increase and the concerns for scholarship are heightened.

It is necessary, consequently, to know more about the academic librarian's activities. This mini-study has given only brief insight into scholarly activities as manifested in the publication of research efforts. As a result, one can begin to understand more fully the extent of this activity but insufficent information is available regarding the causes of these effects. Inasmuch as there was no opportunity to query each librarian personally, the conclusions which follow are derived from the literature, as well as indirectly, from the results of the study. They also include those stated by other persons in the field.

One might pose the question, "Why is there not more evidence of high scholarship in academic librarianship?" There are those who argue that administrative work is of the highest value in the guild. It seems to be a fact, therefore, that many library administrators find it too dificult to combine their duties with any type of teaching or research. There are those who say that administrative work tends to be detrimental to scholarship and professional activity. On the other hand, McAnally states: "Research is also one of the traditional measures of faculty competence. . . . In time there may be no place in the university library for the librarian who is not interested in research."[10]

Another problem appears to be that academic librarians often do not see themselves as scholars. The emphasis on scholarship and research is not a pervasive part of the graduate education for librarianship. Hence, few academic librarians are trained in the skills of research. They do not naturally and normally pursue scholarship as they ply their trade.

It has also been suggested that university administrators and selection committees seeking librarians no longer think of these assignments as scholarly posts. "Research training," states Kaser, "with its emphasis on rigor, exactness, caution, and suspended judgment, often tends to make scholars uncomfortable in administration, where emphasis is more often on haste, compromise, political expedience, and, at best, partial data."[11]

As previously noted, many academic librarians have difficulty meeting their responsibilities as scholars because their professional education has lacked training in research methodology and the skills of writing for publication. Until this gap is closed, there will be a number of librarians who will not be involved in scholarly activity. This will present a frustrating predicament for several librarians, inasmuch as their initial appointments, reappointments, tenure, and promotion may depend heavily upon activities in research and publication.

What can we anticipate from academic librarians? As faculty members, academic librarians are expected "to engage in activities normally associated with scholarship—for example, research and publication," says Dougherty. "But even if successful," he continues, "the rewards will not be reaped easily, for to succeed in academe will require an enormous output of individual dedication and commitment."[12]

It was over ten years ago that Ralph Ellsworth declared: "Our generation has won considerable recognition in many colleges and universities, not just as good librarians, but as good academicians."[13] Librarians are not only engaged in publication as a result of their research activities, of course. They also serve scholarship in several other ways. In some instances, librarians participate as members of the graduate faculty when the library resources can be made known and utilized. The librarian may become involved in the direction of research projects of the students.

The librarian may extend the influence of the library by acting as a teacher in the classroom – particularly in subjects of bibliography. The offering by librarians of lectures or courses in the literature of subject disciplines is another example of scholarly activity. Collaborating with doctoral candidates in conducting research, offers librarians several potential areas of involvement with scholarship.

Librarians' involvement in the organization and direction of academic presses at several universities is also illustrative of the important role which they play in scholarly undertakings. Several librarians serve on boards of directors, editorial committees, or act as referees in reviewing manuscripts.

"Scholarship draws no national boundaries. Inasmuch as its quest is truth, it seeks it wherever it may be."[14] The establishment of scholarship throughout the world has been recognized by American academic librarians. The objective is usually to develop some sort of alliance, such as the International Federation of Library Associations (IFLA), in order to share resources and expertise in the design of new bibliographical tools and products which will ultimately benefit the scholar. The exchange of materials published throughout the world is a prime example, also, of the activity of libraries in the area of international scholarship. The academic librarian is indeed demonstrating all sorts of ways in which librarians are indispensable wherever scholarship is involved.

Perhaps more than all related factors, the quantity and quality of publications in any area are critically important for librarianship, in gaining acceptance as a scholarly field by the other disciplines of academe. Much has been done, by virtue of publications by librarians, to clarify the field of librarianship, particularly in the scholarly community. There is no contribution to the literature which more explicitly illustrates this point than Pierce Butler's *An Introduction to Library Science*.[15] It is a classic in the library field in its delineation of a philosophy of librarianship.

It is hoped that the results of this mini-study have added to the knowledge about the librarian as a scholar. Insight into librarians' publishing patterns has been achieved. We should understand more fully now which academic librarians are doing scholarly research and which ones are not. We tend to grasp more accurately the relationships of the various functions of academic librarianship as well as the status of the librarian in the staff hierarchy.

THE FUTURE

We still need to know more about the academic librarian's attitudes toward scholarship. We need to understand better the librarian's background and the ways he or she reacts to given situations.

This study should be considered exploratory and preliminary. In order for the findings and conclusions to be accepted with even greater confidence, other more extensive investigations should be undertaken. A future effort to validate, to supplement, or to refute the results of this mini-study might be worthwhile.

One can readily conceive of developing a study at other institutions of higher learning. The same kind of inquiry in larger universities, or much smaller colleges, could produce different results. In addition to replicating the present study, other points of inquiry merit attention.

If it is true that the academic librarian tends toward scholarly involvement as he or she climbs the library staff ladder, how can we put this information to its best use? It might be helpful, for example, to try inculcating the need for scholarship while "on the job," and not only during the library school days. This would be particularly important during the initial years of apprenticeship in the field.

It may be in order to consider incentives for academic librarians, beyond the common rewards of promotion, tenure, or salary. Perhaps more efforts toward recognizing in some separate and tangible manner the contributions of individuals to research and scholarship would encourage those who have not yet done so to produce.

What is the relationship of our academic librarian's job performance and his or her contribution or noncontribution to scholarship? Is it the outstanding librarian who does the job well who also is the one involved in research? It would be interesting to determine attitudes of academic librarians about the whole realm of research.

The consideration of relevant studies in other disciplines may have application to the library scene. Motivation research, for example, has introduced new techniques, which could be applied in this arena.

There is a need, finally, for a research study to investigate the characteristics of the librarian/scholar relationship. There remain several components of the system of librarianship and scholarship which are still unknown and unarticulated. Progressive and precise research in the future is certainly one requisite toward a better understanding of librarians as scholars.

FOOTNOTES

1. *Webster's New World Dictionary of the American Language.* New York: World Publishing Company, 1964, p. 1304.
2. "Library Education and Manpower," *American Libraries,* v. 1, no. 4 (April 1970): 343.
3. Gordon Ray, "A Retrospective View," in Edward C. Lathem, ed., *American Libraries as Centers of Scholarship.* Hanover, N.H.: Dartmouth College, 1978, p. 25.
4. David Kaser, "The Effect of the Revolution of 1969-1970 on University Library Administration," in Herbert Poole, ed., *Academic Libraries by the Year 2000.* New York: Bowker, 1977, p. 69.
5. Beverly P. Lynch, "Women and Employment in Academic Librarianship," in Herbert Poole, ed., *op. cit.,* p. 120.
6. "Joint Statement on Faculty Status of College and University Librarians," *College and Research Libraries News,* no. 35 (February 1974): 26.
7. Louis R. Wilson, "The Service of Libraries in Promoting Scholarship and Research," *Library Quarterly,* v. 3, no. 2 (April 1933): 141.
8. Jack Dalton, "Library Education," in Jerrold Orne, ed., *Research Librarianship: Essays in Honor of Robert B. Downs.* New York: Bowker, 1971, p. 121.
9. Leon Festinger and Daniel Katz, *Research Methods in Behavioral Sciences.* New York: Holt, Rinehart & Winston, 1953, p. 241.
10. Arthur M. McAnally, "Status of the University Librarian in the Academic Community," in Jerrold Orne, ed., *op. cit.,* p. 44.
11. Kaser, *op. cit.,* p. 70.
12. Richard M. Dougherty, "Personnel Needs for Librarianship's Uncertain Future," in Herbert Poole, ed., *op. cit.,* p. 113.
13. Ralph E. Ellsworth, "The Library's Life Style" *Michigan Librarian,* v. 36, no. 3 (Autumn 1970): 30.
14. Wilson, *op. cit.,* p. 142.
15. Pierce Butler. *An Introduction to Library Science.* Chicago: University of Chicago Press, 1933.

The moment libraries cease to be problems to university presidents, the time will have arrived when humanistic scholarship is dead. — **Ralph Ellsworth.** *Library Journal, v. 88, no. 7 (April 1, 1963): 1405.*

The Role of the Academic Library Within the Institution

Clyde C. Walton, Director of Libraries
University of Colorado
Boulder, Colorado

The introductory quotation comes from a paper presented by Ralph E. Ellsworth at the Cornell Library Conference and Dedication, in October 1962. The paper was published both in the *Library Journal* (in 1963) and, with other papers from the Conference, in book form.[1]

In his paper, Ralph discussed in greater or lesser detail, some ten topics. Some of these topics dealt with changes that were going on within the university, changes that presumably the librarian might influence or help direct, while others were simply examples of the intrusion of the modern world into the once ivory-towers of academe. It is worth noting that much that influences the role of the library within the institution comes from outside the institution and is almost entirely outside the control of the library director. All of the issues raised in Ralph's 1962 paper bear upon the library's role in the university. This chapter will review, in greater or lesser detail, those points, in an effort to determine, after the passage of twenty years, those that have been resolved and those that have not, and to examine issues that have developed since his article was published.

THE INFORMATION EXPLOSION

The phenomenon popularly known as the information explosion continues unabated; it is but one baffling aspect of a rapidly changing world. Ralph noted that in his lifetime, "the revolution in transportation has carried me through the eras of the horse and buggy, the railroad, the Models T & A, the V-8's, the DC-3's, 4's, 6's, 7's and 8's . . ." We may also add successful small imported cars, the DC-9 and -10, the 727, 737, and 747, the moon landings, the Jupiter and Saturn probes, and the flight from the space laboratory.

In the last twenty years, worldwide production of new books has more than doubled. At the same time, the number of new scholarly books published in the United States increased from 3000 (1960) to 15,000 (1980). Worldwide, the number of scientific and technical serials jumped from about 20,000 to 50,000 titles.[2] To illustrate this growth of information, Ralph noted how the libraries at Harvard, Chicago, Illinois, Cornell, and UCLA had expanded from the time of the First World War to 1961; below are his figures up to date, to show the continued growth of these libraries.[3]

	WORLD WAR 1	1961	1980
Harvard	1,184,000	6,849,000	10,083,000
Chicago	593,000	2,142,000	4,311,000
Illinois	380,000	3,383,000	5,937,000
Cornell	474,000	2,199,000	4,217,000
UCLA	"didn't exist"	1,569,000	4,235,000

A factor that was not of enough significance for Ralph to mention in 1961 clearly is having a major effect on the growth of academic libraries. That factor is inflation. Quite simply, between 1970 and 1980, the average price of a hard-cover book more than doubled, while "periodical prices have risen 13 percent a year or a total of 239 percent over the last ten years."[4] Between 1980 and 1981 alone, the average price of a U.S. serial increased 19.4 percent.[5] Meanwhile, both inflation and the fall of the dollar abroad have caused the prices of foreign publications to rise astronomically. Double-digit inflation in book and subscription prices clearly is eroding academic library materials allocations and is doing so even as the information explosion continues. As a result, academic-library growth rates have slowed. The dollars spent for books and serials by the 75 libraries that were members of the Association of Research Libraries in 1969-70 and in 1979-80 increased by 91 percent over those ten years. During this same period, however, the gross number of volumes added each year decreased by 22.5 percent. That is to say that these libraries now spend almost twice what they did for materials but are adding much less than they did in 1969-70.

Further, the median number of volumes held by this group increased by 44 percent since 1969-70, but the growth rate has
slowed, for the increase in volumes held from 1968-69 to 1969-70
was 7 percent while the rate for the 1978-79 and 1979-80 was only
2.9 percent.[6] Another way of examining the effect of inflation on
academic library growth is in terms of unit costs for library
materials; for example, in the four-year period 1977-1981, unit costs
for library acquisitions at the University of Colorado, Boulder, rose
from $21.18 per item to $27.32.[7] Inflation is indeed a major contemporary issue in academic librarianship, simply by the fact of its persistent existence.

The information explosion, Ralph noted, has made it more and
more impossible for the scholar to obtain the information he or she
needs, by performing the traditional literature search. The scholar
cannot wait for a comprehensive, printed bibliography to be
published, for the need is for instant information, information *now*.
And so it has become common to search for information by accessing a distant, computer-generated data base. To do this
necessitates that librarians acquire new skills – for, to make the op-
timum use of a computerized data base, considerable training and
experience are necessary. But using such a data base is costly:
equipment must be purchased, charges for accessing the data base
must be paid, and staff, who could be performing other duties, must
be trained and available. And so a new issue is born: who pays for
this service? Some argue that the library is doing what it has always
done, providing information, but simply providing it in a different
way. After all, they say, when information was provided from the
card catalog or from reference books and bibliographies, the patron
was not asked to pay any part of the cost of creating and maintaining the card catalog or to pay part of what it cost to purchase, process, and shelve a reference book, or to pay a part of the salary of the
librarian who helped the patron with the card catalog or who taught
him how to use the bibliography. Yet every time a computer-based
data bank is used, an out-of-pocket charge is incurred, which must
be paid promptly, and libraries furnish the terminals and printers
and make available the trained librarians who instruct patrons in its
use.

Here, then, in simple form, is the very emotional issue of whether
a publicly supported library should or should not make a direct
charge for the information it provides its patrons. At the moment, it
appears that many academic libraries have purchased the equipment and trained librarians at their own expense, but require

patrons to pay actual connect-time charges. Others require the patron to pay an overhead charge plus the connect-time charges. Another reason advanced to justify such charges is that, if searching a computerized data base has to be paid for at least in part by the patron, the patron will be restrained from asking for extravagant searches and will tend to be more judicious in his requests. If the service were free for the asking, it is feared that the number of requests for data-base searches would reach such astronomical proportions that it would be absolutely impossible for the library to support them. But, the argument continues, if the library charges, does this not put an end to what might be called the democracy of information? The issue remains unresolved.

BUILDINGS

In his 1962 paper, Ralph was concerned that academic-library buildings were becoming so expensive to build that it would no longer be possible for the library to house all the books the university owned. This implied an increasing use of "cheap storage warehouses" so that when the library shelves were filled, for every new book added, an old one would either be sent to the warehouse or reduced to microform. It is true that, in large part because of our old enemy inflation, academic-library construction costs are very high, currently running between $90 and $100 per square foot, depending on location. But even with these tremendous building rates, there has been no discernable grand rush to build or rent storage warehouses. Further, while more books than ever are being committed to microform, the reason seems to be more related to the need to preserve their intellectual content than to considerations of space.

One effect of the increasing cost of library buildings, Ralph said, might be to force many academic libraries to abandon open stacks and go to some kind of closed stack, with books shelved perhaps by size or by an arbitrary accession number assigned without regard to the subject of the book. Closed stacks with books shelved by size and in the order of their acquisition certainly makes maximum use of space; Ralph notes that for centuries, European scholars have done good work in libraries where books are so shelved. Again, there does not seem to be any concerted rush to convert open-stack libraries to closed-stack libraries or to build new academic libraries with closed stacks. There does seem to be, however, a heightened interest in compact shelving, particularly of the mechanized type; for example, this kind of shelving is used in parts of the new Madison building of the Library of Congress.

COLLECTION DEVELOPMENT

Certainly an issue today related to the information explosion is collection development. Materials budgets in large academic libraries commonly exceed a million dollars a year; of the 99 members of the Association of Research Libraries only three have less, while 35 have materials budgets of over two million, 14 have over three million, and two have more than 4 million.[8] Even though inflation has cut severely into academic-library purchasing power, the sums of money available to libraries can hardly be termed insignificant. But librarians cannot be certain that the money is being spent wisely, largely because it is not yet known exactly what the composition of collections should be, in terms of the advanced-degree programs we are required to support. Is there, for example, a minimum number of volumes required to support a Ph.D. program in chemistry? How many books and journals are needed to support the Ph.D. program in history, and, more particularly, which books and which journals? There is, of course, no set answer to the questions of size and composition, for in spite of the earlier work done by scholars like Herman Fussler,[9] librarians are just now starting to get serious about these matters. The Collection Analysis Program of the Office of Management Studies of the Association of Research Libraries has the potential to teach librarians how to analyze collections and how to plan for their orderly growth, both in terms of internal mechanisms and routines and in philosophical concept; regrettably, so far, only a relative handful of academic libraries have taken advantage of this program.

Then, too, librarians have great difficulty in deciding how to cut up the materials-budget pie. That is to say, how big a slice goes to engineering and how big a slice to anthropology or to English? There are so many schemes and formulas in library literature for dividing up the acquisitions dollars that it is reasonable to conclude that there is no generally accepted method for doing this. Furthermore, it is almost impossible in times of high inflation, when libraries are fortunate if they are able to maintain their buying power, to make any major change in the way the materials budget is allocated, even though it is recognized that inequities exist among the various disciplines. In these years when the library's buying power at best stays level or more likely declines, to increase the dollars allocated for the purchase of books and journals in one program quite simply requires that the amount of the increase has to be taken out of the hide of another program. No library director possessed of a keen sense of self-preservation is likely, in these circumstances, to attempt to reorganize and reallocate the materials funds. Yet another issue related to the growth of libraries is the matter of cooperative acquisitions. Clearly, there is a real potential for savings here, but at what level is it practical to cooperate, and just how is a program of cooperative organizations to be established? Many librarians are used to saying that academic libraries should provide at least 85 percent of what undergraduate students require. The problem with this statement is the automatic assumption that it is known what undergraduates require, an assumption which may be hard to support. Generally, the technique is to examine the catalogs of established undergraduate libraries of good reputation, use the "opening-day" bibliographies as guides, consult with faculty, and then trust to our own instincts. The result is that each library builds a core collection that largely and quite properly is quite similar to that in every undergraduate library in the country. It seems that the very nature of the basic undergraduate collection makes cooperative acquisitions at that level all but impossible.

But at the graduate level, opportunities abound. Several very simple examples: In the Midwest, it would make no sense at all to plan to build a research collection dealing with Latin American colonial history, just as it would be equally foolish to plan to build an exhaustive collection of African materials. The Newberry Library has one of the great collections dealing with the early history of Latin America, and the Melville J. Herskovits Library of African Studies, at Northwestern University, has an unparalleled collection of African materials. To duplicate these would be frightfully expensive; even if the money could be found, it would not be possible to do so totally, and further, there is no logical reason to attempt to duplicate them.

All of this seems quite clear. It is obvious enough that, at least in a generally defined geographical region, special collections of great depth should not be duplicated. The degree to which great special collections should be duplicated even in part is perhaps a matter of argument. In any event, unspoken policies which say that the materials must be brought to the scholar, must be revised with the thought of finding ways of bringing the scholars to the materials. An equally interesting issue to debate is the degree to which an academic library should continue to purchase material to develop and expand one of its special collections when there are at least similar if not identical special collections in existence which also are being developed and expanded. It would be demonstrably cheaper for a library to decide to stop building a duplicated special collection and to send a faculty member who must use these special materials, to one of the other special collections. Even though it would make sense to do this, one rarely hears about a library that has followed such a course of action.

While the possibilities and problems of cooperative activity in the area of special collections are relatively easy to define, less attention has been paid to general cooperative programs of acquisitions. Yet, as inflation each year continues to reduce library purchasing power, it is more and more imperative that libraries address the matter of joint acquisitions. It is indeed little short of scandalous that more has not been done to develop cooperative acquisitions programs long before this. After all, as Ralph pointed out, a kind of rational cooperative acquisitions program was begun after World War II, but for a variety of reasons, not the least of which was financial, there was no follow-through. The Farmington Plan should have proven that it is possible to work cooperatively at the national level, but librarians have not yet used that knowledge to develop the kind of national program needed. Perhaps the Research Libraries Group's (RLG) Research Libraries Information Network's (RLIN) current effort to plan for cooperative acquisitions is a step-child of the Farmington Plan.

But suppose that a group of libraries that share some commonality in programs and patrons decide they would like to begin some kind of program of cooperative acquisitions. How do they start? To begin with, after having made the firm decision to establish the program, they have to have an organizational framework. Either a new organization has to be created or the purposes for which an existing organization was established have to be expanded so that it may become the appropriate vehicle. The libraries involved must have a clear idea of exactly what it is they wish to accomplish and, following that, develop the mechanisms necessary to achieve their goals; finally, the dollars must be found so that the joint purchases may be made. The acid test will come if these dollars have to be taken off the top of an already inadequate materials budget—as they probably will have to be. This poses a severe local political problem for each library director, for it will entail taking dollars that could have been spent for materials on the local campus and, instead, putting them into a cooperative plan. This is why the decision to join a cooperative acquisitions program cannot be entered into lightly.

Seven research libraries in Colorado (Denver University, the Denver Public Library, the Auraria Library, the Colorado School of Mines, the University of Colorado, Boulder, the University of Northern Colorado, and Colorado State University) work together on a variety of cooperative projects, through an organization known as the Colorado Alliance of Research Libraries (CARL). CARL established a committee which it calls COLA (Colorado Organization for Library Acquisitions); its membership is made up of the chief collection-development officers of the seven libraries; COLA is chaired by one of the seven library directors. A formula was developed based on each member's annual materials budget; this formula brings in about $50,000 a year for cooperative acquisitions. The philosophic concept is simple: CARL believes that it must acquire, in one copy only, significant research materials that are required in Colorado. The program is designed both to assure access to these desirable materials and at the same time to avoid expensive duplication. COLA developed rules as it went along, rules such as (1) nothing that costs less than $300 (now $500) would be purchased; (2) no active serials would be purchased; (3) everything purchased would be available on interlibrary loan to CARL libraries, regardless of price or format; (4) the decision to purchase would be made by formal vote; (5) after the decision to purchase was made, the library initiating the request would purchase the item and in turn would be reimbursed by COLA; (6) COLA would decide by consensus where each item should be housed; (7) the library in which the item is housed would catalog it and distribute cards to the other COLA members. This relatively simple arrangement has functioned quite effectively. There have been problems, but they have been solved, one by one, and of course, additional rules and procedures have been adopted. For example, a form was developed which is used to inform COLA members when any COLA library is considering purchasing, or has decided to purchase a particularly expensive item.

At first, COLA was largely reactive, generally making its purchases from among the many current major publishing projects, regardless of form. But after some experience, it became clear that in the long run, COLA needed to do more than just react to what came to its attention; rather, it needed to make a sustained effort to expand existing collections in a planned, logical manner. This meant that each COLA library had to take a hard look, first, at its own collections, in terms of how effectively they were meeting patron needs; and second, at how their collections did or did not relate to the collections in the other six libraries. In fact, COLA now recognizes that its overall approach will be that each of the participating libraries is but one part of a single library.

Cooperative acquisitions programs such as this prevent expensive, unnecessary duplication, generally insure that one copy of an item of significant research value is available in one of the COLA libraries, tends to expand overall CARL purchasing power, and will, in the long run, make it possible for each of the participating libraries to continually enrich its own collections. This is, of course, but one way to get the job done. Cooperative acquisitions may be developed on a regional basis, as a statewide program, or by a consortium of institutions. The point is that it is quite possible to work out a simple but effective program of cooperative acquisitions; clearly, more academic libraries ought to be planning to do so.

THE CARD CATALOG

Another topic that Ralph addressed was the card catalog. In his discussion, he pointed out that the traditional academic subject organization of the university was changing, because of the introduction of area studies programs and because of the increasingly interdisciplinary nature of research. The subject headings in the card catalog reflect the traditional organization of knowledge and do not meet the needs of either the area studies programs or an interdisciplinary approach to research; unfortunately, he said, it was impossibly expensive to make the extensive changes required to keep subject headings current. The same thing was thought to be true of the classification system: it was just too expensive to try to revise the schedules and keep them up to date. The card catalog was, therefore, inefficient, frequently contained outdated information, including location symbols and inadequate or inaccurate subject headings, and was excessively expensive to maintain.

Of course, time has demonstrated that everything Ralph said about the card catalog was true, except, perhaps, concerning the revision of the classification schedules. Now the Anglo-American Cataloging Rules II (AACR 2) are in existence, and it remains to be seen just how expensive it will be for each library to put these new rules into effect and just how well they will serve the needs of patrons. While AACR 2 does make a number of useful changes, the problem with inadequate subject headings for area studies and interdisciplinary research remains with us.

Librarians are now beginning to see some of the problems AACR 2 is creating. One wryly amusing problem that has an unanticipated "snowball" effect is this: the library purchases a new book, coauthored by Mr. Eugene and Mr. Ralph. The library already owns two other books written by Mr. Eugene, so that under the library's current operating rules (redo the cards if five titles or less are involved), the cards are pulled and changed. But the library also owns two books written by Mr. Eugene but which are coauthored by Mr. Jones, so the Eugene cards are pulled and changed. But alas, the library possesses three books written by Mr. Jones, each of them with at least one coauthor. This one book written by Mr. Eugene and Mr. Ralph might well keep one staff member busy changing records indefinitely. The illustration is, of course, overdrawn, but the situation does exist. This amusing but annoying problem is but one of many with which libraries must learn to cope.

It is becoming increasingly obvious that in the long run, only an on-line, public-access catalog is going to be the answer to efficient access to the materials in our libraries. Closing the present card catalog and starting a second card catalog simply confuses patrons, because there are no linkages between the old and the new, unless each library makes them, an almost impossibly expensive task. Another alternative is to file the AACR 2 cards into the existing catalog. But here too, the linkages do not exist and it is far too costly to redo the AACR 2 rules, because of the large number of cards in the catalog that would have to be redone. Once again, the patron will not be well served. Yet another option is to consider the use of computer-produced microform. But closing the card catalog and going to computer-produced microform does not seem to be a particularly good response, since there are no linkages between the old catalog and the new microform, and because the microform is out of date from the moment it is produced.

A number of libraries and organizations are working toward developing on-line, public-access catalogs, and it is surprising that there has not been any sustained, national effort in this direction. Perhaps this is because to make the on-line, public-access catalog completely effective, existing card-catalog records will have to be converted to machine-readable form, and at the present time, retrospective conversion costs are high. Or perhaps it is because there is continuing hope that someone, somewhere, will come up with a cost-effective answer to the problems posed by AACR 2. But wishing will not make it so, and sooner or later, librarians will have to stop wishing and take some action. It is becoming increasingly clear that on-line, public-access catalogs are the wave of the future.

LIBRARY OF CONGRESS

"One of the major crimes that can be charged to the head librarians of American universities of my generation," Ralph wrote, "is our failure to develop, through the Library of Congress, a full, complete and economical system of centralized cataloging."[10] Although to characterize that failure as a major crime seems somewhat extravagant, the problem is still with us. Now the Library of Congress distributes its current cataloging not only in its traditional form but also in machine-readable form, and although it was the Library of Congress that, with help, established the international standard for machine-readable cataloging (MARC), a "full, complete and economical system of centralized cataloging" does not exist. Perhaps librarians are as near as they ever will be to that centralized cataloging, with the distribution of MARC cataloging through the major bibliographic networks, OCLC, RLIN, WLN, and UTLAS. Most librarians believe that MARC distribution by the networks has reduced their individual cataloging costs and if it has not, certainly, at the very least, has retarded substantially the increases in the cost of cataloging. But it is hard to document this, since most academic libraries did not have reliable information about their pre-MARC cataloging costs. Even with all the detailed cataloging information available through the networks, original cataloging still remains one of the most expensive operations in the library.

The Library of Congress remains, by statute, the library of the United States Congress, rather than the national library. But because the Library of Congress, nevertheless, is in effect our national library, it has to play a most difficult and ambiguous role. While the administrators at that library do listen sympathetically to the requests made by the library community, they cannot always make a positive response, since these requests are sometimes at variance with their primary responsibility, which is to the Congress. Were it otherwise, who can doubt that libraries would have a carefully developed plan for a national library network, the network so desperately needed? Ralph suggested that it was because librarians did not know how "to mobilize the backing of our administrations and faculties in our effort to make the Library of Congress a national library."[11] He was absolutely correct, but because there was once failure does not mean that it should not be tried again. The need is obvious and urgent, but little is being done: national library and scholarly organizations should be planning together now, how the goal may be reached. Some way must be found to make a major, concerted effort to have the Library of Congress become the national library of the United States. It is not yet too late, but the continued growth of the national networks suggests that, if action is not soon taken, a less satisfactory and less dynamic de facto response will be in effect. The final resolution to this issue will have a major effect on the role of the academic library within its institution.

Another concern expressed by Ralph was the need for academic libraries to recognize that programmed learning can play a significant role in the educational process and that "wet" carrells (carrells with electrical outlets and direct connections to film and learning centers) should be placed in numbers in our libraries. The newer technological apparatus of wet carells and teaching machines do indeed have a place on the campus, and many academic libraries have installed them. But the trend over the last twenty years seems to be that they are more often found in numbers within the embrace of special remedial programs or in learning centers rather than in the library. The greater use of these kinds of equipment seems to be in the community colleges rather than in university libraries. But the way in which the individual campus decides administratively to handle programmed learning does bear upon the role of the library. If the program is the responsibility of the library, there is serious impact on the library in terms of allocation of funds, space, and personnel, but if the library is, in effect, just one of several "receiving stations" on the campus, the impact is more likely to be minimal. For the moment, this does not appear to be a major issue on most campuses.

HONORS PROGRAMS

Long an advocate of honors courses generally, Ralph wrote:

The mere fact that these Honors Programs exist, is damning evidence of the intellectual depravity of the curriculum of the American university – at least if higher education is education, not training, and if its business is to give young men and women a chance to learn how, as Matthew Arnold once said "To see life steady and to see it whole."[12]

He also believed that they could "restore to the library its role as the learning center of the campus" and that they should be quartered in the library; practicing what he preached, the honors program at the University of Colorado, Boulder, is housed in Norlin Library. But academic libraries generally have not seen fit to house honors programs, and among the most important reasons is one that is not philosophical but a matter of hard reality: the high cost of library construction, which precludes locating anything but library functions in the library. Then too, the great current interest in the core curriculum concept, which on many campuses has resulted in upgrading basic lower-division courses, has lessened the need for honors programs generally. And finally, the revolutionary improvement in high-school curriculum and teaching that seemed so evident in the post Sputnik years has not continued. SAT scores are dropping and are today significantly lower than they were in the mid-sixties, and it is true that "scores on the American College Testing Program, the Metropolitan Achievement Tests and the Iowa Tests of Basic Skills reflect much the same erosion of scholastic achievement."[13] Although there are widely divergent opinions as to why this has happened and what it means, the scores are demonstrably lower. There is a generally felt concern that there "is a growing number of students who – for a wide variety of personal, social, economic and other reasons – are ill-served by the high schools they attend." The same writer suggests the cyclic nature of educational problems by saying: "If early childhood education was the glamour field of the 1960's and 70's, the 80's promise to be the Decade of the High School."[14]

Probably no one knows exactly what changing patterns of education in the high schools means to the academic library. Following increased competition for the better students, significant numbers of less qualified students may be enrolled, with the possibility that there may be more emphasis upon remedial programs and programmed learning, more use of the time-worn method of teaching by using large lists of reserve books, or perhaps, as suggested above, even more attention to structuring a basic core curriculum. But it must be recognized that what happens in the high schools will sooner or later have an impact on the institution and what impacts the institution in turn impacts the library.

PUSH-BUTTON, INFORMATIONAL LIBRARY SERVICE

The idea of a "national system of miniaturized electronic-stored, transmitted and retrieved information" was but a vision twenty years ago and is still little more than a vision today, although elements of such a system are now in place. No one then could possibly have foreseen the creation and rapid development of computer-based library networks and the tremendous impact they have had upon libraries, large and small. But even if a crystal ball had revealed that such networks would come into being and flourish, no one could possibly have imagined that the competition between OCLC and the Research Libraries Group's Research Libraries Information Network (RLIN) would have such a potential for disaster, both to themselves and to the library community generally.

In 1967, the presidents of Ohio colleges and universities founded the Ohio College Library Center, now OCLC, Incorporated. Their initial objective was to retard rising cataloging costs through computer-based, on-line shared cataloging. The spectacular success of OCLC has impacted all libraries, large and small. It is now an international network which in 1980 had 2268 member institutions, and of these members, "1,330 or 58.6 percent were college and university libraries, which included the majority of the large research libraries; 15.5 percent were public libraries; and 11.8 percent were federal libraries," with a variety of institutions constituting the remaining 14.1 percent. A total of 1671 of these institutions used 3402 cathode-ray-tube terminals, while 597 accessed OCLC via dial-up or value-added networks.[15]

In 1979-80 there were 14,179,103 titles cataloged through OCLC which resulted in 10,451,632 chargeable first-time uses (FTUs). The total number of catalog cards billed was 113,102,000, and there were more than seven million bibliographic records in its data base. This was the first year that OCLC charged for participation in its interlibrary loan system, and it processed a total of 565,680 transactions. In this same year, OCLC offered, at a reduced rate, the data bases of the Bibliographical Retrieval Services (BRS), Lockheed's Dialog, and *The New York Times* Information Bank. It has also arranged with the Source Telecomputing Corporation to make the Source, an inexpensive information retrieval system which includes a subset of *The New York Times* Information Bank, the *Official Airline Guide* and *World Almanac,* available to libraries.[16].

OCLC is experimenting with the development of a videotex

system and continues to work with Channel 2000, its system which makes it possible to interface, via an ordinary telephone, computerized data bases with a television set. Also, it is testing its own on-line acquisitions system.[17] OCLC has an ongoing research program, with projects designed to enhance the system, particularly for research libraries. Among these projects are: (1) subject-retrieval capabilities; (2) increased and regular participation by libraries outside the United States; (3) development of local on-line catalogs; and (4) development of an on-line authority system.[18] On June 30, 1980, OCLC had assets of $57,901,582.

OCLC, however, has been challenged by, and is in competition with, another bibliographic utility. This is the Research Libraries Information Network (RLIN) of the Research Libraries Group (RLG). The RLG was formed by Harvard, Yale, Columbia, and the New York Public Library in 1974, and in 1978 it acquired the BALLOTS bibliographic-data system, developed by Stanford University. BALLOTS quickly became the heart of RLIN. Also in 1978, although Harvard left RLG, the group began to receive substantial financial support from a number of foundations as well as from Stanford University. Since then, RLG has conducted an aggressive campaign to get the members of the Association of Research Libraries to join RLIN. According to press releases, RLG describes itself as:

> a corporation owned and operated by its member institutions, [which] was created in 1974 to find solutions to the double problem of dwindling budgets and expanding demands faced by research libraries. Through its four programs — shared resources, collection management and development, preservation and RLIN, the on-line bibliographic tool that forms the basis for other programs — the consortium is working to create solutions that will enable research institutions to make use of the improvements wrought by the information revolution.[19]

As 1980 drew to a close, RLG had 23 members and 2 associate members;[20] with the receipt of loans totalling $2,200,000, RLG now has the money to satisfy the funding requirements it identified in 1979. It had just announced a new on-line message system designed to facilitate interlibrary loan transactions. Its data base had "2.2 million books records, 300,000 other records; 218,000 archive books records; 370,000 serials records, with CONSER; 1.6 million authority records; and 106,000 records in other formats."[21] The current development programs include authority control, an acquisitions system, non-Roman-language support, interlibrary loan, patron access to on-line catalogs, AACR 2 support, and page-form catalogs. Two other bibliographic utilities need to be mentioned here: the Washington Library Network (WLN) and the University of Toronto Library Automation Systems (UTLAS). WLN limits its direct service to the Pacific Northwest (Alaska, Washington, Oregon, Idaho, Montana, and the western provinces of Canada) but does not limit its involvement in nationwide endeavors. Accordingly, WLN has offered its software for sale outside the Pacific Northwest; so far, the Southeastern Library Network (SOLINET), the University of Illinois, and the National Library of Australia have purchased it. Except for research libraries in the Pacific Northwest, and research libraries elsewhere that may wish to purchase its software, WLN is not soliciting ARL libraries to become members. UTLAS, which serves more than 500 libraries on six continents, offers a shared cataloging system (CATSS) and a Library Collection Management System (LCMS), which has been described in press releases as a

> mini-computer package that allows for on-line inventory control, including searching and circulation, at the local level, with no outside hookups; the regional level, for shared management; the UTLAS-centralized level, taking advantage of CATSS bibliographic power; or a combination of these levels.

It recently announced that it had signed a contract with the Rochester Institute of Technology to produce a COM catalog and that it has a memorandum of understanding with RLG to share data bases, collaborate on programs to support on-going functions at their respective libraries, and to share system development projects. At this time, it is impossible to do more than to speculate about the degree to which UTLAS can convince additional United States research libraries to contract for its services.[22]

C. Lee Jones pointed out the basic differences between OCLC and RLIN, in his study, *Linking Bibliographic Data Bases.* He wrote:

> OCLC, Inc., provides services from its data base principally through state or regional network brokers. These organizations handle marketing, training and other services developed by the broker. OCLC also serves some libraries directly. While other utilities view themselves as cooperative operations directly responsible to members or owners, OCLC, at least among its employees, views itself as a company with corporate goals that cannot match all of those of the diverse institutions it serves. OCLC invites all types of libraries to take advantage of its services; it has users in every state of the Union, in Canada, and in Mexico and will soon begin offering services in Western Europe.

RLG, while committed to providing bibliographic services to those institutions that used the old BALLOTS system, is a "program-driven" organization, which uses its bibliographic utility, RLIN, to serve the needs expressed by its owner-members. The utility portion of the RLG operation is simply a tool to help achieve other program goals. RLG does not intend to serve the needs of every kind or size of library. It designs its programs and activities to meet the needs of large research libraries, which are its membership targets. Thus, while there are not geographic limits to RLG, there is a "type of library" limit.[23]

It should be obvious why RLG and OCLC both need the large research libraries—basically, the members of the Association of Research Libraries—in their respective networks. RLG limits its membership, except in the associate membership category, to large research libraries. It must have a minimum number of ARL libraries as members, to achieve financial stability. The number of ARL libraries it needs has fluctuated over the years, but now seems to be set at about 30.

On the other hand, OCLC would find it difficult to survive without having a majority of the ARL libraries in its network. OCLC's basic source of income is from the charge it makes for the first time an institution uses its data base. In 1979-80, OCLC had a total of almost 10,500,000 billable FTUs. Of this total, more than 1,900,000 FTUs were billed to members of the Association of Research Libraries. That is to say that 18.57 percent of OCLC's FTU income came from ARL libraries. Further, OCLC supports a number of reclassification projects, and 13.56 percent of its billable reclassification uses were charged to ARL libraries. ARL libraries directly affect yet another area of the OCLC data base, and that is in terms of nonbillable FTUs, which is to say, contributed cataloging. In this category, there were a total of almost 606,000 titles, of which almost 230,000, or 37.71 percent, were attributable to ARL libraries.[24]

ARL Libraries are involved with OCLC in other ways. A majority of Title IIC grants go to ARL libraries, and a number of these grants involve inputting special kinds or collections materials to the OCLC data base, like, for example, Colorado State University's three-year project to input a particular category of government documents. And, of course, by the very nature of the process, smaller libraries tend to use the OCLC interlibrary loan system to locate and borrow materials from larger libraries, often ARL libraries.

If one looks at the worst possible scenario, which would be that all of the ARL libraries leave OCLC and join RLG and RLIN, it is clear that OCLC would be in desperate circumstances. OCLC would lose 18.57 percent of its billable FTUs and 13.56 percent of its billable reclassification income. In addition, it would lose almost 38 percent of its contributed cataloging; it is the contributed cataloging that especially broadens and enriches the data base. Further, Title IIC projects which involve inputting special materials, would move from OCLC to RLIN, as the libraries receiving these grants move from OCLC to RLG. The OCLC interlibrary loan program would suffer, since there would be no additional ARL library locations or new records entered into the data base. And, of course, where a state or region or network is planning an on-line, public-access catalog using OCLC archival tapes to build its data base, there would be an immediate problem with the machine-readable records from its ARL libraries, since, at least for the present, OCLC and RLIN records are not compatible. Finally, within the library community, what might be described as an era of bad feeling will have begun, for smaller libraries will (with considerable justice) blame ARL-RLG members for putting their perceived needs ahead of the greater good of the majority of the libraries in the United States.

Clearly, if all the ARL libraries leave OCLC for RLG, OCLC is in terrible trouble. It would have a hard time, indeed, in surviving. And if it survived, OCLC would be something very different from what it is today.

The critical question, then, is whether all of the ARL libraries are likely to leave OCLC. At the moment, the answer seems to be that they will not. It is important, however, to remember that if only the dozen largest ARL users of OCLC went to RLG, OCLC would be badly damaged. This, too, seems unlikely at the moment. Yet, it is necessary to recognize that conditions and circumstances change, and that which seems unlikely today, can by tomorrow constitute reality.

At the other end of the spectrum is a very different scenario. This one says that all of the ARL libraries affiliated with OCLC will stay with OCLC. If this happens, RLG will be frustrated continually, because with only 23 members, it barely has the funding to continue at its present level and does not have the rapidly expanding data base it needs. The projections for RLIN indicate expenses will be larger than income through 1982, and that it will be at least 1986 before its outstanding loans can be repaid. Recently, RLG announced that each full member will be assessed a "founders'" fee of

$25,000 annually, and at the same time, raised its charges for FTUs and for cards.

Further, with such a small number of research libraries contributing to the data base, in terms of shared cataloging, the percentage of hits is likely to be lower than if these libraries had stayed with OCLC and were searching the OCLC data base. This suggests that the RLIN libraries in this scenario would have to do more original cataloging than they would have had to do, had they remained with OCLC, which is to say that overall cataloging costs would be higher for RLIN libraries.

In this same scenario, OCLC continues its operations, but because of the loss of FTUs, caused both by the departure of some ARL libraries and the general effect of inflation upon book purchases, will have to postpone development of many of its long-range programs, and in addition, pay greater attention to the kinds of services the large research libraries require.

In all candor, while it seems that either of these scenarios is possible, it is not likely that either will occur. It seems equally unlikely that things will remain as they are today. Because in many parts of the country pressures on state-supported university libraries to stay in OCLC are very strong, it is unreasonable to believe that many of them will go to RLG; currently, only 9 of the 23 RLG members are state-supported universities. But, it does appear that RLG will grow, although not at all as rapidly as it has done in the immediate past. To the degree that RLG grows, OCLC is diminished. OCLC, however, will continue to move into new areas, to the degree that its finances permit, and it may well be that in time, its new initiatives will make substantial contributions to its income.

But if it is true that there is to be some modest growth for RLIN and a slow shift in OCLC's income which reflects new ventures, nothing at all has been solved. The competition will continue and OCLC and RLG will still be toe to toe, a posture which benefits absolutely no one.

Once the American library community recognizes the potentially disastrous effects that may result from the RLIN-OCLC competition, they will also recognize that they cannot allow either scenario to come to reality, nor can they allow the perhaps more realistic assessment of a semi-static situation to occur. Instead, a way must be found to control events, rather than allowing events to control us.

The way out of this dilemma is, in all likelihood, through the national library network that most of us believe is bound to come.

Although one cannot yet perceive exactly what the national network will be, it should be possible for OCLC and RLIN to flourish within it, and in time to share their data bases by allowing each to access the other. This is to say that the American library community, long before now, should have insisted on the formation of a national network, and it is our current failure to do so that has in part created the OCLC-RLIN competition. Somehow, a way must be found to move with all possible speed to establish the network, because if we do not, the OCLC-RLIN problem could be exacerbated to a point of no return.

CONCLUSION

This chapter opened with a quotation taken from Ralph's Cornell Library conference and dedication paper: "The moment libraries cease to be problems to university presidents, the time will have arrived when humanistic scholarship is dead." His argument was that even though there would be an "informational center library, fully automated, highly miniaturized," which would contain "all the books, in microfilm, owned by all the libraries of the country,"[25] which was supported by the national government, our universities will still have to maintain large research libraries. The reason for maintaining these large research libraries was to serve the needs of the humanistic scholar; the "National Center Information Library" could meet the informational needs of scholars generally but could not meet their educational needs.

Ralph put it as well as anyone ever will:

> While we are reading, our mind roams around the thread of thought of the text, like a puppy out for a stroll with his master, and sometimes, from these sashays, which may have nothing to do with our original interest, come the flashes of inspiration, the big ideas, that set us off in a new direction... The side excursions going on in the minds of two people reading the same book will be quite different and they are not predictable... A humanistic scholar does go to a library for specific information, but he may also go to read the current journals, or to look over the new book shelf, or to look again at the Anthony Trollope or Charles Darwin shelves, and he does not want to chart his course in advance, or engage in activities that can be formalized in the form of inquiries that might be fed into a computer... I am talking about the professor as a person who constantly educates himself by poking around in the junkyards of civilization for treasures he may cherish or even find useful.[26]

Although the "National Center Information Library" has yet to be created, Ralph's differentiation between informational needs and the educational requirements of the humanistic scholar remains as valid today as it was when he first discussed it. There can be no question that the humanist – and other scholars, too – needs access to the traditional university library. And even with the many benefits of automation, of increased cooperation and cooperative acquisitions, and in spite of the potentially disastrous competition between OCLC and RLIN, difficulties with AACR 2, the lack of a true national library, the very distressing effect of inflation on acquisitions, the perhaps cyclic problems of the high schools, as well as our failure to develop a national library network, it does appear that academic libraries will continue to play their traditional role within their institutions, and also that they will continue to be problems to university presidents.

FOOTNOTES

1. Ralph E. Ellsworth, "The Changing Role of the University Library," *Library Journal,* v. 88, no. 7 (April 1, 1963): 1405-1411. Cornell University Libraries. *The Cornell Library Conference, Papers Read at the Dedication of the Central Libraries, October 1962.* Ithaca, 1964.
2. Barbara Turlington, Research Universities Project, "Research Libraries." Washington, D.C.: Association of American Universities, March 1981 (draft), p. 1.
3. Carol A. Mandel and Mary P. Johnson, comp., *ARL Statistics, 1979-80.* Washington, D.C.: Association of Research Libraries, 1980.
4. Turlington, *op. cit.,* p. 2.
5. Norman Brown and Jane Phillips, "Library Materials Price Indexes Preliminary Survey of 1981 Subscription Price of U.S. Periodicals," *RTSD Newsletter,* no. 6 (March/April 1981): 13.
6. Mandel and Johnson, *op. cit.,* p. 2.
7. University of Colorado, Boulder. University Libraries. "Cost/Volume for University of Colorado, Boulder Library Materials, 1968-81."
8. Mandel and Johnson, *op. cit.,* p. 37.
9. Herman H. Fussler, "Characteristics of the Research Literature Used by Chemists and Physicists in the United States," *Library Quarterly,* v. 19, nos. 1, 2 (January and April 1949): 10-35, 119-143.
10. Ralph E. Ellsworth, "Another Chance for Centralized Cataloging," *Library Journal,* v. 89, no. 15 (September 1, 1964): 3104.
11. *Ibid.*
12. Ralph E. Ellsworth, "The Quest for Quality in Higher Education," *College and Research Libraries,* v. 23 (January 1962): 7.

13. T. C. Venable, "Declining SAT Scores: Some Unpopular Hypotheses," *Phi Delta Kappan*, v. 62 (February 1981): 443.
14. Edward B. Fiske, "The High Schools: New Shapes for the 80's," *New York Times*, 26 April 1981, Education Spring Survey, p. 28.
15. OCLC Inc. *Annual Report 1979/1980*. Columbus, Ohio: OCLC Inc., 1980, p. 6.
16. *Ibid.*, pp. 4-5.
17. *Ibid.*, p. 8.
18. *Research Libraries in OCLC*. Columbus, Ohio: OCLC Inc., 1980, p. 12.
19. Press Release. Stanford, California: RLG, January 12, 1981.
20. The members were Columbia University, New York Public Library, Stanford University, Yale University, University of Michigan, University of Pennsylvania, Princeton University, Dartmouth College, University of Iowa, Rutgers University, Brigham Young University, Colorado State University, Brown University, Cornell University, Johns Hopkins University, New York University, Northwestern University, Tulane University, the American Antiquarian Society, Pennsylvania State University, the University of Oklahoma, Temple University, and the University of Minnesota. The two associate members were the State University of New York at Binghamton and the Folger Shakespeare Library.
21. Arthur Plotnik, "RLIN, The Bibliographic Utility in Cap and Gown Nears Graduation," *American Libraries*, v. 11, no. 5 (May 1980): 274.
22. Arthur Plotnik, "UTLAS, A Canadian Contender for the U.S. Market," *American Libraries*, v. 11, no. 5 (May 1980): 277.
23. C. Lee Jones, *Linking Bibliographic Data Bases: A Discussion of the Battelle Technical Report* Washington, D.C.: Council on Library Resources, Inc., 1980, pp. 16-17.
24. The actual figures are: billable FTUs, 10,452,830; FTUs billed to ARL members, 1,941,714; 605,845 titles of contributed cataloging, of which 228,468 were attributable to ARL libraries. These figures are derived from OCLC's *Topcat Network Billings* for 1979-1980.
25. Ralph E. Ellsworth, "The Changing Role of the University," *Library Journal*, v. 88, no. 7 (April 1, 1963): 1405.
26. *Ibid.*

The ALA, like the Democratic party of today, represented so many groups with conflicting interests that it could not become, as we academic librarians wanted it to, a truly learned association . . . The result has been that the larger university and research libraries built their own association—the Association of Research Libraries. —**Ralph Ellsworth.** "The Library's Life Style: A Review of the Last 35 Years," Michigan Librarian, v. 36, no. 3 (Autumn 1970): 29.

At home we do not glorify our operations as ends in themselves but only as a means to the kind of library service our kind of libraries expect. The relationship should reflect itself in our national organization—ALA. —**Ralph Ellsworth.** "A Wary Eye to the Future: A Message from ACRL's President," College and Research Libraries, v. 22, no. 4 (July 1961):302.

Much of the sound and fury which we mistakenly think of as the American Library Association would dry up and never be heard from again because it is nothing more than the clanking of the machinery of the association. —**Ralph Ellsworth.** "Critique of Library Associations in America," Library Quarterly, v. 31 (October 1961):384.

The National Organizations—ALA, ARL, ACRL: Meeting Academic and Research Librarians' Needs?

*W. Carl Jackson, Former Dean of
  Library Services**
Indiana University
Bloomington, Indiana

In her survey of library associations in America, Peggy Sullivan commented on the "affinity of librarians to organize," and further noted that a recent *Encyclopedia of Associations* listed some 75 associations of libraries and librarians, excluding state, regional and local associations and groups.[1] Including the latter would quite likely more than double that number. Of the 75, only three, the ALA itself and two of its divisions, have more than 10,000 members.

Yet, in spite of the number and variety of library associations, the published literature of the library field suggests that there is some question as to how well they individually or collectively meet the needs of today's academic librarians. Perhaps it is significant that, with the exception of the National Librarians' Association, all of the larger and more prominent associations are library associations.

Given the conditions and concerns of today's academic librarians, this issue seems fundamental and worth examining, in an attempt to determine if the criticisms by Ellsworth and others have validity, and if so, what alternatives are possible. But any examination of

---

*His untimely death is mourned by his co-contributors.

these associations should be in the context of the profession they purport to serve, since the problems of librarians and the questions of librarianship as a profession are so inextricably interwoven.

Since it would not be practical, or even necessary, to review even all the major and/or the largest of these associations, those which this author believes are most pertinent have been chosen for this discussion: the American Library Association (ALA), the Association of College and Research Libraries (ACRL), and the Association of Research Libraries (ARL). Inclusion of the latter may raise some eyebrows, since the ARL, which is an association of institutional members, obviously does not belong in the same category as the other two associations. However, since its role frequently has been misperceived by numerous librarians, it belongs here for the purposes of this discussion. This purely arbitrary selection is made despite full awareness that many academic librarians devote their allegiance to other associations such as the Special Libraries Association, the Medical Library Association, the Association of Law Libraries, and others.

Let us return to Sullivan's article, where she states:

> A kind of tension drives individuals and institutions to form cooperative groups, and aspects of that tension can cause fragmentation, change of course or identity, and progress. Observers from outside the U.S. library community have commented on this tension, and librarians and others have demonstrated it by their love-hate relationship with associations to which they feel some loyalty and by their willingness to form new associations or to reform old ones.

She also observes that "ALA has had its share of tension and has responded to it in varying ways . . . its history leaves the impression that it is always reorganizing and/or on the threshold of promise or disaster. . . ."[2]

Criticism, both private and public, is inevitably a part of such tension, and persistent critic though he has been, Ralph Ellsworth was not alone in chastising the ALA. Almost from its very beginnings in 1876, articles critical of the association found their way into print, and such articles, finding fault with one or more aspects of the association, continue today to appear on the pages of the profession's journals. The published complaints, of course, do not exist alone, and perhaps represent but the tip of the proverbial iceberg, since the majority seem to prefer to do their complaining in private, complaining to their colleagues, in the corridors of the conference hotels, or through letters to friends. The published complaints are almost all directed at the ALA and tend to vary and change only slightly with the times.

Many of these complaints have recurring themes and include those voiced by Ellsworth: that the ALA is too big, too impersonal, and too bureaucratic; that it spends too much of its time studying its own navel, by focusing on internal and organizational matters; and that it spends too much of its time, energy, and money, keeping its own machinery going. Other themes are that it is not responsive to parts of its membership, regarding particular issues at a given time; that it attempts to carry out too many programs and cannot support those it is already engaged in;[3] and, more recently, that it doesn't care about, or do anything to improve, the financial condition or the status of its librarian members.

Those who have been active in the ALA and/or its sections and divisions, or as elected officers, and have endured the chores of a committee or the Council, would probably agree that a great amount of time seems to be given to the organization itself. But this author is inclined to believe that the same would be true, to some degree, of any membership organization of the size and nature of the ALA, and also does not think that this is a fundamental issue. Therefore, David Clift's homily, "the fleas come with the dog,"[4] is an appropriate one. Neal Harlow has also pointed out that "red tape is a function of size, of the character of the group, and of the amount of activity going on."[5]

The ALA is certainly engaged in a lot of enterprises, more than most members are aware of. In fact, there are few librarians, even those who have been most active in the association, who know of more than a fraction of its programs, and even then, they tend to know only about those in which they have been personally involved.

The ALA's organizational structure of "types of libraries" and "types of activities" brings with it a built-in confusion, overlap, and lack of communication. The result often is conflict, jurisdictional disputes, and a lack of knowledge by one hand as to what the other is doing. It is little wonder that there are disputes, not only between individuals, but between sections, divisions, and, lately, even between Council and membership.

It is, in fact, the very democracy of the ALA which spawns some of these problems and conflicts. Democracy, as is known, is a notoriously "inefficient" form of governance, and too many people want to be involved in running the ALA and want it to operate too many programs. This condition inevitably makes for a messy organization. The ALA could be more "efficient," less costly to operate, and more straightforward if it were left to a few elected officers and the paid staff, although it is doubtful whether many would opt for that approach today. Yet, that is, in some measure, what made the ARL successful. But here again, these are not really fundamental or overriding issues.

Another complaint, voiced by Richard Dougherty, is that the ALA has ignored professional concerns and focused almost exclusively on social issues. As he expressed it, "Another ALA Midwinter has come and gone, and once again I left with a feeling of frustration. The ALA Council had failed to resolve, or even discuss, several important issues. There was plenty of debate about ERA . . . While I am in sympathy with ERA, I remain unconvinced that any social issue should so totally dominate our association's time and attention . . . "[6]

The ALA is not alone in this preoccupation with social issues. Many scholarly associations and societies are facing the same problem as an outcome of the last two turbulent decades. It is interesting, however, that the pendulum has swung so far since Ellsworth complained, in 1962, of the lack of attention to issues beyond the profession's boundaries. As he noted, "A cynic could say that a professional association has no business expressing its views on matters outside its professional competence. Others could say that a national association is exactly the right organ through which professional men and women should express their views on national problems. In recent years, ALA has done little of this."[7] Both are right and are responding to their times. But Dougherty's point does remind us of fiddling while Rome burns.

In recent times, a new, more material note has crept into the complaints, a note which suggests protectionism and is based on the tighter job market, the economic impact of inflation, which has resulted in a declining standard of living for many librarians, and on job environment factors. Many of the recent criticisms reflect these new kinds of concerns, with the result that librarians are increasingly calling for the ALA to become involved regarding the welfare of individual librarians in terms of their economic conditions, their status, and their work environment. Such "bread-and-butter" issues seem to be on the rise.

Hodgins believes that in fact much of the dissatisfaction with the ALA springs from what he describes as the ALA's

> colossal indifference to the plight of the individual . . . [I]n the centennial year of the ALA . . . it seems inconceivable . . . that individual librarians

should be forced to consider themselves as orphans . . . insofar as having a national association concerned with their professional and job-related welfare [is concerned] . . . [T]he ALA has consistently and steadfastly refused to be seriously concerned about the individual librarian.

He goes on to point out that "our profession is not static. It is quietly under siege by the technocrat of the information industry on the one hand and the paraprofessional on the other." He ascribes the blame for the plight of librarians to the ALA, in that "there has never been a strong national voice or professional association which has defined, protected, or promoted the welfare or status of the individual librarian." He adds, "Is this kind of attitude and behavior likely to enhance the status of librarians in the eyes of other professions or the general public?"[8] These are very perceptive questions and comments, and the only wonder is that they have been so long in coming, since this is the real problem with the ALA.

Dougherty showed concern for these issues and also raised the issue of librarianship as a profession. As he put it, "One senses a growing uneasiness about the library profession and its Association." Therefore,

we must clarify our professional identity, our societal roles, and the roles of our professional associations. . . . Gerry Shields . . . proposed an ALA unit whose charge would be to consider the special problems of professional librarians. Unfortunately a unit for professional concerns doesn't fit comfortably, either organizationally or philosophically, into the ALA structure. . . . Changes in the role of professionals will dictate changes in our professional Association. ALA, like most professional groups, derives the bulk of its operating funds from the dues of its members, who, more and more, expect direct, tangible benefits for their money. . . . Bread and butter issues (including salaries, job protection and improved work rules) spark the interests of today's professional . . . After [these] are resolved there will remain the need to identify the unique role of a professional. . . . The need to distinguish between the contributions of professionals and other library workers is no longer an academic issue. . . . Trained library technicians demand salaries equitable to their work responsibilities. They rile at the tendency to equate status and salaries to the holding of an M.L.S. degree . . . Our national Association has an important role to play. . . . The initial task is to define what distinguishes librarianship from other professions and occupations, then to decide how our organization can best serve our objectives.[9]

Those comments open a host of issues: the welfare and status of librarians, librarianship as a profession, and the role of associations, all to be discussed later. But first, the issue of unions or collective bargaining, an issue much discussed in the literature, must be considered. Dougherty was concerned that unions would replace our professional associations, and Schlacter has pointed out that "the social atmosphere in which professionals find themselves is increasingly tolerant of collective bargaining organizations," and therefore "the same factors which created a favorable climate for collective bargaining among nurses and teachers – employment concentration, economic imbalance, limited job advancement, and job insecurity – are increasingly characteristic of the field of librarianship."[10] Boissonas goes further and insists that the "ALA . . . cannot limit its efforts to raising the economic status of its members to the areas of faculty status, tenure and fair employment practices. It must also become . . . concerned about . . . collective bargaining."[11] Gwinup, in a harsh indictment of librarianship, places the blame for the poor benefits and low status of librarians to the failure to achieve either union or profession.[12]

The ALA's Executive Director, Robert Wedgeworth, is aware of the trend and points out that "each of the major groups of library employees – academic . . . public . . . school – have come to realize that for many of them formal negotiations of the terms and conditions under which they will provide their services is inevitable." He further states that "As more library employees . . . become involved in collective bargaining units the question no longer will be whether they should, but under the auspices of what organization it should take place." Noting that effective models exist if the ALA's members choose to use it for collective bargaining, he also believes that under current circumstances, for the ALA to undertake collective bargaining would hardly be feasible or economic, since

> Librarianship is a small universe, composed of several small populations . . . Compared to [other professions] . . . each of the constituent employee populations in the library field tends to be a subordinate professional group within their respective institutions. . . . It is no surprise that most of the experience in organizing library employees has been with organizations such as the American Association of University Professors. . . . To organize small groups of library employees scattered across the country, many of whom are already affiliated with the dominant professional group within their institution, would be exceptionally costly in dollars as well as staff.

He goes on to point out the additional cost to the ALA which would result from the required change of tax status if the ALA were to pursue such a course.[13]

Another factor, if the ALA were to get involved in collective bargaining, would be the separation of supervisory librarians. Boissonas would go even further, maintaining that the issue is collective bargaining or a professional association. As he so strongly expressed it,

> By allowing organizations and their executives to be members, it allows employers of librarians to use the association as a means to influence the future outlook of the profession. . . . As long as management is permitted to have a voice in running the organization, it is unlikely that the association will take a strong stand which will result in librarians becoming more professionalized. It would require individual librarians to be set free from the domination of their employers, by expelling from the association all executives of libraries and libraries themselves.

Clearly, he would see the association as a union, not as a professional association. Collective bargaining is really an issue quite separate from that of a professional association. It can be, but is not necessarily, an essential role that can be played by a professional association. Similarly, his argument for separating executive librarians might have validity in collective bargaining, but not for membership in a professional association.

There still remain two fundamental issues, the status of librarians and the matter of librarianship as a profession.

THE AMERICAN LIBRARY ASSOCIATION

Having enumerated this selection of these many complaints about the ALA, it is appropriate to look at what the ALA is and what it is not. We all know that the ALA, a large, complex membership organization founded in 1876, is what we tend to think of as our "professional" association. I have, for good reason, refrained from calling it such throughout this chapter but have noted when other sources have done so. The organizational facts and figures are unimportant here, but rather, the factors which are pertinent were best described in a perceptive article by Robert Wedgeworth in 1976 as a response to some then-prevalent criticisms. He said, in describing the nature and purpose of the ALA, that its purpose has been the promotion of *Libraries* and librarianship to assure delivery of user-oriented library . . . service to all. . . . ALA is a non-profit *Educational* association whose membership consists of individuals as well as organizations. . . . Contrary to popular belief, the association *has never possessed those unique qualities which characterize the professional association. . . . The association's membership, unlike a professional association, is absolutely unrestricted by any qualification. . . .* This contrasts sharply with bar associations whose membership is confined to lawyers, with medical societies whose membership is restricted to doctors. . . .[15] (my italics)

Clearly, the ALA is *not* a professional association, a matter which is a significant factor in the lack of status or rewards of librarianship. Given the lack of reward or benefit from belonging to the association, one wonders why librarians join and continue to belong to the association and why they pay to attend its meetings.

In an interesting pro and con article entitled "The Value of Professional Organizations," there are some revealing grass-roots arguments on both sides. Virginia Neel, the protagonist of the pro argument, maintains:

Professional organizations are a very important and enriching part of our professional life and are invaluable to librarians by bringing them together for formal and informal meetings . . . where they can discuss their problems, share ideas, exchange information and experiences, and listen to papers and addresses by acknowledged experts. The librarian's responsibility extends beyond . . . his immediate job . . . to include membership in his professional organizations and participation in their programs. Every librarian should continually review his activities and attitudes in determining to what extent he is contributing to the professionalism of librarianship. One of the basic steps is the participation in the professional associations. . . . Participation in professional activities is one of the hallmarks of a professional person. . . . Librarians need each other and must seek to enrich their own personal lives, to broaden their understanding of people. What better way is there than meeting with our colleagues? All professions have associations — why not librarians?"[16]

The debater for the distaff side, who was a long-time member of both the ALA and the Kentucky Library Association, countered:

I consider that I do not belong here. I am not now opposed to library organizations and I have never been opposed to them. . . . The reason such a large percentage of our profession do not join our national association or even our state one is often the cost . . . some prefer to sup-

port *another cause* [my italics] they consider of more value to society. . . .
I've been asked many times, "Do you get your money's worth out of the
A.L.A.?" To me, that has nothing to do with the question. I never joined
to get something for myself but because I believed it was my duty to
support my profession . . .[17]

These are both noble librarians, but the innocence and altruism
demonstrated in those statements, which are representative of too
many librarians, are disturbing illustrations of the problem of
creating a strong professional association.

In relation to this, Ellsworth cites an interesting long-ago conver-
sation at an ALA Conference with Robert Lester, the secretary of
the Carnegie Foundation, who said,

> Yes, but you must understand that the American Library Association
> meetings are a kind of religious experience to them. At home, they work
> hard, are unrewarded, not appreciated, and they feel they aren't getting
> anyplace. They come here in the spirit of a religious pilgrimage. They
> pay 25 cents for a cup of coffee, and they listen to the big shots, and they
> decide things in their committee meetings and they feel they have done
> things. The process becomes a thing of importance in itself.[18]

THE ASSOCIATION OF RESEARCH LIBRARIES

This author does not ascribe motive or meaning to Ellsworth's
complaint that the ALA will not, "as we academic librarians wanted
it to, become a truly learned association."[19] But given the reverence
academic librarians have historically directed toward scholarship
and learned societies, I am pretty sure he didn't really mean a truly
professional association, as I *now* think he should have meant. At
the time, I was in complete agreement that we needed a learned
society, but it is easier to be a "Monday-morning quarterback" than
to have foresight, and my view is quite different from this current
perspective.

In any event, he maintained further, quite mistakenly, I believe,
"The result has been that the larger university and research libraries
built their own association, the Association of Research Libraries."[20]
I disagree with Ralph on this because, while the ARL may have
been an alternative to the ALA, it was not an alternative to a
learned or professional association, at least not for the rank-and-file
academic librarian, even those on the staffs of the association's
member libraries. Undeniably, participation in the ARL provided

certain comforts and some status to its select member representatives, and in its exclusivity offered one of the fundamental
characteristics of a professional association. One can't deny that it
is the most prestigious organization in the library field, and with its
small membership and lack of red tape, along with its power, influence, and, later, resources, which to some extent were based on
its fairly steep institutional dues, it has been able to embark successfully on a number of significant programs, important to
libraries. But if the ARL contributes to any increase in the stature
or in furtherance of the status of academic librarians in general, it is
only indirectly, through the value of its programs to universities
and scholars; through the collaboration of its members (who are
leaders in the profession) with prestigious educational and scholarly
organizations such as the American Association of Universities and
the American Council of Learned Societies; and through its work
with foundations and government agencies. This is not intended to
detract in any way from the accomplishments of the ARL, but to
point out that it never was intended as an agency for furtherance of
the professionalization of librarianship in general.

In discussing much this same issue in 1962, Frank Lundy described the ARL as follows:

> The ARL is a group of institutions usually represented in its meetings
> by the directors of these libraries. There are at present forty-two univer-
> sity libraries in ARL and seven non-university libraries of a research
> nature. It is now entirely possible and even probable that within this
> year and next the university library members will be increased to forty-
> five or more and the non-university members to ten or twelve. If so, its
> semi-annual meetings will be participated in by about one hundred direc-
> tors of libraries and guests instead of the present fifty. Obviously, this is
> not a membership organization in the sense that ACRL is. . . . The ARL,
> small as it is, has managed its own affairs during the past thirty years
> with a so-called Advisory Committee which was really a five-man self-
> perpetuating oligarchy, a real live functioning benevolent dictatorship.
> It yet remains to be seen if the ARL can survive and thrive with an
> openly elected nine-man board and with a chairman selected by the
> device of getting the most votes in the annual election.[21]

What Frank didn't say was that attendance at an ARL meeting
by a substitute for the director, usually an associate or assistant
director, required prior permission from the association, and may
still do so. In its earliest days, it was, in fact, a totally undemocratic
"old boys' club," and its prestige was greatest when it was at its

smallest. Although it became somewhat more democratic as it widened its membership, neither factor was always warmly embraced by some of its members. I remember the occasion of leaving my first meeting with that august group in the company of a friend who was an early, if not original, member, and remarking on how much I had enjoyed the meeting. His view of the meeting was considerably less positive, and he lamented that, "they now let everyone in and it's grown too big." (Not, I think, referring to me or my institution, but who knows?) That occurred in the mid-sixties, shortly after the expansion referred to by Lundy but before the membership reached anything like its current level.

So the exclusivity or selectivity factor had at least something to do with the prestige the ARL enjoyed. But while it may have been perceived by some of its members as a "learned association," it clearly is not that for academic librarians at large.

In examining the background of overtures toward an elite association by the directors of the larger university libraries which finally culminated in the organization of the ARL, one is conscious of a perhaps innate human predilection for elitism and exclusivity. However, one can but wonder whether, if academic librarians had then had a fully professional association, the need for a separate exclusive association would have existed. Certainly, the ALA of that time was not a likely base for either an "action-oriented" group or a true professional association. Regardless, Ellsworth's complaint reflected a perhaps subconscious and continuing concern for recognition of the professional status of librarianship, and I believe that he and others perceived the development of a "truly learned" association as playing a useful role in boosting that status. It is hardly surprising that these men who formed the ARL, all prominent male library directors, most of whom possessed the Ph.D. would desire respectability and full acceptance by their teaching faculty colleagues, for this was where their natural relationships and friendship stemmed, and it isn't inconceivable that some might have thought that such an association would help their own status in that regard.

But whatever the motives, and in spite of the accomplishments of the ARL in service to university *libraries*, it is perhaps regrettable that the founders didn't have a larger window to the future and instead established a really professional association for all academic librarians. The consequences today might have been far more significant than even the great achievements of the ARL, since the individual and collective leadership, abilities, and influence of these able men could have produced a powerful professional association which might have significantly altered today's conditions.

THE ASSOCIATION OF COLLEGE AND RESEARCH LIBRARIES

The ACRL, one of the largest divisions of the ALA, is the agency to which most academic librarians direct their loyalty. As a "type-of-library" division, it lends to them an identification of their academicism.

Currently, its members seem to exhibit a quite positive attitude toward the association, as a result of the first "breakaway" Boston ACRL Conference, which was sanctioned by ALA. This positive spirit appears to be based on the notion that this was a more "professional" meeting, in that it focused on "papers" and topics of "substance" and eliminated the maze of committees and business meetings that so dominate ALA conferences. But while the ACRL may be seen by some, based on that Boston Conference and that scheduled for Minneapolis in the fall of 1981, to be playing the role of a "learned" association, an objective which has so long been sought by academic librarians, its perceived role may in the long run be a cruel hoax. While I applaud and support a learned association for academic librarians, I believe there is the need for a professional association to have far greater urgency, and if one is ever established, it should play both roles.

Almost from the beginning, the role and relationships of college and university librarians in the ALA was uncomfortable and often troubled. Early on, there was a valid basis for belief among academic librarians that the ALA was almost completely oriented toward the public-library sector. As a consequence, a small group of people met during the 1889 ALA Conference in St. Louis to discuss and explore, and out of this came the College Libraries Section, in 1890. It is interesting to note that the ALA did not officially acknowledge, welcome, or recognize the Section until 1900. It was not until eight years after its establishment that a program specifically for college librarians was allowed, in 1898, and that came only after widely voiced complaints from academic librarians and threats by them to hold separate meetings.[22] Sound familiar?

The 1920s saw the adoption of the first constitution for the College Library Section, and rising pressure for a college library "specialist" at ALA headquarters. Discontent with the ALA's focus continued to escalate. The report of the ALA's First Activities Committee included, among many issues, the following: "In the opinion of many librarians of college and reference libraries, the ALA has been guilty of neglect in attention to scholarly and bibliographic work. This feeling has gone so far as to threaten, at times, actual withdrawal of the College and Reference Section from the ALA . . ."[23] Despite a continuing campaign for representation of academic libraries at the ALA headquarters, it was not until 1931 that a College Libraries Advisory Board was appointed, but since this was part-time and volunteer group, the complaints continued. It wasn't until 1947 that a much larger and much changed ACRL got its first executive director. This long-delayed success was credited to a committee report which became known as the "Ultimatum," because of its blunt threat to separate from the ALA.[24]

Ironically, about the same time that the College Libraries Advisory Board was established, the meeting which led to the formation of the ARL a year later took place. This may have been because of increasing democratization of the CLS, since, as one ARL member said, "we are not interested in the problems of junior colleges." It may or may not be significant that 53 percent of the libraries represented among the original members of the CLS became charter members of the ARL.[25] In fact, throughout its early history, the very small CLS exhibited the characteristics of a fraternal society, which is not particularly surprising, since it was comprised principally of library directors. Membership, which did not exceed 100 until the mid-thirties, took a jump to several hundred in the late thirties and has continued to grow. As the growth continued in the 1940s and 50s it became noticeable that the association's programs shifted to an emphasis on committee work. The majority of these committees focused on *library* concerns, and of the large number of such committees, only one, that on faculty status, reflected a direct concern for librarians. But in spite of this change, other things remained the same. Unhappiness with the parent ALA continued through several reorganizations and into the 60s. Ellsworth, in his presidential message, left no doubt where he stood on the matter.[26]

Frank Lundy shared that concern in a letter to Neal Harlow, in which he said,

Ralph and I are obviously concerned about the state of mind and state of health of our professional organizations of college and university librarians . . . I don't know how to explain this lack of organizational strength in associations of university librarians . . . if we are to improve matters within the ACRL . . . if I am right in my present impression that the ACRL is actually "dying on the vine" . . . it is up to the "leadership" to solve the problem. . . . The environment of higher education is a primary conditioning factor which shouldn't be . . . ignored.[27]

Not everyone shared this attitude, and Neal Harlow himself expressed opposition to any separation from the ALA, in the following words, "College and university librarians are said to have a 'profound disgust' with the ALA. There is nothing easier than disgust, and profound is usually the lightest case. Academic librarians take to it most naturally—many are unhappy on their own campuses, they do not work together well in groups, and they are inclined to regard themselves as an elite . . ."[28] He continues, "I cannot recollect that the ACRL has performed more wisely and well under earlier ALA organizational schemes. . . . Has ACRL ever settled down to any program which would seriously affect or benefit academic libraries. . . ? *College and Research Libraries* . . . has been magnificent, but it is not program in the real sense of the word. . . . We have no list of what is to be done, and this is what ACRL needs more than anything else."[29]

A more recent and formalized gauge of the attitudes of ACRL members was provided in a 1975 survey by the association's Subcommittee on Goals, Priorities, and Structures, in which sophisticated sampling techniques were used.[30] It is difficult to assess the responses in context of this discussion other than to make a few observations: (1) History may be distorted in interpretation, through reliance on published sources, since those who make the effort to write for publication are a minority and their views may well be the same; (2) an amazingly high number of respondees to this survey expressed "no opinion" to most questions; and (3) an equally amazing number of respondees were new members; that is, almost 52 percent had been members less than 5 years, and over 72 percent had been members less than 11 years. This is worth considering in reviewing the results.

Over 40 percent of the respondents believed that ALA's support for the ACRL office was satisfactory, and only 13.5 percent thought it was poor, but 45.8 percent had no opinion.

In regard to possible ACRL independence, there were a number of options, with 31.3 percent suggesting a federation and less than 10 percent choosing disaffiliation, but 31.1 percent had no opinion.

Nevertheless, 61.7 percent thought that the ACRL could respond better to the needs of academic librarianship if the organizational structure were altered.

A most surprising finding was that a significant 71 percent indicated satisfaction with the ACRL's response to the issues and problems of *librarians* and libraries. Under the specific category of the welfare and status of librarians, 57 percent were satisfied. Whatever the cause of these responses, they seem to be at odds with both the published record and with the condition and status of librarians.

In reflecting on this long history of complaints about the ALA, one can look past the specifics and see that many seem to be based on the lack of a real professional association. This concern seems also to be much more prevalent among academic librarians, perhaps even exclusively. This, no doubt, is because of the environment in which they function, as pointed out by Lundy. That environment is important, and in spite of Melvil Dewey's optimistic declamation of 1876 that the "time has at last come when a librarian may without assumption, speak of his occupation as a profession."[31] Most academic librarians are often uncomfortably aware that not all scholars and administrators with whom they work and associate in their campus communities share the view that librarianship is a valid profession. They are even more aware that, in comparison with the rewards and compensation of the teaching faculty of most colleges and universities, librarians tend to fare quite poorly.

As Gwinup describes it, "the public recognizes no profession at all and its image of the occupation is brutally frank and uncharming."[32] Hodgins adds a similar complaint: "The public and professional role of the individual librarian remains largely undefined, unappreciated, and, in most instances, under-rewarded."[33]

Ennis points out that "almost every occupation aspiring to a higher place in the sun has, at one time or another in recent years, scrutinized itself critically. Librarianship does so constantly, but rarely in an extensive way."[34] Indeed, this question of professional status remains before the field of librarianship almost all the time. The charge that it is but an occupation, or a non-profession, has been raised by practitioners and nonpractitioners alike. Most academic librarians have likely been exposed to some uncomfortable situations and encounters in this regard, and few would be deluded into thinking it is held in high esteem even on the campus. As someone once said, "*Libraries* are important, but librarians aren't." Many years ago, in a graduate seminar, I told my highly and affectionately regarded professor I was going to be a librarian, upon which he cried out almost as if in pain, "Don't waste yourself on that."

Even Dougherty has raised the question of what librarians do, a question which in turn unavoidably forces the further question, is librarianship a profession?[35] A brief look at the background of the profession may be useful.

THE PROFESSION

The classic definition of a profession was given by Alexander Carr-Saunders in his pioneering work on professions. "A profession may perhaps be defined as an occupation based on specialized intellectual study and training, the purpose of which is to supply skilled service or advice to others for a definite fee or salary."[36] Since that definition, other sociologists have developed characteristics of professions, so in spite of Johnson's claim that "the field is littered with largely sterile attempts to define what the special 'attributes' of a profession are," others believe there is a sufficiently large consensus to provide a model.[37] As Goode says, "If one extracts from the most commonly cited definitions all the items which characterize a profession . . . a commendable unanimity is disclosed."[38] The following seem to be those to which he refers:

A Systematic Body of Theory
A Professional Authority
A Regulative Code of Ethics
A Professional Culture
A Service Orientation
The Sanction of the Community

Those most important to this discussion seem to be the second and third, although reference to some of the others will be made.

> The practitioners realize they possess a certain craft . . . but the public does not accord them an exclusive right to that description. Not only may the poorly equipped call themselves by these titles and attain public recognition, but so also may those without any equipment whatever. The better equipped desire that they should somehow be distinguishable, and to that end they form associations, membership of which is *confined to those possessing minimum qualifications.*[39]

This exclusivity is a fundamental characteristic of a professional association and its control over entrance into the profession itself. This important characteristic is notably lacking both in our profession and in our so-called professional associations. It is interesting that seemingly so few librarians, academic or otherwise, have appeared to be concerned over that lack. Of course, it should be noted that all professions, semi-professions and occupations possess some or all of these characteristics to varying degrees, in a continuum, with the long-established and influential professions such as law and medicine at the top of the ladder and the lesser professions placed at various lower rungs of the ladder. That continuum is reflected as well in the significant status and reward gradations among the professions. It is not my intention to try to answer the unresolvable question of whether librarianship is a profession, but to demonstrate some possible reasons why we are on the bottom of the ladder.

A SYSTEMATIC BODY OF THEORY

According to the experts, a professional body of theory is a system of abstract propositions from which the profession derives and develops its skills and on which it bases and rationalizes its daily operations. Parsons declares, "To generate valid theory that will provide a solid base for professional techniques requires the application of the scientific method to the service-related problems of the profession. Continued employment of the scientific method is nurtured by, and, in turn, reinforces, the element of rationality . . ."[40]

Some librarians and others have denied that librarianship has a systematic body of theory. Pierce Butler maintained that librarianship could not become a profession, because there were no abstract principles behind library science. It is easy to agree with this statement – until one comtemplates Butler's next contention, that librarianship is too quickly learned, this in acknowledgement of the factor of prolonged intellectual training in the body of knowledge which must consist of those abstract principles and not mere details, "however vast in quantity. . . ."[41] But Butler, who was neither a librarian nor a sociologist, could be seen as correct in his view that librarianship is too quickly learned only if one assumes that the M.L.S. degree provides full training for librarianship. I recall the comment of the "grand dame" who directed the library where I went to library school, in reference to the most able, mature M.L.S. graduate that year, whom she hired, that "he might become a documents librarian in five years, if he really applied himself to learning the documents field." Few would argue that most M.L.S. graduates have been exposed to and have assimilated all they need to know in every area they will encounter during their careers. The medical profession would hardly consider giving medical students an introduction to the field and then turning them loose with the title of doctor, to learn the majority of their needed knowledge on the job. But the time available in the M.L.S. program is obviously too short. Discussions about extending the program usually run up against the "chicken or egg" proposition, owing to the low salaries and, now, job shortages. The main point of raising this is, however, to make a link later with the Shaw proposal.

SANCTION OF THE COMMUNITY

As Greenwood says,

> Every profession strives to persuade the community to sanction its authority . . . by conferring upon the profession a series of powers and privileges. . . . Among its powers is . . . control over its training centers . . . The profession also acquires control over admission into the profession . . . via two routes. . . . First . . . no one should be allowed to wear a professional title who has not been conferred it by an accredited professional school . . . Secondly, the profession persuades the community to institute on its behalf a licensing system for screening those qualified . . . A *sine qua non* for the receipt of the license is, of course, a duly granted professional title.[42]

Clearly, the library profession is not just weak in regard to this important characteristic; it is totally deficient. It is this characteristic which controls entry both into the profession and into its professional association. While the ALA accredits library programs, the practice appears to have little force behind it, and since this is about our only controlling authority, seemingly we have little control of our profession. There are reputedly some states which offer some kind of certifying or licensing process for librarians. If this is true, there has been little evidence of their existence, let alone effectiveness. So not only do we lack a counterpart of state bar examinations, we librarians as practitioners have been guilty of many sins toward our profession by disregarding educational or qualifying criteria within our libraries. How many university libraries, in their employment practices, make a firm distinction between the graduates of accredited versus unaccredited library schools? How many libraries over the years have "promoted" a staff member into a professional position? How often have we, whether passively or grumblingly, accepted the appointment of a nonlibrarian to a key post in a major university library or a national library? During my years as a director of university libraries and then as dean, I frequently had no other recourse than to cringe in private as some unit or department of my university publicly gave the title of "Librarian" to some clerk or secretary who was assigned to "supervise" a departmental collection or reading room. Recently, newspapers carried the headline that Jean Harris, the newly convicted murderer of the *Scarsdale Diet Book* author would become the "librarian" at the prison which is her new home.[43]

In my younger days, not having much political savvy, I used to try to persuade the unit to change the title, but I soon found such efforts impolitic. Lacking support from any agency or statute, the notion of changing the title was rightly thought of as a personal opinion which I held as a member of a minority. This abuse of our title is not a thing of the past but continues today all over the country, in universities, governmental agencies, public libraries, corporations, and elsewhere. Until there is an authority that can provide us the power to restrict the use of our title to those who are qualified, it will evoke little respect.

This lack of community sanction is also demonstrated by the many leading library educators and practitioners who were not trained as librarians. Ellsworth unfortunately defended this practice, and thus seemed as uncertain as most of us about how to strengthen the profession. This is not to detract from individuals but to make the point that if ours is a profession, entry into it ought to be controlled. It certainly raises questions when an individual comes, completely untrained, into the directorship of an important library. Some would say that we do not have within the profession individuals with the necessary stature and leadership qualities and would agree with Gwinup, who said, "The occupation is accorded such a slight degree of social honor that even its moguls emerge as hardly more than the pick of a poor crop."[44]

This author would not agree! I have known many in this field who were a lot more able than many of the university faculty, deans, vice-presidents, and presidents with whom they are associated or from whom they take orders. Gwinup has a point, but he misses it.

The problem is indeed the slight honor accorded the profession, so that few in any community perceive or believe that our best are, in fact, able. On most campuses, it is seen as a subservient profession by most students, faculty, and administrators, the latter paying lip service to their libraries but wanting only for them not to make waves and to stop costing so much. I find it hard to imagine the American Bar Association allowing even the Congress or the President of the United States to appoint a nonlawyer to one of their key posts such as the Supreme Court, or the American Medical Association allowing the same for, say, the Surgeon General's office. It is hard to imagine any other profession acquiescing as we do in such situations. If we have no regard for our professional training and for our profession, then how can we expect others to have respect for it?

Quite clearly, in this category of community sanction, librarianship has failed totally. We have no community sanction and, as a result, no control over entry into the profession or into our so-called professional associations. We often seem not to care, but when we do, we lack the necessary strength or influence to have any effect.

A REGULATIVE CODE OF ETHIC

Greenwood suggests that

> a profession's ethical code is part formal and part informal, of which the formal is the written code to which the professional swears upon being admitted to practice . . . exemplified by the Hippocratic Oath of the medical profession. The informal is the unwritten code, which nonetheless carries the weight of formal prescriptions . . . the profession's commitment to the social welfare . . . self-regulative codes are characteristic of all occupations, non-professional as well as professional . . . While the specifics of their ethical codes vary among the professions the essentials are uniform . . . may be described in terms of client-professional and colleague-colleague relations . . . colleague relationships demand behavior that is cooperative, equalitarian, and supportive . . . colleagues must support each other vis-à-vis clientele and community . . . formal discipline is exercised by the professional associations, which possess the power to criticize or to censure, and in extreme cases to bar recalcitrants . . . membership in the professional associations is a *sine qua non* of professional success.[45]

That description certainly gives us cause to reflect on our own associations.

As I have pointed out, in the earlier days, complaints focused exclusively on the problems of *libraries* and of "librarianship," and only recently have concerns for librarians been expressed. Ralph Shaw did not, in this case, speak for librarians' benefits, but he did address the concern for professional status. Like so many before him and since, he acknowledged the dissatisfaction with the ALA, the threats to break away, and the drop-outs. Concerned that these actions would weaken the ALA and thus the profession, he proposed some solutions. To bring the association closer to its members, he first proposed a system of local or regional chapters, but more important, he suggested a system of professional classification of members of the ALA as other professional associations have done. As he said, "No good purpose is served by the admission of unqualified or indifferent members," and he went on to suggest that members "will esteem membership more highly if convinced that qualifications . . . are sufficiently strict to command his respect," and that this "would clearly demonstrate to the public . . . that librarianship is a profession . . . for librarians would have a strictly professional organization . . . and that it would be possible to establish a professional code of ethics and to enforce it."[46]

He maintained:

> In the matter of state certification of librarians, there could be no better basis for a universal scheme which might be adopted uniformly by all states, than the self-certification of the profession upon the highest professional lines, so that the attainment of a certain grade of membership in the American Library Association would automatically confer certification of that grade in the various states.[47]

What better prescription would we want for acquiring these vital but missing processes for our profession?

Recognizing the financial implications of eliminating friends, libraries, corporations, and others from the membership, Shaw proposed nine classes of membership, with only full and associate membership being exclusive, while the subsidiary memberships would be inclusive. He proposed, as an example, that a full member, at the time of his admission, "shall be qualified to organize, direct and operate a library . . . have been graduated from an accredited library school . . . have been active . . . in the profession . . . for not less than ten years . . . five in a responsible position . . . and shall be not less than 35 years of age." Further, "an associate member would as well have been graduated from an accredited library school . . .

been active not less than five years with at least one year in a responsible position and not less than 29 years of age."[48]

Whether these specific criteria are appropriate is open to discussion, and Shaw would have been the first to welcome such discussion, since he did not propose these as hard and fast but as the basis for a beginning. He proposed this scheme in recognition of the difficult struggle for professionalism and because neither the ALA nor the ACRL, or any other library association, for that matter, was doing anything to improve the situation. His principal point, that we must establish a fully professional association, is still valid. It is a point to which Ellsworth and many others came very close without fully articulating it and, perhaps in some cases, even recognizing it. I believe that it is not totally illogical to suggest that many of the frustrations and complaints about our associations have been based on this unstated, undefined and unidentified need for a real professional association. That need exists today with even greater urgency. I am personally convinced of the need for such an association and believe strongly that its creation is a key ingredient in strengthening the status of the profession and the status of librarians. However, I have little confidence that the ALA membership would support such a move. I believe that the only existing agency that could effectively convert to a professional association is the ACRL, if it chooses to do so, but it will be unlikely to choose that course unless its members come to recognize this as a necessary step toward professional status. Since the record shows that very few librarians have really focused on this issue, wide support is unlikely without a prior educational effort.

One first step in that direction could be the appointment of a blue-ribbon committee or task force, as suggested so long ago by Frank Lundy.[49] The committee's studies should focus on *how* to accomplish the conversion, and its report should consist of a full-blown plan, including the criteria for membership and all steps necessary to achieve a real professional association. Until we have achieved this goal, academic librarians can expect little more improvement in their status and conditions than they experienced over the last hundred years.

FOOTNOTES

1. Peggy Sullivan, "Library Associations," *Library Trends*, v. 25, no. 1 (July 1976): 135-152.

2. *Ibid.*
3. Jean Key Gates, *Introduction to Librarianship.* New York: McGraw-Hill, 1976, p. 85.
4. David Clift, cited in Philip H. Ennis, "Seven Questions about the Profession of Librarianship, Introduction," *Library Quarterly,* v. 31, no. 4 (October 1961): 304.
5. Neal Harlow, letter to Maurice Tauber, 9 April 1962.
6. Richard M. Dougherty, "Who Will Speak for the Library Profession?" *Journal of Academic Librarianship,* v. 5, no. 1 (March 1979): 3.
7. Ralph E. Ellsworth, "Critique of Library Associations in America," *Library Quarterly,* v. 31, no. 4 (October 1961): 382-395.
8. Ellis Hodgins, "Orphans Without a Home," *Library Journal,* v. 102, no. 15 (September 1, 1977): 1722.
9. Richard M. Dougherty, "Professionalism," *Journal of Academic Librarianship,* v. 2, no. 3 (July 1976): 119.
10. Gail Ann Schlacter, "Professionalism vs. Unionism," *Library Trends,* v. 25, no. 2 (October 1976): 451-468.
11. Christian Boissonas, "ALA and Professionalism," *American Libraries,* v. 3, no. 9 (October 1972): 972-979.
12. Thomas Gwinup, "The Failure of Librarians to Attain Profession: The Causes, the Consequences, and the Prospect," *Wilson Library Bulletin,* v. 48, no. 6 (February 1974): 482-490.
13. Robert Wedgeworth, "Organizing Librarians: Three Options for ALA," *Library Journal,* v. 101, no. 1 (January 1, 1976): 213-215.
14. Boissonas, *op. cit.*
15. Wedgeworth, *op. cit.*
16. Virginia Neel, "The Value of Professional Organizations: Pro," *Kansas Library Association Bulletin,* v. 41, no. 1 (Winter 1977): 4-6.
17. Elizabeth Clofelter, "The Value of Professional Organizations: Con," *Kansas Library Association Bulletin,* v. 41, no. 1 (Winter 1977): 7-8.
18. Robert Lester, cited in Ralph E. Ellsworth, "Critique of Library Associations in America," *Library Quarterly,* v. 31, no. 4 (October 1961): 382-395.
19. *Ibid.*
20. *Ibid.*
21. Frank Lundy, letter to Neal Harlow, 18 April 1962.
22. Charles F. Hale, *The Origin and Development of the Association of College and Research Libraries, 1889-1960.* Doctoral Dissertation, Indiana University, Bloomington, 1976, pp. 38-167.
23. American Library Association, "Report of the Committee on A.L.A. Activities," *Library Journal,* v. 55, no. 21 (December 1, 1930): 964.
24. Charles Harvey Brown, "The ACRL and ALA," *Library Journal,* v. 71, no. 14 (August 1946): 1009.
25. Hale, *op, cit.*
26. Ellsworth, *op, cit.*
27. Frank Lundy, *op, cit.*

28. Harlow, *op. cit.*
29. *Ibid.*
30. LeMoyne W. Anderson, "Report of the ACRL Subcommittee on Goals, Priorities, and Structures," *College and Research Libraries,* v. 37, no. 3 (May 1976): 111-113.
31. Melvil Dewey, "The Profession," *Library Journal,* v. 1, no. 1 (September 30, 1876): 5-6.
32. Gwinup, *op. cit.*
33. Hodgins, *op. cit.*
34. Ennis, *op. cit.*
35. Dougherty, *op. cit.*
36. Alexander Carr-Saunders, *Professions: Their Organization and Society.* Oxford: Clarendon Press, 1938,.p. 7.
37. Terence J. Johnson, *Professions and Power.* London: Macmillan, 1972, p. 10.
38. William J. Goode, "The Librarian: From Occupation to Profession?" *Library Quarterly,* v. 31, no. 4 (October 1961): 306-320.
39. Carr-Saunders, *op. cit.*
40. Talcott Parsons, "The Professions and Social Structure," *Social Force,* v. 17 (May 1939): 457-467.
41. Pierce Butler, "Librarianship as a Profession," *Library Quarterly,* v. 21, no. 4 (October 1951): 235-247.
42. Ernest Greenwood, "Attributes of a Profession," *Social Work,* (July 1957): 45-55.
43. "Jean Harris Working as Prison Librarian," *Indianapolis Star* (February 27, 1981): 3.
44. Gwinup, *op. cit.*
45. Greenwood, *op. cit.*
46. Ralph R. Shaw, "The American Library Association – Today and Tomorrow," *ALA Bulletin,* v. 29, no. 8 (August 1935): 483-488.
47. *Ibid.*
48. *Ibid.*
49. Lundy, *op. cit.*

I will begin to rejoice when I see the library schools stop pretending that one kind of program meets the needs of all kinds of libraries. – **Ralph Ellsworth.** "The Quest for Quality in Higher Education," College and Research Libraries, v. 23, no. 1 (January 1962): 10.

The Education of
Academic Librarians

Robert D. Stueart, Dean
Graduate School of Library and Information
  Science
Simmons College
Boston, Massachusetts

The sentiment prefacing this chapter, expressed by Ellsworth 20
years ago, has never been a reality in library education, although
many librarians were and still are advocated of such an approach.
Indeed, the *Standards for Accreditation, 1972* of the American
Library Association do make provisions for single-purpose schools
to become accredited. Such a dichotomy not only is unrealistic but
probably unnecessary as one looks at how professional education
has developed. However, the idea of specialization in its broader
sense, which may be what was implied in the argument, has become
a very important aspect of graduate professional education today.
  In fact, "the deepening and narrowing of focus, the specialization
characteristic of graduate education, is one of its two hallmarks
compared to the broader spectrum of studies in undergraduate
education (the other is the research effort or independent project,
and this is exactly a characteristic of professional education)."[1] One
of the major issues facing library education today is how much
specialization there should be, when should it occur, and whether it
is feasible or even desirable to reduce the number of courses which
are considered "core" in order to accomodate specialization in a one-
year master's program. Asheim points out that "there are many who
see – or affect to see – library service as consisting of a congeries of
specialties in which there are some small areas of minor overlap,

perhaps, but no single core."[2] However, most library educators and practitioners alike would agree that there is some identifiable "core of knowledge" common to all types of librarianship and that all students, no matter what their declared eventual career aspirations might be, should be exposed to it. From the beginning of Dewey's program in library service, just as from the beginning of some other professions' programs, the intent was to produce practitioners who were to be uniform, standardized individuals put through a series of courses that the profession required. This approach "brought about a highly prescribed curriculum stressing more application than theory with little or no time in the curriculum for any liberalizing subjects."[3] It was not until the founding of the University of Chicago's Graduate Library School, in the late 1920s, that the scales were tipped "in favor of theoretically based professional education over the vocational type training which had prevailed prior to the publication of the Williamson Report" earlier in that decade.[4] The basic idea of a core curriculum was preserved and has continued until today with a strong belief that an identified core, supplemented by elective courses of both substance and technique, is central to *all* of librarianship, and that the core is so central that all students are required to master it, no matter what type of library they are interested in studying. Some have mistakenly interpreted this approach to required courses as being narrow, traditional, inflexible, and one which restricts graduates to a common professional goal. Among the several aspects of library education which have a pendulumlike quality, the issue of how much "core" seems to be one of the more prominent. Most schools have a core requirement, although it might have nuances of differences and may be approached differently, depending upon the school's particular philosophy.

That "core" most often consists, basically, of an introduction to the profession and to its tools and techniques. This introduction usually includes a social/historical background for the profession, a philosophy of reference, cataloging and classification, and the management process, including a research component which has been assimilated into many programs "in order that the practitioner may be a contributing scholar along with the delivery of professional services. It is here that some educational programs include heavy doses of research design and research methodology."[5] Certainly for academic librarians, struggling for recognition as "faculty" or at least as "academics," the need for a research component is as great as for any other area of librarianship.

Some schools have introduced a unified core concept into their programs, wherein a single course, team-taught by faculty with ranging expertise, encompasses all of the aspects identified as absolutely necessary for any type of library work. Those schools which have adopted this approach have assumed that most students will attend full-time but, failing that, have also introduced an alternative which is basically the same as that of other programs with a series of core courses. Over the years, the number of hours of required courses has varied greatly from a totally prescribed program (particularly for those choosing certain specializations such as school librarianship) to one which is rather flexible. Such a flexible program, which is more common today than ever before, is not unique to librarianship. As Mayhew points out, "even in those professions which traditionally have produced generalists, there is a loosening of course requirements and a widespread reaction against a large core curriculum required of all students."[6]

Despite the variation in core requirements and the tremendous changes in curriculum content and methodology, library education's purpose has not changed dramatically over the years, although it is sometimes misunderstood or misinterpreted. The purpose is not to impart a narrowly defined set of skills but rather to define a set of criteria which individuals entering the profession should meet – this conceptual understanding being the foremost consideration, not skills and techniques which easily become obsolete. There must be an intellectual orientation to skills and methods, both technical and behavioral, before there can be an application of skills. The educational process for the profession is no longer strictly the transmission of knowledge and skills from the teacher to the student, but rather is the acquisition of knowledge, skills, and attitudes by the learner, with the help of a facilitator.

There are some recognized characteristics of the profession that have a direct bearing on these curricular problems and needs which are facing formal professional education for librarianship.

There is a systematized body of knowledge related to each profession which entails its recognition as a learned profession. Thus the professional school must do more than develop technical competencies. However, each profession does use an accepted and unique set of standardized procedures for practice. Hence the school must develop skill in using these techniques.[7]

Schools are constantly reviewing and revising the curriculum in an attempt to remain on target with developing trends and techniques to cope with both long-existing problems and recently emerging ones. For instance, several schools, in addition to requiring a "core," are also changing graduation requirements to include knowledge of a computer language, knowledge of statistics, knowledge of media hardware, knowledge of on-line searching techniques, and some knowledge of on-line cataloging. These skills and techniques may be part of regular preadmission courses, offered on a "test-out" basis, or may be acquired through additional noncredit modules while in the program.

Part of the problem is in winning the debate as to whether the schools should concentrate on preparing for initial job competence or on providing students with a broad base of principles to pursue long-range development. It is hoped that library education is preparing the latter type of student.

SPECIALIZATION

Specialization is such a prominent feature of librarianship today. In library education programs this emphasis is usually represented by type of clientele or subject rather than by type of library, although specialization by type of library is represented in course offerings, particularly administration courses, for academic, public, school, and special librarianship, and some schools do identify specializations by type of library and do track the students through those programs. Almost any student in any school, should he or she so desire, can construct, with faculty approval, a specialization by type of library. This sometimes almost subconscious specialization is probably more evident to the outside world than to librarians. A sociologist once observed that "most librarians are either public librarians or academic librarians first, before they are librarians as such."[8]

The flexibility for individual programs, mentioned before, has opened the way to greater specialization, and this, combined with the explosion of knowledge and technology, has had an impact on library education programs. Specializations have been further refined by faculty competencies, the university environment, which encourages specialization, and through the identified needs of clientele. Some specializations have developed through pressures from the field, and are often taught either by alumni of the schools or other professionals working in the general geographical area of the school.

There remains the real question as to how extensively a school can offer specializations. As Taylor points out, "no single school can or should cover in depth all . . . subjects. We will have to specialize among the various schools, without losing our generalist base."[9] The generalist program is still the backbone of professional preparation and probably will remain so, but we must find ways of balancing that with the introduction of new knowledge which previously didn't exist or was considered esoteric.

The name change, which has occurred in almost half of the accredited schools in the last ten years, is only a formal acknowledgement of one specialization which has developed in the educational programs. Information science and technology has been integrated into the total curriculum of most programs. Since there is no doubt that technology is one of the strongest factors in the future of academic libraries, as well as other types of libraries, most schools have introduced courses related to automated systems, information technology, networking, and media. This has meant that faculty are being recruited with specialized knowledge in electronics, communications, computer design, operations research, media technology, and other allied fields. More schools are emphasizing technology with hands-on experience, for students in a variety of courses. On-line experience in schools is now commonplace and integrated into courses such as reference, cataloging, abstracting and indexing, and some of the literature courses, and is also offered in some special courses relating to on-line data base searching. Access to OCLC, RLIN, Lockheed, SDC, and BRS is not uncommon. About one-half of the schools offer specializations in information science and another one-fourth offer upward of two courses in the area.

There have been developments of other specializations, both through individual courses and as whole programs. For instance, there are currently a variety of specializations offered in accredited programs, including the following. (1) Archives Management is offered by about one-fourth of the accredited programs, with eight of the schools offering joint degree programs with history departments; one school even offers a special degree in Archival Studies, (2) Health Sciences/Medical Librarianship is offered as a specialization by about one-third of the schools, with another one-fourth offering at least one course in the subject, (3) A Law-Librarianship specialization is offered by about one-fourth of the schools, with nine offering joint-degree programs in conjunction with law schools, and two others having designated special-degree programs for Law Librarianship, leading to a Master's in Law Librarianship (M.L.L.);

another one-third of the schools offer at least one course in law librarianship, (4) Other specializations include Music Librarianship, Art Librarianship, Business Librarianship, and Map Librarianship, to mention only a few. The combination of special courses, independent study, and cross-registration of courses from other disciplines can provide tailored "specialized" programs in a variety of areas for students in most library-education programs. In addition, almost every school, besides offering a basic management course, also offers a type-of-library course, and many offer several management courses either within the school or through another academic unit of the parent institution.

One variant of this interdisciplinary work is the joint-degree program mentioned before. There is now, more than ever before, a greater attempt to use materials from the social and behavioral sciences in the preparation of librarians. Librarianship, by its very nature, is interdisciplinary, allowing students to learn in depth while developing broad attitudes. Currently almost 40 percent of the accredited programs offer possibilities for joint-degree programs, either with other departments in their own institution or with other institutions. Several other schools are now beginning to develop such possibilities for new curricula and new career paths which are interdisciplinary. The most popular programs are in combination with art or art history, music or music history, education, communications, educational media, law, history, or business, where students receive both the M.L.S., or some variation thereof, and an M.A., M.S., M.B.A, or J.D. degree – in all cases, the subject degree being a career-oriented one along with the library degree. Other schools provide subject concentration in such programs as area studies or one of the other dozen or so subject areas which have been cited as joint-degree offerings in the schools' catalogs. All of these combinations have import for academic librarianship, because there is more and more a question as to whether or not the straight master's degree is the optimal credential for entering academic librarianship. One is aware of the fact that large numbers of entering students already have subject-master's degrees, and many of those are interested in academic librarianship. Current statistics indicate that between one-fourth and one-third of students being admitted to accredited programs already have subject master's and a goodly number also have doctorates. While it is true that some of those are dropouts from other professions, many have also gotten the word that a second master's may be required in some areas of academic librarianship. Anywhere from 20 to 30 percent of each library school's graduates are entering academic librarianship, and about 20 percent of the entering students already have had substantial experience in academic libraries before they were admitted to the program, and still others gain valuable experience by working full- or part-time while attending school part-time. Approximately 1,000 academic librarians are being educated each year. When one considers the eventual attrition rate and the current average age of academic librarians, one might well question what the picture will be even five years from now.

On the point of specialization, if utilization of available knowledge were used as the test of content and length of programs, then the curricula would need to be structured over the lifetime of an individual. Recognizing that as the need for some specialization develops, as basic knowledge expands, and as the profession further matures, it is probably not possible to compact into a one-calendar-year program, all of the information necessary to function as a professional, several approaches have been taken to broaden and expand the educational experience. As noted before, some prerequisite knowledge and training have been moved back into a prerequisite or prematriculation mode in some schools; the joint-degree option has been introduced widely; and in some cases the master's program has been expanded into more than one full calendar year. This has come about because of the feeling on the part of some that it is impossible to compact everything into one year and that by doing so, one must either neglect the core or neglect specialization. This "expanded" program approach has been taken by only a few schools, mostly Canadian ones. Librarianship is certainly not the only profession which now has programs of varying lengths, and it is doubtful whether all schools will even consider this option. In looking at other professions, there doesn't seem to be available evidence to indicate that the lengthening of a program makes for more effective practice, a more marketable individual, or higher salaries for graduates of those programs. Time will tell whether the current experiments in a few library schools are successful.

EXTENDED PROGRAMS

The rationale for extending the length of the master's degree program in library education focuses on three basic factors. First is the expanded basic knowledge now required for librarianship; the second is the increasing pressure to achieve some competence in specialized areas while in library school.[10] Another component in this extended program is fieldwork experience. Part of the reason for reintroducing the practicum concept into a formal academic curriculum is to stem the criticism that comes to library education, as it seems to come to all other programs for educating professionals, that the schools do not help students acquire "skills" essential to practice in the "real world."

The major problem of implementing a high-quality formal practicum is that it is expensive if it is good, and the expense must be borne by the host library as well as the school. If it is to be carefully structured, with broad exposure to operations under a skilled supervisor, it is going to cost money. Many also feel that, although such experience is important, it should not be part of an academic program but should be accomplished through a noncredit mode.

The question as to which of the two aspects of professional concern—theory or skills—should be emphasized has had an almost seesaw history. Some would maintain that the field experience has, indeed, entered its Renaissance. That it has, again, become an important issue is evidenced by the fact that the 1981 Association of American Library Schools' annual conference had as its theme "Issues in Field Experience as an Element in the Library School Curriculum." Too, the Council on Library Resources has recently announced a program for master's-level internships in academic libraries, and a few select schools are participating in this program. Most library schools now offer opportunities for practicums, either as part of a program or through some other independent study means. The arguments "for" and "against" the reintroduction of a practicum follow both extremes, from McGrath—who points out that "a plan for an ideal professional education cannot overlook the value of practical experience courses having to do with the techniques of daily practice . . . have in the past been prominent in all professional curricula"[11]—on the one hand, to McGlothlin—who argues that "much of the conflict over professional schools centers around the curricula, mainly over whether the schools focus so sharply on 'vocational ends' that their graduates emerge . . . as superb technicians."[12] One thing is certain: the line between vocationalism and professionalism is held in a delicate balance which must be carefully monitored.

The practicum development does present opportunities for stronger relations between academic librarians and library educators. There is no reason why the college or university library could not provide resources similar to those of a teaching hospital.

These resources could take a variety of forms: internships, assistantships, observation points for students, case-study examples, special projects beneficial to both the library and the student, and available personnel resources of librarians to teach in the schools. Many schools are enriched by the use of practitioners as part-time faculty and by the entry of recent practitioners into library education. Opportunities for experience, either formally or informally, could be provided through such associations. Although a large percentage of students have had substantial experience in libraries, either prior to admission or during their library-education program, many schools do require some type of experience for individuals without previous experience. This means that if a student has not worked in a library before graduation, he or she probably chose not to do so. One special program which provides extensive formalized experience is the apprenticeship program which has been initiated by several Association of Research Libraries members, including the Library of Congress, the National Library of Medicine, Northwestern University, Iowa State University, and the University of New Mexico. The advantage of this apprenticeship approach – which gives recent graduates the opportunity of working in a number of areas in a large academic/research library or to sharpen expertise by concentrating in one specialized area – over that of an internship or an assistantship has not yet been fully explored.

As far as experience is concerned, many courses in the curricula have field components, and this is in addition to hands-on courses such as cataloging, on-line data bases, and the design and production of instructional materials. For instance, a concept which takes the problem-solving approach is simulation, which is a logical substitute for field experience. "Simulation is valuable because it can be slowed down, diagnosed, and repeated; it offers practice under the control of the student with the easy intervention of the faculty; it is psychologically safe for the student; and it protects the clients from being misused in the name of education."[13]

CONTINUING EDUCATION

Like the question of fieldwork – practicum, assistantship, internship, or whatever the term for an experiential course that one pursues – the issue of specialization concerns when it should occur. Some would say that specialization should come during the master's program, which must be expanded to accomodate it; others would maintain that a formal advanced-certificate or degree-granting program, after an appropriate interval of experience, is the appropriate vehicle; and still others would push for continuing education, in any form, as the proper approach to specialization as career goals are refined or revised. Those who advocate the latter two examples would maintain that it is only after an individual has been out of school for a period of time that he or she is able to identify career goals and can begin to establish a pattern of specialization which will allow him or her to achieve those goals.

Professional library education, like all education, must be a continuing process. If one's experience is to be 40 years of constantly changing, more responsible activity, one cannot expect that one year of formal professional education, at the outset of a career, is enough. Someone has suggested that the "half-life" of knowledge in the professions has shrunk to about five years, and therefore, in order to continue to function effectively, one must seek continuous education. A former U.S. Secretary of Health, Education, and Welfare once suggested that one should look on degrees as decreasing about 6 percent in value each year, so that after about 16 years, a degree would be worth nothing if there hasn't been continuing growth. Competencies do become dated with time or become inadequate to cope effectively with the demands of new clienteles and unconventional technologies. Obsolescence is one of the most serious problems facing academic librarianship today. By obsolescence is meant the degree to which librarians lack up-to-date knowledge or skills necessary to maintain effective performance in current or potential future roles. The causes of obsolescence are many, but include 1) the information explosion and dynamic change stimulated by the knowledge revolution, 2) personal characteristics, particularly those which are psychological in nature, and 3) the work environment and clientele.[14]

Academic librarians should recognize signs of obsolescence as being 1) less and less inclined to keep up to date, which reveals a real lack of motivation for self-education, 2) having increasing difficulty in reading new materials, 3) finding that new concepts are confusing, 4) realizing that new tasks and assignments look too difficult to be practical, thus bringing a greater reliance on the status quo, 5) recognizing lack of broader education for the development of conceptual skills, and failure to perceive potential future change, and 6) becoming aware of the fact that contemporaries no longer seek advice, which indicates a lack of awareness of change on the individual's part.

To reduce or reverse the obsolescence trend, continuing education must be integrated into the professional life. According to Houle,

> if the term "continuing education" has any meaning at all, it implies sequential experience in which one module of learning, however independently valuable it may be, gains force and direction from the cumulative impacts of its integration with other modules. At present, the most startling and ironic characteristic of continuing education is its discontinuity in the experience of the professional. Sequence is seldom planned at least in the entrepreneurial professions or in the organizational professions (such as librarianship).[15]

The organized learning must be related to the individual's career goals and, to an extent, the organization's objectives if academic librarianship is to advance. Systematic strategies must be developed and implemented to raise consciousness regarding the need for continuing professional development and to reward self-development.

On the degree-granting level, several formalized advanced programs have been designed specifically to meet the needs of specialists, and academic library managers in particular. In 1961, the first sixth-year specialist certificate program was introduced to provide preparation for a particular kind of professional activity. Its purpose has been to allow practicing librarians to return to school for further education in areas which have been identified by them as important to further development of their careers. By now, almost one-half of the accredited programs offer some type of post-master's program. Its impact, during the last 20 years, has not been what was originally hoped; therefore, other avenues for career development have been designed along with the sixth-year programs. The expansion of the doctoral programs, first offered at Chicago, in 1930, primarily for educators but also for practicing librarians, has been a significant trend which "will likely have the greatest impact upon librarianship for the remainder of the century."[16]

Another still relatively new program concept is that of the Doctor of Arts in Library Administration, which was introduced at Simmons College in the mid-1970s to prepare practitioners specifically for higher-level administrative positions in libraries. Other schools have explored the concept, and some may follow suit to provide advanced education for academic librarians. A recent announcement of a Certificate of Advanced Study in Library Management at

Chicago, being funded by the Council on Library Resources, is an example of further development of such programs.

CONCLUSION

There is currently a great deal of activity in library-education programs, with the belief that changes which are occurring will better prepare librarians for the challenges of the decades ahead as managers of information. From the beginnings of Dewey's school in 1887, to the founding of the Graduate Library School at Chicago in 1926, to the master's-level preparation first offered at Denver in 1947, to the current scene, almost 100 years later, there has been an evolution in the preparation of academic librarians. In that history, some would agree that one of the turning points in the development of library-science education was the founding of the Chicago school, with its early doctoral program.[17]

Interestingly, Ralph Ellsworth was enrolled in the doctoral program at Chicago during that early formative period, between 1934 and 1937, and he had as classmates outstanding academic librarians, including Robert Miller, Stephen McCarthy, Benjamin Powell, Lewis Stieg, J. Periam Danton, and Ralph Parker. Ralph attributes much of his own development to those early associations with people who were to become leaders in the profession, but, in the judgement of many, no one overshadowed Ralph himself.

Over the years, Ellsworth's contributions to academic librarianship have been sustained. His influence on the education of academic librarians has been more subtle, yet significant. The role model that he provides for students aspiring to become academic librarians is immeasurable. His innovations in organizational planning and staffing, in building planning and development, in scholarship and cooperation, have provided thousands of students with outstanding examples of innovation and change, and has greatly enriched the educational process.

FOOTNOTES

1. McAllister H. Hull, Jr., "Place of the Professional (Library) School in the Graduate School Structure," in Mary B. Cassata and Herman L. Totten, eds., *The Administrative Aspects of Education for Librarianship.* Metuchen, N.J.: Scarecrow, 1975, pp. 66-67.

2. Lester Asheim, "The Core Curriculum," *Journal of Education for Librarianship*, v. 19 (Fall 1978):153.
3. Lewis B. Mayhew and Patrick J. Ford, *Reform in Graduate and Professional Education.* San Francisco: Jossey-Bass, 1974, p. 12.
4. C. Edward Carroll, "History of Library Education," in Cassata and Totten, *op. cit.,* p. 12.
5. Lloyd H. Elliott, "Some Observations on Graduate and Professional Education," in Richard L. Darling and Terry Belanger, eds., *Extended Library Education Programs*, Columbia University School of Library Service, 1980, pp. 15-16.
6. Lewis B. Mayhew, "Curricular Change in the Professions," in Herbert Goldhor, ed., *Education for Librarianship: The Design of the Curriculum for Library Schools*, Urbana, Ill.: University of Illinois Graduate School of Library Science, 1971, p. 57.
7. Mayhew and Ford, *op. cit.,* p. 2.
8. K. Naegle and E. Stolar, "The Librarian in the Northwest," Morton Kroll, ed., *Libraries and Librarians in the Pacific Northwest*, Seattle: University of Washington Press, 1960, p. 65.
9. Robert S. Taylor, "Curriculum Design for Library and Information Science," in *Education and Curriculum Series #1.* Syracuse: Syracuse University School of Library Science, 1973, p. 82.
10. Kay Murray, "The Structure of MLS Programs in American Library Schools," *Journal of Education for Librarianship*, v. 18 (Spring 1978): 279.
11. Earl J. McGrath, "The Ideal Education for the Professional Man," in Nelson B. Henry, ed., *Education for the Professions.* Chicago: University of Chicago Press, 1962, p. 290.
12. William J. McGlothlin, "Insights From One Profession Which May Be Applied to Educating for Other Professions," in G. Kerry Smith, ed., *Current Issues in Higher Education.* Washington, D.C.: Association for Higher Education, 1961, p. 120.
13. Chris Argyris and Donald A. Schön, *Theory in Practice.* San Francisco: Jossey-Bass, 1978, p. 186.
14. H. G. Kaufman, *Obsolescence and Professional Career Development.* New York: Amacom, 1974.
15. Cyril O. Houle, "To Learn the Future," *Medical Clinics of North America*, v. 54 (January 1970):8.
16. William Summers, "The Emergence of Library Education," *American Libraries*, v. 3 (July-August 1972):792.
17. Louis R. Wilson, "Historical Development of Education for Librarianship in the United States," Bernard Berelson, ed., *Education for Librarianship.* Chicago: American Library Association, 1949.

Appendix I

Publications by and about
  Ralph E. Ellsworth
Compiled by Edward R. Johnson

BOOKS

Academic Library Buildings: a Guide to Architectural Issues and Solutions. (Boulder, Colo.: Colorado Associated University Press, 1973.)

The American Right Wing: a Report to the Fund for the Republic. (Urbana, Ill.: University of Illinois, Graduate School of Library Science, Occasional Papers, no. 59, 1960.) (Sarah M. Harris, joint author.)

The American Right Wing: a Report to the Fund for the Republic. (Washington, D.C.: Public Affairs Press, 1962.) (Sarah M. Harris, joint author.)

Buildings. (New Brunswick, N.J.: Rutgers University, Graduate School of Library Service, The State of the Library Art, vol. 3, 1960.)

The Economics of Book Storage in College and University Libraries. (Washington, D.C.: Association of Research Libraries, and Scarecrow Press, 1969.)

Ellsworth on Ellsworth: an Unchronological, Mostly True Account of Some Moments of Contact Between "Library Science" And Me Since Our Confluence in 1931, with Appropriate Sidelights. (Metuchen, N.J.: Scarecrow Press, 1980.)

Modular Planning for College and Small University Libraries. (Iowa City, Iowa: Private Printing by the authors, 1948.) (Donald E. Bean, joint author.)

Planning the College and University Library Building: a Book for Campus Planners and Architects. (Boulder, Colo.: Pruett Press, 1960, 1968.)

Planning Manual for Academic Library Buildings. (Metuchen, N.J.: Scarecrow Press, 1973.)

The School Library. (New York: Center for Applied Research in Education, 1965.)

The School Library: Facilities for Independent Study in the Secondary School. (New York: Educational Facilities Laboratories, 1963.) (Hobart D. Wagener, joint author.)

ARTICLES

"ALA Celebrates Its Seventy-fifth Anniversary," *Stechert-Hafner Book News,* 5(February, 1951), pp. 79-80.

"ALA's Anniversary: an Appraisal," *Library Journal,* 78 (April 1, 1953), pp. 547-550.

"Academic Library Buildings in the United States," in *Advances in Librarianship,* vol. 3. (New York: Seminar Press, 1972), pp. 119-136.

"Activities of the Colorado Conference of Librarians of Institutions of Higher Learning," *College and Research Libraries,* 4(June, 1943), pp. 233-238.

"The Administrative Implications for University Libraries of the New Cataloging Code," *College and Research Libraries,* 3 (March, 1942), pp. 134-138.

"Another Chance for Centralized Cataloging," *Colorado Academic Library,* 1(Fall, 1963).

"Another Chance for Centralized Cataloging," *Library Journal,* 89(September 1, 1964), pp. 3104-3107. (Reprint of 1963 article.)

"Appearance as Modern as the Best Store in Town," *Library Journal,* 74(December 15, 1949), pp. 1852-1853. (First appeared in *Kansas Library Bulletin,* December, 1949. See section on presented papers.)

"Are Our Architects Letting Us Down?" *Library Journal,* 72(December 15, 1947), pp. 1723-1725.

"Bibliographic Control," *American Council of Learned Societies Newsletter,* 22(January, 1971), pp. 9-13.

"Buildings and Architecture," *College and Research Libraries,* 6(June, 1945), pp. 279-281.

"Centralized Cataloging," *Library of Congress Information*

Bulletin, (November 16-22, 1948), appendix, pp. 1-13.

"Centralized Cataloging for Scholarly Libraries," *Library Quarterly,* 15(July, 1945), pp. 237-243.

"College and University Libraries of the State Begin Plan of Cooperation," *Colorado Library Association Bulletin,* 11(February, 1941), p. 7.

"The College and University Library as a Building Type," *American Institute of Architects Journal,* 43(May, 1975), pp. 79-82.

"Colorado Libraries in the Defense Effort," *Colorado Library Association Bulletin,* 15(Summer, 1942), p. 8.

"Colorado University's Divisional Reading Room Plan: Description and Evaluation," *College and Research Libraries,* 2(March, 1941), p. 103-109.

"Comments on Censorship," *Stechert-Hafner Book News,* 4(October, 1949), p. 17.

"Communications Study and University Librarians: Comment by Ralph E. Ellwsorth," *College and Research Libraries,* 6(September, 1945), pp. 402-404.

"Consultants for College and University Library Building Planning," *College and Research Libraries,* 21(July, 1960), pp. 263-268.

"Contribution of the Library to Improving Instruction," *Colorado Academic Library* 4(Summer, 1968), pp. 15-19.

"Correction Notes on the Ellsworth Report," *Library of Congress Information Bulletin,* (February 8-14, 1949), pp. 24-25.

"Critique of Library Associations in America," in *Seven Questions About the Profession of Librarianship.* (Chicago: University of Chicago Press, 1962), pp. 84-102. (Originally appeared in *Library Quarterly,* 1961. See section on presented papers.)

"Critique of Library Associations in America," in *Landmarks of Library Literature, 1876-1976.* (Metuchen, N.J.: Scarecrow Press, 1976), pp. 98-109. (Reprint of 1961 article.)

"Determining Factors in the Evaluation of the Modular Plan for Libraries," *College and Research Libraries,* 14(April, 1953), pp. 125-128, 142.

"Discussion," *College and Research Libraries,* 1(December, 1939), pp. 50-56, 96.

"Elements in Planning a Library Building Program," in *Library Buildings and Equipment Institute,* Kent State University, 1961, Planning Library Building for Service. (Chicago: American Library Association, 1964), pp. 9-12.

"An Evaluation of Pharmacy Journals," *American Journal of Pharmaceutical Education,* (January, 1940), pp. 14-19.

"The Greatest Waste" (by a former president of the American Association of Collegiate and Reference Libraries), in John M. Henry, ed. *The Articulates*. (Indianapolis: Bobbs-Merrill, 1957), pp. 105-111.

"How Buildings Can Contribute," in John Lubans, ed. *Educating the Library User*. (New York: Bowker, 1974), pp. 415-422.

"Introduction to the School Library," in P.L. Ward and R. Beacon, comps. *School Media Center: A Book of Readings*. (Metuchen, N.J.,: Scarecrow Press, 1973), pp. 2-11. (Hobart D. Wagener, joint author.) (Reprint from the authors' *The School Library: Facilities for Independent Study in the Secondary School.*)

"Is Intellectual Freedom in Libraries Being Challenged?" *American Library Association Bulletin*, 42(February, 1948) pp. 57-58.

"John Cronin and Centralized Cataloging," *Library Resources and Technical Services*, 12(Fall, 1968), pp. 394-395.

"The Legislature is Not Convinced," *Library Journal*, 90(May 15, 1965), pp. 2199-2203.

"A Librarian Looks at General Education: an Indictment with Constructive Criticisms," *Journal of Higher Education*, 34(April, 1953), pp. 177-181. (Published anonymously "By One Who Knows.")

"Library Architecture and Buildings," *Library Quarterly*, 25(January, 1955), pp. 66-75.

"Library Architecture and Buildings," *Bogens Verden*, 37(May, 1955), pp. 191-192. (Danish Abridged Version.)

"Library at a Crossroad," *Library Journal*, 90(December 15, 1965), p. 5344.

"A Modular Library for the State University of Iowa," in *American School and University: a Yearbook Devoted to the Design, Construction, Equipment Utilization, and Maintenance of Educational Buildings and Grounds*. 18th ed. (New York: American School Publishing Corporation, 1946), pp. 98-105. (Reprint from *The School Library: Facilities for Independent Study in the Secondary School.*)

"New Architecture Dimensions," *Library-College Journal*, 1(Winter, 1968), pp. 68-69; (Spring, 1968), pp. 54-56; (Summer, 1968), pp. 53-54; (Fall, 1968), pp. 58-59. (Richard Dougherty, joint author.)

"Notes on the Lubetzky Report," *Journal of Cataloging and Classification*, 9(September, 1953), pp. 130-131.

"Our American Heritage," *General Federation Clubwoman,* (March, 1951), pp. 4, 21.

"Place of College and Reference Library Service at ALA Headquarters; a Symposium; General Statements" *College and Research Libraries,* 7(April, 1946), pp. 166-167.

"President's Report: Colorado Libraries in 1938/39," *Colorado Library Association Bulletin,* 7(October, 1939), pp. 8-9.

"The Promise of Microprint; a Symposium Based on the Scholar and The Future of the Research Library; Brief Comments: Eight Librarians," *College and Research Libraries,* 6(March, 1945), pp. 179-180.

"Proposed Printed Catalog of the Library of Congress," *Colorado Library Association Bulletin,* 15(Summer, 1942), p. 12.

"Publishing Doctoral Dissertations," *Higher Education,* 9(September 15, 1952, pp. 19-20.

"Reading Patterns Among High School Students in Colorado," *Colorado Library Association Bulletin,* 12(June, 1941), pp. 6-8.

"Some Aspects of the Problem of Allocating Book Funds Among Departments in Universities," *Library Quarterly,* 12(July, 1942), pp. 486-494.

"Some Notes on Law Library Buildings," *Law Library Journal,* 61(May, 1968), pp. 67-68.

"Some Observations on the Architectural Style, Size, and Cost of Libraries," *Journal of Academic Librarianship,* 1(November, 1975), pp. 16-19.

"Summary of Current Practices in Colleges and Universities with Respect to the Management of Book Funds," *College and Research Libraries,* 3(June, 1942), pp. 252-255.

"To What Extent Can We Integrate?" *College and Research Libraries,* 8(October, 1947), pp. 401-404.

"The Training of Divisional Reading Room Librarians," *College and Research Libraries,* 6(December, 1944), pp. 4-7.

"Trends in Higher Education Affecting the College and University Library," *Library Trends,* 1(July, 1952), pp. 8-19.

"Trends in University Expenditures for Library Resources and for Total Educational Purposes, 1921-1941," *Library Quarterly,* 14(January, 1944), pp. 1-8.

"The University Library and the Lifetime Reader," in University of Michigan and the National Book Committee. *Reading for Life.* (Ann Arbor: University of Michigan Press, 1959), pp. 224-240.

"Why Librarians Should Participate in the ALA Anniversary

Contest," *American Library Association Bulletin,* 45(February, 1951), pp. 48–49.

ENCYCLOPEDIA ARTICLES

"Architecture, Library Building," *Encyclopedia of Library and Information Science,* vol. 1, pp. 491–515.

Ellsworth also contributed articles on college and university libraries and library buildings and architecture to the *Encyclopedia Americana,* from the early 1950s to the early 1970s.

PUBLISHED PRESENTED PAPERS

"Academic Libraries in an Uncertain Future," *Texas Library Journal,* 39(Summer, 1963), pp. 47–51. (Texas Library Association, March 27–30, 1963.)

"The Changing Role of the University Library," *Library Journal,* 88(April 1, 1963), pp. 1405–1411. (Cornell University Library Conference and Dedication, October, 1962.)

"College Library in the Next Decade: Problems and Prospects," *Missouri Library Association Quarterly,* 19(June, 1958), 56–59. (Missouri Library Association, 1958.)

"College Students and Reading," *American Scholar,* 27(Autumn, 1958), pp. 473–481. (National Conference on the Undergraduate and the Lifetime Reading Interest, University of Michigan and National Book Committee, Ann Arbor, Michigan, 1958.)

"Comprehensiveness Versus Selectivity," in *Changing Patterns of Scholarship and the Future of Research Libraries: a Symposium in Celebration of the 200th Anniversary of the Establishment of the University of Pennyslvania Library.* (Philadelphia: University of Pennsylvania Press, 1951), pp. 73–79.

"Critique of Library Associations in America," *Library Quarterly,* 31(October, 1961), pp. 382–395. (26th Annual University of Chicago Graduate Library School Conference, 1961.)

"Educational Implications of the New Ideas in Library Construction," *College and Research Libraries,* 7(October, 1946), pp. 326–329. (Association of College and Research Libraries, Buffalo, New York, June 18, 1946.)

"Extra-Curricular Activities of Libraries," *Quarterly Journal of*

Speech, 36(December, 1950), pp. 471-475. (Speech Association of America Convention, Chicago, December, 1949.)

"The Institutional Environment," in John T. Eastlick, ed. *Changing Environment of Libraries, Papers Delivered at the 1970-71 Colloquium Series, Graduate School of Librarianship, University of Denver.* (Chicago: American Library Association, 1971), pp. 30-38.

"Libraries, Students, and Faculty," in *The Cornell Library Conference: Papers Presented at the Dedication of the Central Libraries, October, 1962.* (Ithaca, N.Y.: Cornell University Library, 1964), pp. 67-83.

"Library Architecture Today," *Kansas Library Bulletin,* 18(March-December, 1949), p. 305. (Kansas State Library Association, October 6, 1949.)

"Library's Life Style: a Review of the Last 35 Years," *Michigan Librarian,* 36(Autumn, 1970), pp. 29-39. (First G. Flint Purdy Memorial Lecture, American Library Association, Detroit, Michigan, June 29, 1970.)

"Midwest Reaches for the Stars," *College and Research Libraries,* 9(April, 1948), pp. 136-144. (Norman L. Kilpatrick, joint author.) (Conference of Eastern College Librarians, Columbia University, November 29, 1947.)

"MPLA: What of Its Future?" in *MPLA Conference on Inter-Library Cooperation, Lyons, Colorado, 1973.* (Mountain-Plains Library Association, 1974), pp. 59-60.

"Now That We Have Built," *Louisiana Library Association Bulletin,* 22(Summer, 1959), pp. 39-41. (Louisiana Library Association, March 19, 1959.)

Planning the Academic Library: Metcalf and Ellsworth at York. Harvey Faulkner Brown, ed. (Newcastle upon Tyne, England: Oriel Press, 1971.) (Course on Academic Library Planning, York, Institute of Advanced Architectural Studies, 1966.)

"The Quest for Quality in Higher Education," *College and Research Libraries,* 23(January, 1962), pp. 7-10. (Association of College and Research Libraries, Cleveland, Ohio, July 12, 1961.)

"Scholarly Publishing and the University Librarian," *Library Journal,* 96(November 1, 1971), pp. 3568-3572. (American Association of University Presses, May 1971.)

"Second 200 Years: the Peaceful Revolution," *Illinois Libraries,* 58(May, 1976), pp. 347-351. (Illinois Library Association, December 4, 1946.)

"Tasks of the Immediate Future," *Library Quarterly,*

22(January, 1952), pp. 18-20. (Dedication ceremony Midwest Inter-Library Center, October 5, 1951.)

"The University Library, Center of Study and Development," *Southeastern Librarian*, 3(Winter, 1953), pp. 117-128, 137. (University of Georgia Library dedication, November 19, 1953.)

"University Library in Violent Transition," in University of Tennessee. *Library Lectures, nos. 13-15, 1961-1963.* (Knoxville, Tenn.: University of Tennessee Library, 1963), pp. 15-22.

"University Library in Violent Transition," in *The Library in the University: the University of Tennessee Library Lectures, 1949-1966.* (Hamden, Conn.: Shoe String Press, 1967), pp. 236-244. (Reprint of 1963 paper.)

"What Does the American Heritage Mean?" A radio discussion over WGN and the Mutual Broadcasting System in cooperation with the American Library Association, on the occasion of its 75th anniversary (with Ralph E. Ellsworth, Clarence R. Decker, and John A. Wilson), James H. McBurney, Moderator, *The Northwestern University Reviewing Stand*, 16(July 15, 1951), pp. 3-9.

"What's Happening in the School Library," in *What's in a Library? School Function Present and Future.* (Denton, Texas: unpublished pamphlet, the Selwyn School, 1968 [?].) (Selwyn School Library Planning Conference, April, 1-2, 1968.)

REVIEWS

Lee Ash, comp. Subject Collections, in *Library Resources and Technical Services*, 4(Winter, 1960), pp. 94-95.

Lester Asheim, The Humanities and the Library, in *Journal of Higher Education*, 29(February, 1958), p. 114.

Charles H. Baumann, Influence of Angus Snead McDonald and the Snead Bookstack on Library Statistics, 1939-1940, in *Library Quarterly*, 15(January, 1945), p. 90.

College and University Library Statistics, 1939-1940, in *Library Quarterly*, 15(January, 1945), p. 90.

Committee for New College, Amherst, Mass., Student Reaction to Study Facilities with Implications for Architects and College Administrators, in *College and Research Libraries*, 22(March, 1961), pp. 165-167.

Council on Library Resources, Annual Reports, 1957-1959, in *Library Quarterly*, 30(October, 1960), pp. 289-290.

Herman Fussler, ed. The Function of the Library in the Modern

College, in *Journal of Higher Education,* 27(April, 1956), pp. 230-231.

General Specifications for a Library Building for the University of Toledo, in *Library Journal,* 75(February 15, 1950), pp. 272-273.

How to Locate Education Information and Data, Alexander Library Exercises, in *Journal of Higher Education,* 7(June, 1936), pp. 341-342.

Library Handbook, Olin Memorial Library, Wesleyan University, in *Library Quarterly,* 13(July, 1943), pp. 277-278.

J. Morris, Managing the Library Fire Risk, in *Journal of Academic Librarianship,* 2(September, 1976), pp. 192-193.

Non-Professional Library Instruction in Teachers Colleges, in *Library Quarterly,* 5(July, 1935), pp. 356-357.

Organization and Personnel Procedure . . . a Suggested Plan, in *College and Research Libraries,* 2(March, 1941), p. 162.

Periodical Checklist for a Teachers College Library, in *Library Quarterly,* 5(January, 1935), pp. 141-142.

Lawrence Clark Powell, Passion for Books, in *College and Research Libraries,* 20(May, 1959), pp. 255-256.

Frank L. Schick, ed. Future of Library Service: Demographic Aspects and Implications, in *Library Journal,* 87(May 15, 1962), pp. 1878-1879.

Scholar and the Future of the Research Library, in *College and Research Libraries,* 6(March, 1945), pp. 179-180.

Survey of the University of Notre Dame, in *Library Journal,* 77(August, 1952), pp. 1284-1285.

Maurice F. Tauber and Louis Round Wilson, The University Library, in *Journal of Higher Education,* 27(October, 1956), pp. 406-407.

Anthony Thompson, Library Buildings of Britain and Europe, in *Library Journal,* 88(December 1, 1963), pp. 2529-2530.

LETTERS

"C.U. Library Expansion Program" *Mountain Plains Library Quarterly,* 4(Spring, 1959), p. 21.

"Comments on the American Right Wing," *American Library Association Bulletin,* 56(January, 1962), p.7.

"Coordinated Research," *Library Journal,* 92(May 15, 1967), p. 1901.

"Letter to Kirk," *National Review*, 14(January 15, 1963), p. 38.

"Librarians Need to Know More," *Library Journal*, 88(January 1, 1963), p. 40.

"MacLeish Appointment," *Saturday Review of Literature*, 20(July 1, 1939), p. 9.

"Microphotographing Service at University of Colorado," *Journal of Documentary Reproduction*, 4(December, 1941), p. 259.

"To The Editor," *College and Research Libraries*, 31(January, 1970), pp. 55–57.

"A Wary Eye to the Future: a Message from ACRL's President," *College and Research Libraries*, 22(July, 1961), p. 302.

ARTICLES ABOUT ELLSWORTH

"ACRL President Attacks ALA Policies," *Wilson Library Bulletin*, 37(September, 1962), p. 26.

Miller, Robert A., "Dr. Ellsworth 'Retires to Become More Active,'" *Wilson Library Bulletin*, 46(April, 1972), p. 684.

"Prof. Ralph E. Ellsworth, Director of Libraries at the University of Colorado, Will Retire," *Mountain Plains Library Quarterly*, 16(Winter, 1972), pp. 25–27.

"Professor Ralph E. Ellsworth, University of Colorado Director of Libraries for the Past Fourteen Years, Retired February 1, 1972," *College and Research Libraries News*, 7(July, 1972), pp. 203–204.

"Ralph E. Ellsworth, Director of Libraries at the University of Colorado in Boulder, Retired," *American Libraries*, 3(April, 1972), p. 346.

"Ralph E. Ellsworth, Formerly Director of Libraries, University of Colorado, Boulder, Retired," *Library Journal*, 97(March 1, 1972), p. 821.

Tauber, Maurice F., "Ralph E. Ellsworth," *College and Research Libraries*, 18(November, 1957), p. 498.

"Untitled," *American Library Association Bulletin*, 42(February, 1948), p. 93.

– – –, *College and Research Libraries*, 11(April, 1950), p. 187.

– – –, *Library Quarterly*, 25(January, 1955), pp. 127–128.

REVIEWS OF ELLSWORTH'S WORKS

Academic Library Buildings

J. Orne, *Library Journal*, 98(June 15, 1973), p. 1895.

G. J. Novak, *College and Research Libraries*, 34(September, 1973), pp. 386–387.

R. P. Youngren, *Library Quarterly*, 44(April, 1974), pp. 157–159.

M. J. Leprovost, *Bulletin of Documentation and Bibliography*, 19(July, 1974), pp. 535–536.

The American Right Wing

R. Zumwinkle, *College and Research Libraries*, 22(September, 1961), p. 401.

H. Margolis, "Right Wingers Seem to Be Almost Everywhere: Notes on a Report to the Fund for the Republic," *Science*, 134(December 22, 1961), pp. 2025–2057.

E. T. Moore, "Why Do the Rightists Rage?" *American Library Association Bulletin*, 56(January, 1962), pp. 26–31.

D. V. Black, *Library Journal*, 87(February 15, 1962), pp. 745–746.

R. Kirk, "License They Mean at Colorado," *National Review*, 13(November 20, 1962), p. 393.

Buildings

K. D. Metcalf, *Library Journal*, 86(January 15, 1961), pp. 220–222.

G. E. Pettengill, *Special Libraries*, 52(February, 1961), p. 106.

W. H. Jesse, *College and Research Libraries*, 22(March, 1961), pp. 165–167.

R. S. Smith, *Journal of Documentation*, 17(September, 1961), pp. 173–174.

Economics of Book Storage

J. Orne, *Library Journal*, 95(April 1, 1970), p. 1299.

B. Stuart-Stubbs, *Canadian Library Journal*, 27(May, 1970), pp. 239–240.

J. E. Levis, *RQ*, 9(Summer, 1970), pp. 360–361.

P. Spyers-Duran, *Drexel Library Quarterly*, 6(July–October, 1970), pp. 343–345.

J. W. Kraus, *College and Research Libraries*, 32(January, 1971), pp. 50–51.

R. F. Doust, *Australian Library Journal*, 20(March, 1971), pp. 47-48.

J. H. Meister, *Zentralblatt für Bibliothekswesen*, 86(February 7, 1972), pp. 106-107.

Modular Planning

W. H. Jesse, *Library Journal*, 73(June 1, 1948), pp. 874-875.

W. M. Randall, *College and Research Libraries*, 9(October, 1948), pp. 373-374.

R. E. Enthoven, *Journal of Documentation*, 4(December, 1948), pp. 209-210.

H. H. Fussler, *Library Quarterly*, 19(January, 1949), pp. 66-68.

J. P. L. *Library Association Record*, 51(May, 1949), pp. 164-165.

W. W. Parker, *Journal of Higher Education*, 20(May, 1949), pp. 277-278.

Planning Manual

J. Orne, *Library Journal*, 99(April 1, 1974), p. 968.

J. A. Cunningham, *Catholic Library World*, 46(February, 1975), p. 313.

R. P. Youngren, *Library Quarterly*, 46(January, 1976), pp. 81-83. (Rejoinder: *Library Quarterly*, 47(January, 1977), pp. 109-110.

Planning College and University Library Buildings

J. Orne, *Library Journal*, 86(March 1, 1961), pp. 982-983.

E. F. Patterson, *Library Association Record*, 63(June, 1961), p. 223.

L. Kaplan, *Library Quarterly*, 31(July, 1961), pp. 277-278.

R. S. Smith, *Journal of Documentation*, 17(September, 1961), pp. 173-174.

J. Orne, *Library Journal*, 94(October 15, 1969), p. 3628.

The School Library

J. A. Rowell, *Library Journal*, 90(September 15, 1965), p. 3716.

J. A. Rowell, *School Library Journal*, 12(September, 1965), p. 78.

E. Youngmeyer, *School Libraries,* 15(October, 1965), p. 72.

R. L. Darling, *College and Research Libraries,* 26(November, 1965), pp. 530–531.

T. Mowbray, *New Zealand Libraries,* 29(October, 1966), pp. 183–184.

The School Library: Facilities for Independent Study

R. H. Hektoen, *Senior Scholastic,* 83(October 4, 1963), p. 5T.

R. A. Gibboney, *Library Journal,* 88(November 15, 1963), pp. 4452–4453.

R. A. Gibboney, *School Library Journal,* 10(November, 1963), pp. 44–45.

M. R. A. Johnson, *School Libraries,* 13(March, 1964), p. 51.

S. I. Fenwick, *Library Quarterly,* 34(April, 1964), pp. 215–216.

M. H. Grazier, *School Libraries,* 13(May, 1964), pp. 60–62.

R. A. Edelfelt, *School Libraries,* 14(October, 1964), pp. 69–70.

B. Buick, *Australian Library Journal,* 14(September, 1965), p. 156.

Appendix II

*A Partial Listing of Consultantships
of Ralph E. Ellsworth
Compiled by Robert D. Stueart*

This is a partial listing of Ralph E. Ellsworth's consultantships on new buildings, additions to old buildings, and remodeling projects, compiled from the archives at the University of Denver, as of November 1980. Dates relate to the contact letters on file. The list only contains contracts for which there is evidence in the archives, but does not include the planning Ellsworth did in the two major university libraries he directed – the University of Colorado and the State University of Iowa. It exists as an incomplete record because Ellsworth is unsure of the exact number of his consultantships.

1957
California Institute of Technology (Pasadena, Calif.)   March 4

1959
Earlham College (Richmond, Ind.)	May 2
St. Benedict's College (Atchison, Kans.)	September 8

1960
Stephens College (Columbia, Mo.)	February 2
Temple University (Philadelphia, Penn.)	July 6
Beaver College (Glenside, Penn.)	September 28

1961
Colorado Women's College (Denver, Colo.)	January 31
Colorado State University (Fort Collins, Colo.)	April 17
Reed College (Portland, Ore.)	November 27
Western State College (Gunnison, Colo.)	December 31

1962

Fairleigh Dickinson University (Rutherford, N.J.)	March 5
University of Bridgeport (Bridgeport, Conn.)	March 7
Bowling Green State University (Bowling Green, Ohio)	April 5
University of South Dakota (Vermillion, S.D.)	May 10
Park College (Parkville, Mo.)	May 10
San Diego State College (San Diego, Calif.)	May 12
Fort Lewis College (Durango, Colo.)	May 2
Austin Peay State University (Clarksville, Tenn.)	June 12
University of Utah (Salt Lake City, Utah)	August 7
Cazenovia College (Cazenovia, N.Y.)	August 14
Southern Colorado State College (Pueblo, Colo.)	September 17
Hofstra University (Hempstead, N.Y.)	December 4

1963

Syracuse University (Syracuse, N.Y.)	January 8
Oberlin College (Oberlin, Ohio)	February 26
Drake University (Des Moines, Iowa)	March 8
Centre College of Kentucky (Danville, Ky.)	March 31
University of Otago (Dunedin, New Zealand)	May 1
Saint Johns College (Santa Fe, N.M.)	May 17
Arizona State University (Tempe, Ariz.)	September 20
Simon Fraser University (Vancouver, British Columbia, Canada)	October 23
San Fernando Valley State College (Calif.)	December 9

1964

Saint Norberts (West DePere, Wis.)	January 24
Brooklyn College (Brooklyn, N.Y.)	April 23
Hunter College, City College of New York (New York, N.Y.)	April 27
Occidental College (Los Angeles, Calif.)	June 15
University of Rochester (Rochester, N.Y.)	July 29
Ohio University (Athens, Ohio)	September 11

1965

Prescott College (Prescott, Ariz.)	February 8
Wells College (Aurora, N.Y.)	February 15
Augustana College (Rock Island, Ill.)	March 17
University of Tulsa (Tulsa, Okla.)	April 14
Rice University (Houston, Tex.)	May 6
Cleveland State University (Cleveland, Ohio)	July 2

West Valley College (Campbell, Calif.)   September 14
Gustavus Adolphus College (Saint Peter, Minn.)   December 11

1966
Cochise College (Douglas, Ariz.)   January 4
Santa Fe College (Santa Fe, N.M.)   July 7
Western Washington State College (Bellington, Wash.)   July 7
Calvin College and Seminary
   (Grand Rapids, Minn.)   September 20

1967
Baptist College at Charlestown (Charlestown, S.C.)   January 17
Friends University (Wichita, Kans.)   January 26
Wayne State University (Detroit, Mich.)   February 2
California State University (Chico, Calif.)   February 7
Adams State College (Alamosa, Colo.)   August 28
Sacred Heart College (Wichita, Kans.)   October 7
University of Arizona (Tucson, Ariz.)   October 23
University of Georgia (Athens, Ga.)   December 7
Southern Methodist University (Dallas, Tex.)   December 12

1968
Selwyn School (Denton, Tex.)   March 12
Doane College (Crete, Nebr.)   April 10

1969
Illinois State University (Normal, Ill.)   February 2
Arizona-Thunderbird Graduate School of
   Management (Tucson, Ariz.)   February 3
Washington and Lee University (Lexington, Va.)   February 5
Washington State University (Pullman, Wash.)   February 12
University of Delaware (Newark, Del.)   February 18
Southwestern Medical School (Dallas, Tex.)   August 7
Eastern Washington State College (Cheney, Wash.)   August 13

1970
University of Akron (Akron, Ohio)   January 15
Rensselaer Polytechnic Institute (Troy, N.Y.)   April 29
Hardin-Simmons University (Abilene, Tex.)   June 3
Webber College (Babson Park, Fla.)   June 17
Randolph-Macon College (Lynchberg, Va.)   July 6
University of California, Berkeley
   (Berkeley, Calif.)   November 23

1971

University of Texas, Dallas (Dallas, Tex.)	June 3
Edinboro State College (Erie, Penn.)	June 18
Fairmont State College (Fairmont, W. Va.)	October 19
Temple University (Philadelphia, Penn.)	November 5
Kentucky Wesleyan College (Owensboro, Ky.)	November 30

1972

Gettysburg College (Gettysburg, Penn.)	August 12
California State College, Sonoma (Sonoma, Calif.)	October 4

1973

Pahlavi National Library (Teheran, Iran)	June 2

Index

Compiled by William H. Webb